179. 3
S587m

Unleashing Rights

}

Law, Meaning, and Violence

The scope of Law, Meaning, and Violence is defined by the wide-ranging scholarly debates signaled by each of the words in the title. Those debates have taken place among and between lawyers, anthropologists, political theorists, sociologists, and historians, as well as literary and cultural critics. This series is intended to recognize the importance of such ongoing conversations about law, meaning, and violence as well as to encourage and further them.

Series Editors:

Martha Minow, Harvard Law School
Michael Ryan, Northeastern University
Austin Sarat, Amherst College

Narrative, Violence, and the Law: The Essays of Robert Cover,
    edited by Martha Minow, Michael Ryan, and Austin Sarat

Narrative, Authority, and Law, by Robin West

*The Possibility of Popular Justice: A Case Study of Community Mediation
    in the United States,* edited by Sally Engle Merry and Neal Milner

Legal Modernism, by David Luban

*Surveillance, Privacy, and the Law: Employee Drug Testing and the
    Politics of Social Control,* by John Gilliom

Lives of Lawyers: Journeys in the Organizations of Practice,
    by Michael J. Kelly

Unleashing Rights: Law, Meaning, and the Animal Rights Movement,
    by Helena Silverstein

Unleashing Rights

Law, Meaning, and the
Animal Rights Movement

Helena Silverstein

Ann Arbor

THE UNIVERSITY OF MICHIGAN PRESS

Copyright © by the University of Michigan 1996
All rights reserved
Published in the United States of America by
The University of Michigan Press
Manufactured in the United States of America
⊛ Printed on acid-free paper

1999   1998   1997   1996   4   3   2   1

No part of this publication may be reproduced, stored in a retrieval system, or transmitted in any form or by any means, electronic, mechanical, or otherwise without the written permission of the publisher.

A CIP catalog record for this book is available from the British Library.

Library of Congress Cataloging-in-Publication Data

Silverstein, Helena.
    Unleashing rights : law, meaning, and the animal rights movement / Helena Silverstein.
        p.   cm. — (Law, meaning, and violence)
    Includes bibliographical references and index.
    ISBN 0-472-10685-6 (hardcover : alk. paper)
    1. Animal rights.   2. Animal rights movement.   3. Animal welfare—Law and legislation.   4. Natural law.   I. Title.   II. Series.
HV4708.S555   1996
179'.3—dc20   96-10321
                                                                        CIP

For Wayne

Preface

Over the past few years, many people have asked me about the research project that appears in the following pages. In responding, I always began by saying that my research concerned the relationship between law and social change and that I was studying the animal rights movement to examine this relationship. Almost everyone reacted to this brief summary of my work by focusing on the fact that my research deals with the animal rights movement. Most thought, initially, that I was dealing with the philosophical question: Do animals have rights? In addition, most assumed that I must have been an animal rights supporter before choosing this topic; after all, why else would I have selected the movement as my focus?

In fact, my work does not seek to answer the philosophical question of whether animals have rights. Rather, it is concerned with how rights language is deployed by social movements and how the language constitutes and is constituted by movement activism. Moreover, my knowledge of and interest in the animal rights movement was minimal prior to the research and writing of this work. I had never contributed to an animal rights or welfare organization. I had never read any of the literature concerning the animal rights movement. My diet consisted of beef, chicken, and fish; and my closet was filled with leather shoes. Indeed, like most people, I had never really considered in any depth the experiences of the animals that made up a part of my everyday life. I had never even had a pet of my own until two months before this research project was born.

Prior to my research on this subject, the closest I ever came to considering the issue of animal rights was during conversations with a few vegetarian friends. I recall grilling one of these friends about her diet, asking her how she could feed her cat meat while not eating meat herself. I clearly remember my own feelings regarding her general ethical choice to be a vegetarian: not only were her actions inconsistent with her views, but she was confused to think that animals have rights because animals are not the kind of beings that can have rights. Only beings capable of rationality have rights.

My decision to study the animal rights movement, then, did not grow out of activism or prior interest in the movement. Rather, it developed out of my theoretical interests in three particular topics: natural rights theory, legal theory, and theories of social change. In courses I had taken while a graduate student, I continually considered several questions relating to rights. Why did natural rights theory develop historically when it did? Why are rights so prominent in our country? Why do social movements continually deploy rights to advance their goals? Is such deployment beneficial for marginalized groups seeking to advance social change? Or are rights a tool used by the ruling class to maintain its position of power?[1]

These were the questions I was interested in pursuing. And I was interested in exploring these issues within the context of social movement activism. Over many years I had examined these questions within the context of various social movements, including movements for civil rights, women's rights, Native American rights, rights for the mentally ill, and worker's rights. However, I was not sure how I would further probe these issues within the context of a more extensive research project.

It was not until a fateful day in January 1989 that I stumbled upon the topic that takes form in this book. On that day, I happened to be watching the television program *Crossfire* on CNN with the person to whom this book is dedicated. This half-hour news debate show covers a different topic each day and, in doing so, brings in people with divergent views on the topic. That day, the topic happened to be animal rights. I think the discussion centered around scientific experimentation using animals, but I cannot recall for certain. Regardless of the subject matter, I remember listening to the two guests debate the issue. At some point, the animal rights activists began to speak the language of rights, arguing that animals should be protected because their rights were being violated. I turned to my partner and said something like the following: "Isn't it interesting how here is yet another social movement using rights to advance its cause?" As I spoke the words, a light bulb flashed over my head and a research topic was born.

After thinking more about my remark, I decided that the animal rights movement might provide a good empirical case for evaluating the deployment of rights by progressive social movements. Given my background and research interests, I thought I had discovered a potentially wonderful way to explore the relationship between law, rights, and social change. Still, I was concerned about the selection of the animal rights movement as an empirical case, and my concerns were echoed by others. My primary concern was whether a study of the animal rights movement would be viewed as too marginal. After all, the animal rights movement itself remains on the margins. It is not uncommon to hear animal rights supporters called human haters, animal fanatics, and the like. Moreover, I was hesitant to study this movement out of fear that I would be labeled an animal rights activist masquerading as a scholar. Although I knew my original motivations were not driven by a desire to advance the animal rights movement, the worry was that others would incorrectly assume that I was biased and would not view my work and my position as sufficiently "objective."

Despite these concerns, I chose to go forward with the project. I made this decision largely because of the context within which I was studying the animal rights movement. Given my focus of attention, I have not had to address the issue of whether or not the animal rights movement is a worthy cause. As such, my own personal feelings about the cause of animal rights—whatever they may be—are not directly relevant to the focus of this work.

Now that this project is complete, I am glad that my concerns did not inhibit me from proceeding with the topic. I think this work, with its examination of the animal rights movement, contributes to our understanding of law, rights language, litigation, and the construction of legal meaning. In addition, I am now less concerned about whether people think that this must be something written by an animal advocate. Although my views about the *language* of animal rights certainly do come into play in the following pages, my personal attitudes toward how we, as a society, should treat animals do not. I expect that those who read what follows will agree.[2]

More importantly, this work may help scholars recognize the value of studying what is popularly viewed as marginal, excluded, and illegitimate. Rather than becoming more inhibited about examining the marginal, I have discovered over the course of my research and writing that it is important to take up issues on the margins. Studying what has been excluded is crucial because it helps us understand not only the margins but the mainstream as well. As Martha Minow suggests,

"Making central what has been marginal remakes the boundaries of knowledge and understanding and sheds new light on the whole" (Minow 1990, 16). I know that this work has helped me to better understand the margins and the whole, and I hope that others will also, through this work, increase their appreciation of both.

Acknowledgments

A project like this one is never the work of one individual. Many people have contributed directly and indirectly to this work, and my appreciation goes out to all of them.

I cannot overstate my gratitude to Michael McCann, the most direct contributor to this work. In guiding me throughout this project, Michael combined the qualities of critic, supporter, and friend. For that, I cannot thank him enough. A number of other people lent their valuable time to this project. Stuart Scheingold deserves special thanks for his counsel and critical feedback. So too does John Gilliom who provided meaningful commentary on the manuscript as well as an important friendship. In addition, Austin Sarat, Martha Minow, Christine Di Stefano, Steve Hanson, and Joshua Miller each read the entire manuscript and offered substantial advice on how to improve the work.

This book would not have been possible without the assistance of the animal advocates who agreed to be interviewed. They gave their time and energies to a stranger, and offered their views with candor. Their insights taught me a great deal about the animal rights movement and about the legal system. I am indebted to each of the participants.

My appreciation goes out to Robert Van Dyk, Bill Lyons, Linda Cornett, Lee Overton, David Haugen, Michael Oppenheim, Amy King, and Lori Stevens. In various ways, these colleagues and friends provided me with essential intellectual and moral support. My appreciation also goes out to the Political Science Department at the University of Washington and the Government and Law Department at Lafayette College. Both furnished conducive environments for the completion of this work.

The members of my family deserve credit for their support and encouragement: my father, Zelig, for egging me on all my life to make something of myself; my mother, Lea, for her sensitivity and patience, and for reading and understanding my work; and my brothers David and Dubi for providing me with a standard against which I could compete. I would especially like to thank Dubi, who first listened to my ideas for this work on the way home from a Rangers hockey game, who sent me newspaper clippings, and who commented on various parts of the written product.

The person to whom this work is dedicated provided me with the crucial emotional and intellectual sustenance needed to take on and carry out such a project. Wayne Fishman, my spouse and best friend, was with me throughout and, nevertheless, has not left. He helped me think through many of the ideas that have made their way into this work. He cheered me on as I completed each hurdle and encouraged me every step of the way. He was a combination of coach, fan, and friend. I only hope that I can be to him what he has been to me.

Finally, I must extend my thanks to Jerry, Schroedinger, and Shadow, who spent their days on my lap, on my desk, or sprawled out comfortably somewhere nearby. I thank them not only for keeping me company during the long hours spent at my computer but for never accidently stepping on the keyboard and destroying what I had written.

Contents

Chapter 1

Constituting Legal Meaning

"[L]aw," here, there, or anywhere, is part of a distinctive manner of
imagining the real.

— Clifford Geertz

In 1987, 15-year-old Jenifer Graham sued Victor Valley High School in
California. At issue was a frog and the First Amendment of the Constitution. Refusing to fulfill her biology class assignment to dissect a frog,
Graham claimed that the dissection requirement infringed upon her
moral beliefs protected by the First Amendment. Arguing that her position stemmed from "a strong, sincerely held and longstanding belief
that dissection is morally wrong," Graham requested that the school
provide her with an alternative to dissection (*Los Angeles Times*, June 12,
1987, 35). When the school rejected her request, Graham brought suit. A
year later, U.S. District Court judge Manuel Real came up with a solution to the conflict: the school would have to locate a frog that had died
of natural causes for Ms. Graham to dissect (Murphy 1988).

Bringing suit on behalf of a dead frog is certainly unusual, even in
what is often viewed as an overly litigious society. But this odd lawsuit
displays a very common reality in American society: in attempts to produce social change, resort to legal institutions and languages has
become the norm. Propelled in part by the seeming successes of the
civil rights movement during the 1950s and 1960s, reform advocates on
both the right and the left now regularly adopt legally oriented strategies in the hope of achieving their goals.

The deployment of legal tactics by social movements has provoked
extensive investigation. Some have examined the potential problems of
using courts to produce reform policy (Rosenberg 1991; Horowitz
1977). Others have questioned whether this deployment reinforces
existing power structures (Medcalf 1978; Bruun 1982; McCann 1986;
Bell 1985). Many have explored whether or not turning to the legal sys-

tem has proven successful for the movements and their reform-oriented goals (Scheingold 1974; Handler 1978; Olson 1984; McCann 1994).

The following pages have also been inspired by social movement efforts to advance change through existing legal structures. Using social movement activism as the starting point, this book seeks to explore the dynamic interrelationship between law and the practical activism of social movements. In particular, the focus of this exploration rests in legal meaning: how legal meaning constitutes and is constituted by social movement practice. To examine the constitutive character of legal meaning, this work employs a "decentered" approach to the study of the law and applies that approach to an investigation of the animal rights movement.

A Decentered View of Law

Law is commonly defined and studied as a system of rules established by the governing institutions of a society.[1] This understanding of law encourages investigation into the rules themselves, the actors who make the rules, and the processes within which the actors and the rules work (Carp and Stidham 1990; Murphy and Pritchett 1986; Richardson and Vines 1970). Studies of law thus frequently begin with the courts and the processes of adjudication. Research emphasizes judges and lawyers as the key players and then moves beyond these to address the individuals and groups involved in the litigative process, especially government officials, individual citizens, and interest groups (Abraham 1974; Rosenthal 1974; Shapiro 1990). This kind of academic study stresses how cases get to the courts, the factors that influence judicial decision making, the decisions themselves, and the impact of decisions.

From this angle, law can be examined as either the dependent or independent variable of analysis. When investigating the input side of the judicial system (e.g., the manner in which litigation makes its way through the judicial system, the variables affecting judicial decision making, and judicial opinions), law is taken to be the dependent variable. Legal rules are created and defined by legal players acting through and within official institutions and processes.[2] When exploring the output side of the judicial system (e.g., the impact of judicial decision making), law is the independent variable. Judicial impact studies, for instance, move from the judicial arena outward to see how judicial decisions affect particular populations (Johnson and Canon 1984; Tarr 1977; Rosenberg 1991).

These studies generally take an instrumental approach, viewing law "as a tool for sustaining or changing aspects of social life. . . . However it does its work, law's job is to regulate effectively the activities of legal subjects, what they do or abstain from doing" (Sarat and Kearns 1993, 23). Whether these analyses focus on how judges arrive at decisions or on the degree of compliance with these decisions, the primary concern of instrumentalism rests on the effectiveness of the law.

> So conceived, legal scholarship begins and ends with a specifically legal focus: it begins with legal rules (or with cognate legal standards) and ends in an examination of their effectiveness in regulating or changing everyday life, that is, in a study of the extent to which this law has, or has failed to have, *the intended role* in shaping the domain of activity in question. (Sarat and Kearns 1993, 26)[3]

It is not surprising that the bulk of legal analysis takes such an approach. There is good reason to question and investigate the effectiveness of the law, and examining legal players and institutions is the obvious place to begin an analysis of effectiveness. Nevertheless, these studies miss important insights as a result of their view of law and their focus of attention.

Defining law narrowly as a system of rules created and enforced by the governing institutions of society is problematic. Such a definition wrongly assumes and suggests that law is precise and definitive; it assumes that we can look at the written rules and straightforwardly comprehend the meanings, implications, and intentions of those rules. This definition also neglects the construction, interpretation, and enforcement of law beyond official state institutions. It may lead us to disregard other arenas in which law plays a significant role and to ignore the specific contexts in which people understand, act upon, develop, and challenge law. As such, too narrow a focus on judicial institutions may cause us to misread the overall workings of law and misunderstand the connections between law and social change.

The research presented here suggests an alternative to the standard approach taken within public law literature and recommends that we begin with a broader view. This broader, or decentered, view does not focus on what is often taken to be the centerpiece of law, that is, the courts. Instead, the decentered view stresses the importance of looking at law as it is manifest in the wider spheres of society. Law from this perspective is defined not simply as a set of rules elaborated and enforced by state institutions. Rather, law is the agglomeration of cultural beliefs, norms, languages, and practices that reflects and constructs social relationships, regulates social interaction, and establishes and maintains order. From this perspective, law should be "understood less as abstract, impersonal rules established by the state than as cultural conventions that shape and facilitate practical social interaction" (McCann and Silverstein 1993, 133). Understanding law in this way means noticing that law is located not only in judicial and state institutions but in nonjudicial and nonstate realms. Although the official state institutions remain important to analyses of the legal system, it is by exploring the broader, unofficial realm of social interaction that we can develop a more subtle, complex, and expansive understanding of the law.

A decentered approach recommends that we proceed with an examination of law by exploring the continuous and dynamic interaction between the judicial and the nonjudicial. In examining the interaction between these two realms, we look to the way each informs and shapes the other. The creation, definition, and implementation of law continually occurs within these realms and within the complex linkages that bind them together.

It is therefore important not only to examine the instrumental effectiveness of law, but also to explore the constitutive character of law. A constitutive approach looks at law not as something external to society, acting upon, regulating, and concretely affecting social activity. Rather, law is manifest internally, for it "shapes society from the inside out, by providing the principal categories that make social life seem natural, normal, cohesive, and coherent" (Sarat and Kearns 1993, 22). On this view, a study of law requires that we move beyond the exploration of law's effectiveness, narrowly construed, to an examination of "law's effects more broadly conceived" (23). This broad conception includes investigation of both legal and nonlegal effects; but, more, it means that we must look to the law as it shapes the beliefs, norms, and practices of social beings. Law, then, does more than establish rules and impose sanctions; it is implicated in the creation of meaning.

> Our gaze fastens on meaning, on the ways in which [people] make
> sense of what they do—practically, morally, expressively. . . juridi-

cally—by setting it within larger frames of signification, and how they keep those larger frames in place, or try to, by organizing what they do in terms of them. (Geertz 1983, 180)[4]

The constitutive perspective entails a decentering of legal analysis, and many scholars who study law and society have begun to adopt such a perspective, shifting to a broader focus of analysis (Gordon 1984; Brigham 1987; Harrington and Yngvesson 1990; Hunt 1985). This shift is to the many "local" levels of practical activity where law is at once imposed from above and created from below. Much scholarship on alternative dispute resolution makes this shift, exploring the move away from formal judicial avenues to informal and extrajudicial methods of handling disputes.[5] In addition, recent conflict management studies have taken this alternative perspective in exploring law from below, thereby providing "a more complex portrayal of law and courts in shaping and reflecting local practices and understandings" (Yngvesson 1988, 410; see also Engel 1984; and Merry 1985). Likewise, the new legal pluralism investigates the local and nonjudicial realms that shape and are shaped by law. Indeed, the new legal pluralism, as defined by Sally Engle Merry, highlights one of the important insights of a decentered approach: the plurality and multiplicity of law.

> According to the new legal pluralism, plural normative orders are found in virtually all societies. This is an extraordinarily powerful move, in that it places at the center of investigation the relationship between the official legal system and other forms of ordering that connect with but are in some ways separate from and dependent on it. The new legal pluralism moves away from questions about the effect of law on society or even the effect of society on law toward conceptualizing a more complex and interactive relationship between official and unofficial forms of ordering. Instead of mutual influences between two separate entities, this perspective sees plural forms of ordering as participating in the same social field. (1988, 873)

The approach pioneered by these and other scholars provides the foundation for the present study (Silbey and Sarat 1987). Although courts, judges, lawyers, and litigation remain important components of the analysis, the move is away from court-centered study.[6] "The concern is to document other forms of social regulation that draw on the symbols of the law, to a greater or lesser extent, but that operate in its shadows, its parking lots, and even down the street in mediation offices" (Merry 1988, 874). In examining these nonjudicial forms of social regulation in relation to judicial forms, the goal is to see how they are mutually constituted. This approach leads us to

> understand law not as something removed from social life, occasionally operating upon and struggling to regulate and shape social forms, but as fused with and thus inseparable from all the activities of living and knowing. (Silbey and Sarat 1987, 173)

The Constitutive Character of Legal Meaning

What is crucial in this decentering is an exploration into the constitutive nature of legal meaning. *Legal meaning* here refers not only to the meaning of specific laws but to the meanings attributed to the expressions, understandings, and practices that constitute legal and moral behavior. Legal and moral behavior manifest within and beyond state institutions is interpreted within a legal context. When the interpretations assigned to such behavior are shaped by legal consciousness, languages, symbols, or specific laws, legal meaning is constructed.

Three points should be stressed about this definition of legal meaning.[7] First, legal meaning is attributable to a broad range of perceptions, vocabularies, and activities. When individuals conceive of themselves as rights-bearing beings, for instance, legal meaning may be assigned. When an abortion protester expresses the view that we have a moral obligation to protect the unborn, legal meaning may be construed. When a peace activist locks herself to the gate of a nuclear weapons facility, we may find legal meaning in the act. And, certainly, when Congress passes a statute, we may interpret the meaning of the law.

Second, legal meaning so defined requires a broad understanding of the sources of meaning. The meanings attributed to legal and moral behavior find their sources not only in state-sanctioned institutions. Legislators writing statutes, judges interpreting statutes, and police officers enforcing statutes are central but not exclusive sources of legal meaning. Legal meaning is constructed by neighbors who argue over whether one should cut down a tree, by an employee who demands paid leave to care for a sick relative, and by an employer who refuses such a demand. The sources of legal meaning thus go well beyond government entities; they are located in average people who think, speak, and act within the legal context of society.

Third, the various sources of legal meaning interact in a complex manner; that is, legal meaning, as articulated within state institutions, constitutes and is constituted by legal meaning as articulated in nonjudicial and nonstate realms of social interaction. Hence, legal meaning is not simply created and dispersed from above; it is constructed from below.

There is no doubt that legal meaning, as articulated in state-sanctioned institutions, permeates society, shapes perceptions, and structures actions. Legal edicts, formulated by and received from government institutions, frame and define social consciousness and action. When legislatures and courts articulate specific laws, their words carry intent and content. On occasion, the intentions and substance of statutes are unambiguous, and certainly it is not uncommon for the public, legislators, and judges to ascribe the same meaning to written laws.

Nevertheless, we must recognize that the articulation of written law is rarely unequivocal. Words, and thus laws, contain multiple and diverse meanings. It is a mistake to think that it is always possible to fix the meaning of a linguistic form antecedently, in advance of its implementation and practical usage (Wittgenstein 1962). The indeterminate nature of language in general, and legal language in particular, results in the likelihood, maybe even the necessity, of various and often conflicting interpretations.[8]

In addition, it is a mistake to think that legal behavior, and thus legal meaning, begins and ends with written law. Legal images, vocabularies, and practices, derived from written laws, unwritten norms, cultural traditions, and so forth, are pervasive. The meanings assigned to these are surely subject to diverse interpretations.

Given the indeterminate and malleable nature of language, and the various manifestations of legal symbols and actions, the process of constituting legal meaning is frequently characterized by imagination and re-creation. Imagination and re-creation do not occur solely within the purview of official legal institutions. To be sure, legislatures, courts, and administrative agencies communicate, sanction, and enforce particular understandings of legal meaning; in essence, the state "polices" the boundaries of law. What's more, these understandings may well be prevalent and defined as "the law." Still, popular perceptions may differ from official perspectives. The flexibility of legal language offers maneuvering space for competing interpretations of meaning. These competing interpretations may challenge official definitions, influence perceptions and practices outside of official institutions, and find their way back into those institutions. Within the contested terrain of legal meaning, alternative images can shape, structure, and redefine the law.

We can thus speak of legal meaning as being constituted by and constitutive of society. Legal meaning is constituted by and in state institutions during the processes of drafting, interpreting, and enforcing specific laws. Various players influence these official processes, including legislators, judges, lawyers, administrators, lobbyists, interest groups, media, the public, and so forth. Legal meaning becomes constitutive of society as it permeates, informs, and structures the social realm, that is, as it becomes a part of the way people think, understand, and act. But the constitutive process is neither unidirectional nor determinate. People do not simply absorb legal meaning into their consciousness. Incorporating legal meaning into thought and action involves reconstruction of legal meaning. Hence, just as legal meaning constitutes individual and social identity, so too does individual and social identity constitute legal meaning. Understanding, speaking, and acting in legal ways can re-create and redefine legal meaning. Such reconstruction reverberates back through state institutions where meaning is continually constituted and reconstituted.

The battles over legal meaning ensue in legislatures, courtrooms, government agencies, and police stations, but they also emerge in schools, churches, community organizations, on the streets, and in the home. Debates over legal meaning can be heard on the radio and seen on television; they are communicated in newspapers, books, pamphlets, and magazines; they are articulated in law books and advertisements; and they are expressed in protests, rallies, and sit-ins.

To examine law, then, entails investigation into the constitutive nature of legal meaning. Such investigation involves exploration of the various realms of constitution. We must look both within and beyond state institutions, to both official and unofficial manifestations of law, to both the written and spoken word, and to both thought and practice. Overall, the investigation boils down to the following: How is law part of "imagining the real"? (Geertz 1983, 184).

Legal Meaning and Legal Consciousness

If we are to understand the constitutive character of legal meaning, we must explore the realm of understanding. Due to the flexible and indeterminate nature of legal language, meaning will be perceived and defined differently by different people. One of the battlegrounds in which the struggle over meaning is fought exists within the realm of consciousness.

Legal consciousness can be defined simply as "the way people think about law and legality" (Merry 1990, 4). When a person ascribes legal meaning to an event, the ascription is founded upon legal consciousness. Generally speaking, we can say that legal consciousness consists of attitudes, definitions, and expectations concerning matters of law. These components of legal consciousness, like legal meaning, vary greatly from person to person.

One's attitudes toward law may be characterized by such things as hopefulness, trust, confidence, indifference, skepticism, suspicion, and fear. An individual, for example, may view legal structures as necessary for the maintenance of order and stability in society. Such an individual may be disposed to a law-abiding view of legal matters. Alternatively, an individual may conceive of legal entities as repressive tools of the powerful. This conception may foster suspicious and fearful attitudes. A third individual may perceive of legal forms as the embodiment of morality and thus hold a hopeful and faithful attitude.

Legal consciousness also includes definitions. Individual understandings of legal definitions tend to be comprised of specific legal rules (e.g., traffic regulations, drug laws, and tax laws) and of specific legal procedures (e.g., trial by jury and habeas corpus). Legal definitions also consist more broadly of understandings of justice. An individual may define *justice* in terms of such things as the right to a fair trial, freedom from government interference, equal pay for equal work, and so on. Legal definitions further include an interpretive component. For instance, a member of the National Rifle Association may define the Second Amendment of the Constitution as protecting the right to own an automatic weapon, whereas a gun control advocate may define the same amendment as affording no broad-based right to gun ownership.

Finally, legal consciousness consists of expectations regarding the proper and effective functioning of the legal system and legal claims.

Expectations include such things as whether legal violations will be discovered and enforced and whether "justice" will be served. Some individuals presume that written laws will be effectively or fairly enforced while others expect ineffective or discriminatory enforcement. Some may expect that rights assertions will lead to justice whereas others may more skeptically expect rights claims to be ignored.

The content and extent of an individual's attitudes, definitions, and expectations depend greatly upon the context of an individual's experiences. "The law looks different, for example, to law professors, tax evaders, welfare recipients, blue-collar homeowners, and burglars" (Merry 1990, 5). Moreover, legal consciousness is not static; instead, it shifts with experiences. Experiences involving legal education or interaction with the law often foster changes in legal consciousness. Especially important are experiences that result in outcomes contrary to one's expectations. If an individual has faith that the legal system will produce just outcomes but then experiences a perceived injustice not remedied by law, attitudes, definitions, and expectations may shift. Thus, consciousness "changes with contradictory experiences" (5).

It is important to note that not all perceptions of legal meaning carry the same weight or power. Some perceptions will be privileged; for example, some perceptions will have the authority of the state behind them, and some will be widespread and accepted, and some will be heralded as the "true" and "correct" perceptions. Other perceptions will be marginalized; for example, some will be viewed as radical or invalid or, more simply, as unsanctioned understandings. Still others will compete somewhere in the middle for the privileged position. Legal consciousness is shaped largely by privileged or prevailing legal meaning. Yet, within contested terrains of legal meaning, competition flourishes regarding which meaning should prevail. Legal consciousness is influenced by these contests. Furthermore, legal consciousness shapes these contests and may, as a result, influence accepted legal meaning.

Legal Meaning and Language

Legal consciousness and legal meaning both take shape in the form of language. Although legal language is renowned for its characteristic technical jargon, what is more important for understanding the constitutive nature of legal meaning is the complex, open, and flexible quality of legal language.

Consider the language of such legal concepts as equal protection, contractual obligation, due process, liability, and rights. The meaning of these concepts has been and continues to be the subject of extensive debate. Each concept invites diverse interpretations; each can be used in a variety of contexts. Equal protection, for instance, can be understood in terms of equal opportunity, equality of results, equal treatment, political equality, social equality, economic equality, and more. On the one hand, equal protection is thought to imply sameness, but on the other it is thought to suggest similar treatment of difference. The issue of who deserves to be considered under the principle of equal protection is another subject of dispute. In short, the meaning embodied in equal protection and other forms of legal language is neither singular nor definitive.

Constituting legal meaning involves a discursive process aimed at defining the central concepts of legal vocabularies. This discursive process takes place largely in the official realms of the courts and legislatures and in the arena of legal and philosophical scholarship. In these locations, judges, lawmakers, and scholars interpret and construct the meaning of legal language and then attempt to put forward definitive interpretations.

These interpretations, while frequently purported to be "true," are hardly irrevocable or immutable. Indeed, the dissemination of legal language and its meanings from these realms is incomplete and imprecise. Few people read legal opinions, legislative debates, or scholarly interpretations of legal concepts (Brigham 1990). Even if legal and scholarly interpretations were widely read, they would still be indeterminate since they are themselves diverse and subject to interpretation.

None of this means that the average person fails to use or develop conceptions of legal language. To the contrary, the language of equal protection, due process, liability, rights, and more is ubiquitous within public discourse. Within this ubiquity we can discern the further constitution of legal language. The use of legal language on the streets, in protests, at union meetings, and at work offers constructions of legal language that shape legal meaning.

It is therefore important to recognize that the meaning of legal language is constituted not only within the judicial, legislative, and scholarly realms but within the realm of public discourse. Legal language as it is constituted in the former arenas informs public discourse. It provides the frames of reference for perceiving and defining legal meaning. But the communication of legal language and its meaning is partial and ambiguous. In the process of translation into public discourse different understandings develop and new meanings are articulated. Within public discourse these meanings may become more prevalent than official meanings. Furthermore, these interpretations of legal language may offer new frames of reference for official definitions of meaning.

The discursive process that constitutes the meaning of legal language can therefore be seen as a dialectical one. It is a process of interaction and communication, of formulation and reformulation. The malleability of language results in dialogue out of which legal meaning is continually constructed and reconstructed.

Legal Meaning, Practice, and Strategy:
Instrumental Constitutivism

Legal meaning does not reside solely in the mind and the word. It resides also in action. A complete understanding of legal meaning must therefore consider law in practice. This suggests that we should look not only to written law and its interpretation in judicial opinions. We should look not only to legal consciousness and the articulation of legal language. We should look also to actions taken in response to, in support of, and in reaction against legal conceptions and articulations. Law, from this perspective, must be seen

> not as a set of rules to be memorized, but as an *activity*, as something that people do with their minds and with each other as they act in relation both to a body of authoritative legal material and to the circumstances and events of the actual world. The law is a set of social and intellectual practices that defines a universe and culture in which you will learn to function. (White 1985a, 52)[9]

The practical activities that contribute to law and thus to legal meaning take many forms and occur in many arenas. They include actions to influence legislation, such as lobbying and campaigning; actions that directly involve the judicial sphere, such as litigation; practices that broadly seek to advance certain principles and reforms, such as protests and education campaigns; and practices of resistance, including ignoring and defying the law. These practical activities shape and are shaped by legal meaning. Existing perceptions of legal meaning guide, structure, and constrain social and political practice. In addition, social and political practice, often aimed at challenging law, shapes legal meaning. "[L]egal norms and conventions are constantly reconstructed in content, meaning, and tactical significance through political practice" (McCann and Silverstein 1993, 133).

The relationship between practice and legal meaning highlights the importance of examining strategic uses of legal forms. If, as suggested here, legal meaning structures and is structured by action, then exploration of strategic action is crucial to an exploration of legal meaning. Attempts to strategically deploy, for example, legal languages, legal statutes, or litigation are shaped and informed by legal meaning; in turn, these attempts shape and redefine legal meaning.

Law therefore must be understood as a political and strategic resource. This view, elaborated in Stuart Scheingold's *The Politics of Rights* (1974) and expanded upon by others, holds that litigation and legal rights should be seen as resources for groups seeking change (see Milner 1986; and Olson 1984). As Michael McCann suggests,

> Legal knowledge can be a resource in that it facilitates interaction and participation in different institutional sites and social spaces. It contributes to "common sense" expectations and understandings through which citizens routinely negotiate relations with each other. Such participation does not necessarily just induce conformity and reproduce existing relations but may also enable resistance to, or reconstruction of, those relations. (1994, 283)

In viewing law, and therefore legal meaning, as political resources, we can discern both promises and drawbacks. Assertions of law and legal meaning can be mobilized to promote social change and to redistribute power, but such assertions are also limited in their capacity to redistribute power. Used as a strategic tool, alternative expressions of legal meaning can confront prevailing expressions. Law, more generally, can challenge the existing system in attempts to advance reform. But those using law must be wary of the potential dangers and costs inherent in this type of enterprise.[10] Users of the law must recognize that changes in the law and alterations of predominant legal meaning occur, if at all, at the margins, in the gaps and cracks of the prevailing legal edifice.

Examining legal meaning in light of strategic practice thus points us toward investigation of the strategic choices made by those who resort to legal forms. The connection between meaning, practice, and strategy also highlights the importance of considering instrumentalism within a constitutive analysis. Incorporating instrumentalism within a constitutive analysis reveals the way strategic choices and the effects of these choices are implicated in the construction of meaning. Connecting instrumentalism and constitutivism leads to the investigation of several important questions. How do users of the legal languages, meanings, and practices choose their actions? How does legal meaning constitute those choices? Do users act with an awareness of the implications their actions may have for legal meaning? If so, how does such awareness influence choices and legal meaning? If strategic action is significantly constituted by prevailing legal meaning, to what extent can such action challenge and alter legal meaning?

Legal Meaning and Social Movements

To explore these questions, a further question arises: How might we go about such a study of legal meaning? If, as suggested above, legal meaning is constitutive of and constituted by society, where should we look to investigate the constitutive character of law? There are, of course, numerous places from which to start, including sites within and beyond the state. The present study chooses one of these places and begins there—with the study of social movements.

Social movements provide an excellent point of departure for a decentered study of law and an analysis of the interaction between the official and unofficial realms in which law is constituted. We can locate the practical activity of social movements in multiple locations. These include locations internal to the state and internal to the courts. Social movements lobby legislatures, become active in electoral politics, and often use litigation to advance movement goals. In addition, social movements frequently act in locations beyond the state and the courts, using such tactics as boycotts, protests, and civil disobedience. Furthermore, these multiple sites are importantly related. For example, protest activities in nonstate realms influence and are influenced by activities within courts and legislatures.[11]

Social movements also provide an excellent point of departure for a study of legal meaning in the United States. A study of movement

activists and practices is likely to reveal insights into legal consciousness, the use of legal language, and practical activity involving the law.
With their increasing turn to the legal system, social movements can
help to illustrate the constitutive character of law as well as the often
contested nature of legal meaning.

Several scholars have examined the relationship between social
movements and the legal system in light of the constitutive character of
the law. According to John Brigham, for instance, "Movements are constituted in legal terms when they see the world in those terms and organize themselves accordingly. . . . Legal forms are evident in the language, purposes, and strategies of movement activity as practices"
(1987, 306). In a more specific examination, Amy Bartholomew and
Alan Hunt suggest the constitutive character of rights language.

> One potentially fruitful way of transcending instrumentalist con-
> ceptions of rights is by reconceptualizing them as the crystalliza-
> tion of past struggles and the resulting balances of forces or power.
> They are thereby legitimated and play a role in constituting the ter-
> rain for subsequent social action and interaction. Rights thus typi-
> cally constitute arenas of struggle or contestation. (1990, 551)

Along these lines, the present study investigates law and legal
meaning as they constitute social movements. But, more than this, the
analysis here seeks to examine the ways in which social movements
constitute law and legal meaning. When social movements, as Brigham
states, see the world in legal terms and organize themselves in accor-
dance with those terms, one side of law's constitutive character can be
discerned. The other equally important side can be seen when we consider that as social movements see and organize themselves in legal
terms they are redefining and re-creating the law and its meaning. As
social movements express alternative conceptions of legal meaning, the
law is reconstituted.

A study of the relationship between social movement activism and
legal meaning can helpfully highlight several important issues. First,
such a study can highlight the impact of legal meaning on society. It can
indicate how official articulations of legal meaning are received and
understood. In so doing, this type of analysis may reveal the extent to
which law is effectively imposed from above or resisted from below.

Second, and relatedly, an examination of legal meaning and movement activism can help to illustrate the construction of legal meaning and the influence society has on this construction. Movement percep-tions, definitions, and articulations of legal meaning may, at times, challenge official views of law or prevailing conceptions of legal mean-ing. In advancing alternative constructions of legal meaning, social movements may succeed in adjusting official law. On the other hand, attempts to alter official law or prevailing conceptions of legal meaning may fail. Exploring such attempts and the extent to which they succeed should offer insight into the constitution of legal meaning.

Third, such a study can provide insight into the opportunities and barriers produced as social movements constitute and are constituted by the law. In this regard, an examination of legal meaning and social movements may help us assess the effectiveness of turning to the law in attempts to advance social change. As such, this type of study follows a line of research that focuses on the effectiveness of using law to advance reform (Medcalf 1978; Bruun 1982; Tushnet 1987; Rosenberg 1991). However, this line of research does not generally emphasize the constitutive character of legal meaning as it has been defined above, and thus it does not examine effectiveness in light of this constitution. I shall argue that exploring social movements with an eye toward the constitutive character of legal meaning offers a more comprehensive assessment of the effectiveness of a legal strategy.

Legal Meaning and Rights Language: The Case of
the Animal Rights Movement

This book explores the constitutive nature of legal meaning through an in-depth analysis of a contemporary social movement: the animal rights movement. There are a number of reasons why animal rights advocacy should provide an interesting case study for examining legal meaning through the particular approach to law discussed above.[12] For one thing, this movement has not been studied much. While the con-cept of animal rights has received a good amount of philosophical attention, the movement has not; and, although groups seeking to pro-tect animals are not new, over the past two decades the movement has gained considerable momentum.[13] Thus, animal rights groups are part of a rapidly growing movement that has received little academic atten-tion.

Lack of attention, however, is not a sufficient reason to delve into a case study. The primary reason for exploring a particular case rests in whether it provides special insight and evidence for analysis. For the purposes of this study, what is at issue is whether the movement is informative about law and legal meaning.

Given that animal rights activism increasingly involves the law, a study of this movement should prove informative. Like other social movements, the animal rights movement has increased its reliance on the judicial system. Turning to the courts to halt hunts, to prevent vivisection, and to alter various practices involving nonhuman animals,[14] movement organizations are becoming seasoned users of a litigative strategy. Animal rights lawyers, although still few in number, have become important players in this movement's attempts to advocate reform.

While the increasing employment of a litigative strategy should provide interesting insights into the constitutive nature of legal meaning, what is more significant for the present study is an analysis of this movement's use of rights language. The language of rights in the United States is a central element of law and legal meaning. Rights language is also prevalent within public consciousness, discourse, and practice. We live in a society in which people see themselves as rights-bearing beings and in which legal, political, and social relationships are commonly defined in terms of rights. Appeals to rights are regularly heard both within and beyond the courtroom. In short, rights language is a dominant component of the legal, political, and social realms, and it is embedded within thought and practice.

Animal advocates have increasingly defined their cause in terms of rights. In doing so, movement activists have relied partly on philosophical grounding in rights theory to appropriate rights language and to attribute meaning to rights. This philosophical foundation attempts to extend the meaning of rights, calling for the application of moral rights to animals. It further translates this demand for moral rights into a demand that legal rights be extended to animals.

At the same time, individuals and groups within the animal advocacy movement are divided over the rights label and are wary of its use. Many within the movement worry that rights language has become a "red flag" or a buzzword. Others are uncomfortable with attempts to apply rights to animals because the prevailing meaning of legal and moral rights associates rights with humans and excludes nonhuman animals. Moreover, the debate over rights parallels a conflict between the traditional animal welfare movement and the newer, more radical, animal rights movement. The label of animal rights has only been popularly applied to the movement over the past two decades. Although the movement now calls itself the animal rights movement and is depicted in the media and in politics as a rights movement, many proponents of animal welfare avoid the rights terminology because of its connections to the perceived extremism of animal rights claims.

The debate and conflict over the issue of rights make the animal rights movement an interesting case. What we see in this case is a marginalized movement that has deployed a prevailing legal language and tried to apply this language to a new group of beings and interests. The movement is therefore attempting to expand the language of rights to a realm of relations in which rights generally have not been applied. The movement has, like others, appropriated a dominant way of speaking and making meaning in attempts to gain credibility, acceptance, and transformative power. Yet this appropriation is fraught with difficulties, including, but not limited to, the conflict, contention, and division that the idea of animal rights has caused within the movement itself.

The appropriation of rights language by this marginalized movement is important for another reason. The animal rights movement, in using rights talk, seeks to leave the margins by appealing to mainstream beliefs and languages. But at the same time, the movement challenges the prevailing conception of legal meaning, questions the concept of rights, and seeks to adjust and revise it in significant ways. By applying rights to nonhuman animals, activists are not simply extending the notion to a previously excluded group. More than that, they are calling into question the long-established meanings of rights. In particular, as we shall see, the call for animal rights seeks to infuse the values of sentience, relationship, caring, responsibility, and community into the meaning of rights.

Thus, we have a movement that is at once constituted by and seeking to reconstitute the language of rights and prevailing legal meaning. The movement has unquestionably been shaped by rights, that is, shaped by common understandings, definitions, and usages of rights. Concomitantly, this movement has sought to re-create and redefine the meaning of rights. This is what may be most important about a study of the animal rights movement: it may help to demonstrate the effects of a movement's appropriation of rights talk on the construction of legal meaning.

In demonstrating these effects, we will see that the appropriation of rights language by a social movement does not begin or end with that movement. The use of rights language by one social movement and the constitution of legal meaning that results often affect other movements. A study of the animal rights movement illustrates the connections between social movements by uncovering the influence earlier movements had on the construction of rights language. Activists within the animal rights movement continually note their connections to other social movements, including movements for civil rights, women's rights, and gay and lesbian rights. As attorney Gary Francione stated, these movements "made it acceptable for people to talk about animals having rights. If you had started talking, say, in 1950 of animal rights, people would have thought you were completely out of your mind. They still had segregated bathrooms."

There is another very interesting dimension to the animal rights movement that makes it an intriguing case. As already noted, the movement uses both rights language and litigation to affect change. However, the language of rights ironically is used more frequently outside of judicial institutions than within them. That is, lawyers in the movement rarely speak of animal rights in the courtroom. This is not surprising since the courts and legislatures have not recognized legal rights for animals and are far from amenable to the concept of animal rights. Yet the language of animal rights plays a significant role in the movement, and lawyers frequently speak of animal rights outside the courthouse. Thus, we have an unusual case in which animal rights talk is frequently used outside of judicial institutions and rarely used inside them. At the same time, activists and lawyers attempt to use rights in the nonjudicial realm to eventually make animal rights acceptable in the judicial realm.

Equally intriguing, rights talk itself is not out of bounds in the courtroom. When rights talk is used, however, it is not in the form of animal rights but in the form of human rights. Lawyers and movement advocates have come to realize that human rights claims can be strategically effective in advancing the cause of animal rights. As a result, lawyers and movement organizations advance human rights claims such as the First Amendment right to freedom of speech in order to promote animal rights.

These ironic relationships between animal rights and human rights, and between litigation and rights in general, may offer further insight into the constitutive character of legal meaning. For instance, using human rights in court to advance animal rights beyond the courts may have interesting implications for the construction of the meaning of rights and the meaning of litigation. In short, an analysis of these relationships may help to illustrate the construction of legal meaning as it develops along the nexus of language and litigation and as it occurs when political practice and judicial action are interwoven.

Overall, the animal rights movement provides an excellent case for exploring the connections between rights language, legal activity, and social change in American culture. The case presents an example of practical activity in both judicial and nonjudicial realms that attempts to shape and influence the judicial and the nonjudicial. This activity has been, and continues to be, shaped by prevailing legal meaning. All of this should then add to an assessment of legal meaning in general and rights talk in particular. As such, this study can join the scholarly debate on the relationship between rights language and social movement activism and the more general discussion regarding the effectiveness of using law, litigation, and legal discourse to foster social change.[15]

By offering additional insight into the implications of rights talk, an analysis of the animal rights movement can contribute to the general debate over rights language. It can help us obtain evidence as to whether, in what ways, and under what conditions the use of rights language constitutes legal meaning and, in turn, contributes to social change. Moreover, it can help us determine whether and in what ways the vocabulary of rights is capable of challenging existing institutions and prevailing understandings of law. Thus, the particulars of this case should help shed light on the limits and possibilities of deploying law and legal meaning, that is, on the potential for using rights language to transform prevailing social conditions.

Methodology

Attempts to answer questions on law and legal meaning are greatly aided by in-depth analysis of specific movements. Past movement examinations attest to this point (Handler 1978; Scheingold 1974; Tushnet 1987; Olson 1984; McCann 1994). Several social movements have been explored within the context of legal analysis. The civil rights movement is, not surprisingly, the primary one, since this movement's appeal to the law achieved some degree of success—at least in the attainment of a formal recognition of rights—and provided significant inspiration for other movements. In fact, the civil rights movement may be cited as the major instigator of the study of the relationship between law and social movement activism. The dispute over the purported success of the civil rights movement has led many scholars to question the effectiveness of using the legal system (Scheingold 1974; Bell 1985; Tushnet 1987; Rosenberg 1991). As a result, the controversy over whether or not legal tactics are effective has been applied to other movements, including movements for women's rights, the rights of the mentally disabled, workers' rights, the rights of Native Americans, and so on (Schneider 1986; Rose 1985; Milner 1986; Klare 1982; Medcalf 1978).

Many of these studies demonstrate that we can better understand law and legal meaning by looking at the workings of law within and upon particular groups and relations. Understanding the effects of law does not come solely from looking at the courts, lawyers, judges, and case precedents. It comes also from looking at how the people—in this case people within a movement and people responding to the movement—are influenced by law and how they, in turn, affect law through their actions. Understanding law comes from exploring how people who are educated by a social movement are affected by legal meaning and how movement activists make strategic choices based on their views of law. Thus, the study of particular social movements provides a kind of social laboratory for exploring the legal system.

Investigating these issues within the animal rights movement requires an in-depth analysis of the movement, its deployment of rights language, and the interaction between its activities within the legal and extralegal realms. This interpretive analysis with its decentered approach leads to a research methodology that is multidimensional.[16] I employ what has been referred to as a "triangulating" approach (McCann 1994). This approach recognizes that, when direct measures are difficult or impossible to obtain,

> one sensible response is to rely on a variety of techniques that supplement one another. . . . The basic assumption is that multiple techniques can, to some degree, compensate for each other's defi-

ciencies; furnish a broader foundation for critical analysis of interpretive constructions; and provide more plausible support for
arguments confirmed by common findings. (16)

I employ this multidimensional approach by using multiple techniques
and multiple sources that include the following.

Content Analysis

This work is concerned specifically with the constitutive character of
rights language. To examine the use and constitutive character of rights
language, I look to the way activists, organizations, and the media
apply the vocabulary. To this end, content analysis of diverse published documents, including newspapers, popular periodicals, and
movement literature, is utilized to explore how the appeal to rights is
made by movement insiders and outsiders and how the meaning of
rights is constructed.

Analysis of Philosophical Writings

The rights language employed by the movement is founded upon
philosophical writings that deal with the moral question of whether
animals have rights. Using this literature, I explore the historical development of rights talk and its application to animals. I combine this
analysis with the content analysis of movement literature to demonstrate the construction of legal meaning that results from connections
between theory and movement practice.

Analysis of Litigative Experiences and
Legal Writings

To examine how judicial and extrajudicial arenas are mutually constitutive and how the meaning of rights takes shape along this nexus, I
investigate the diverse litigative experiences of the animal rights movement and the legal writings that have been generated from these experiences. Included in this analysis are examinations of judicial opinions,
law review articles, media presentations of litigation, and movement
portrayals of litigative activity.

Participant Observation

The fourth component of this approach draws on my own experiences in observing the activities of animal rights groups. I have attended numerous meetings of animal rights organizations, observed protest activity, listened to speeches given by animal activists, and talked informally with group members. In addition, I attended a seminar on how to become an animal rights activist. From these experiences I have been able to observe a great deal regarding the perception of rights and how the language of rights is employed within the movement. In short, participant observation offered the opportunity to witness the constitution of legal meaning as it occurs within everyday political practice.

In-Depth Interviews

The final and maybe most significant component of my research comes from information gathered through intensive, open-ended interviews conducted with 25 movement activists and participants from a variety of groups across the country. I began the interviews in the spring of 1990 and completed most of them by the spring of 1991. These interviews were conducted with the goal of understanding movement tactics regarding rights, litigation, and the various motivations for appealing to rights and the legal system. As such, these interviews inquired into activists' perspectives on a variety of issues involving the appeal to rights, the strategic use of litigation, and the effectiveness of movement strategies. I used the interviews to explore how activists and participants think about rights: how they define and perceive rights, the sources of these definitions and perceptions, and their overall faith in the concept of rights. I also used the interviews to investigate whether activists are aware of the purported risks and costs of rights language. Combining these interviews with other data provides important additional information for examining the construction and strategic deployment of legal meaning.

Looking Ahead

Through the use of these varied techniques and sources, and using a decentered approach, the chapters that follow examine the various articulations and definitions of legal meaning that are salient to the animal rights movement and constitute the consciousness, language, and strategies of movement participants. In addition, this analysis investigates the effects that legal perceptions and practices of movement proponents have on the continual construction of legal meaning. Through an exploration of this mutual constitution, this work further examines whether and in what ways the deployment of the law may be effective in advancing reform.

The methodological techniques outlined above are useful because they focus attention on the workings of rights in the minds and practical activities of people who act in realms both internal and external to the judicial system. The approach thus provides insight into the workings of rights and the legal system both within and outside of judicial institutions. In the end, I use the evidence acquired from this study to reevaluate questions regarding how far rights can be extended without losing their power; how far rights can be altered to advance values of relationship, responsibility, and community; and how rights can be used to mobilize movement activism.

Toward these ends, the remainder of this work proceeds as follows. Chapters 2 through 4 focus on rights language by examining two central questions: (1) Does the extension of rights language to animals diminish the meaning and power of rights? and (2) Are animal rights activists misguided by a naive faith in rights to deploy a language that impedes social change? To examine these questions, chapter 2 reviews the philosophical foundations of rights and examines the extension of these foundations to animals. Chapter 2 also reviews philosophical approaches that compete with animal rights theory. Based on the exploration of these theoretical foundations, I argue that the philosophical expansion of rights to animals has strengthened rather than undermined the power of rights by infusing the language with alternative meaning.

Chapter 3 proceeds to examine whether the extension of rights to animals in the political realm has diminished the power and meaning of the language. I argue, as I do in chapter 2, that the extension of rights has bolstered the language by imbuing it with new meaning. In particular, I suggest that rights talk, as it is used within movement literature and activities, moves away from the traditional emphasis on individualism and separation toward an emphasis on the alternative values of relationship, responsibility, care, and community. As such, I contend that the experience of the animal rights movement counters critics who suggest that the meaning of rights talk necessarily undermines egalitarian and communitarian values. Indeed, I assert that the very extension of rights to nonhuman animals poses a challenge to the liberal individualistic underpinnings of rights and thus reconstructs the meaning of rights.

Chapter 4 continues the focus on rights, exploring how movement activists understand and deploy the language in strategic action. In this chapter I offer an alternative perspective on the deployment of rights, suggesting that activists are not misguided by a naive faith in the discourse. Instead, I provide evidence supporting the view that activists have a sophisticated, flexible, and critical understanding of rights that leads them to deploy the language in a strategic and productive manner. In addition, I put forth a variety of arguments suggesting that, in the context of present-day American political culture, it makes a good deal of sense to strategically deploy the powerful, albeit limited, language of rights. In sum, chapters 2 through 4 explore the philosophical and practical activism of this movement. In light of this exploration, these chapters suggest that the strategic mobilization of rights language reconstitutes the meaning of rights in ways that challenge the standard underpinnings and implications of the language.

Chapters 5 through 7 move beyond rights language to examine the litigative experiences of the animal rights movement. I argue that to understand litigative activity and the legal meaning of such activity we need to combine instrumental and constitutive perspectives regarding the law. These perspectives when properly informed by each other offer important insights into the effectiveness of litigation and the broad effects the litigative process has for the construction of legal meaning.

Each of these chapters provides in-depth analysis of several legal cases brought by the movement to advance the cause of animals. Chapter 5 examines these cases by means of the standard instrumental approach, emphasizing the direct consequences of this litigative activity such as movement access to the courtroom, judicial victories, the establishment of precedent, and the translation of court decisions into effective implementation. The chapter concludes by noting that, in terms of instrumental effectiveness, litigation on behalf of animals has had only mixed success.

Chapter 6 moves beyond these direct effects and makes the case

that when instrumentalism takes constitutivism seriously we can see
that litigation has multiple, indirect consequences for movement activity. In particular, I argue that litigation has important implications for
education, movement building, and movement leverage against opponents. I further suggest that once we consider both direct and indirect
effects litigation appears to be a much more effective tool for advancing
social change.

Chapter 7 returns to legal meaning by offering a constitutive interpretation of litigation but one that is informed by instrumentalism. Litigation, I suggest, is importantly connected to the constitution of legal
meaning. Judicial rulings offer certain constructions of the meaning
and value of animals, rights, individualism, autonomy, and more.
However, these constructions are challenged and resisted by animal
advocates who, through a strategically instrumental approach, put forward alternative constructions of litigative meaning. Thus, I assert that
litigation has important implications for the constitution of legal meaning but that these implications are importantly connected to the strategic deployment of litigation.

Chapter 8 concludes the work by examining how the meaning of
rights influences social movement identity and the public's perceptions
of that identity. I suggest that by challenging the prevailing meaning of
rights, the animal rights movement constructs its identity in terms of an
altered vision of rights. However, I further contend that, since the public's understanding of rights remains bounded by traditional conceptions, the turn to animal rights fosters a negative public perception of
the movement's identity. The relationship between rights and identity
is therefore a double-edged sword that gives the movement the power
to define itself but is constrained by public constructions of meaning.

Chapter 2

Expanding the Circle: The Evolution of Animal Rights

Once we acknowledge life and sentiency in the other animals, we are bound to acknowledge what follows, the right to life, liberty and pursuit of happiness.

—Brigid Brophy

[T]here is such a thing as an evolving ethic where the norms of stewardship and responsibility to class to sex to race are now moving to its logical whole, and that is to sentient creatures.

—John Kullberg

The contemporary animal rights movement has a strong philosophical foundation that is primarily derived from Western liberal political thought. The philosophical underpinnings and controversies within the movement come largely from two schools of thought developed during the Enlightenment: natural rights theory and utilitarianism.[1] In addition, more recent theoretical approaches such as feminism, ecofeminism, and ecological analyses that stress holistic views have gained increasing prominence in the dialogue regarding animals.

Despite the various theoretical approaches that have been applied to animal issues, the language of rights has become dominant within the philosophical debate over animals. Several philosophers have attempted to find a basis for animal rights. Moreover, theorists using alternative approaches continue to frame their work in terms of the debate over rights,[2] and scholars opposing the various attempts to increase respect for and liberation of animals generally have responded by entering the debate over animal rights.

The ascendance of rights talk in the philosophical realm has been matched in the political realm. Over the past two decades, activists concerned about animals have taken up rights talk. The 1970s and 1980s

witnessed a move away from the discourse of compassion that had
been the primary mode of conversation concerning animals for more
than a century.[3] This move away from compassion—and away from
the animal welfare movement, which employed the discourse—was
inspired by philosopher Peter Singer's 1975 work, *Animal Liberation*.
Prompted by Singer, activism surrounding animals moved beyond
attempts to treat animals more humanely and took on a more radical
form calling for the abolition of all animal exploitation. However, the
movement did not become the "animal liberation movement," nor did
the fact that Singer's work was based on utilitarianism inhibit activists
from turning to rights. The ironic result for Singer and utilitarianism
has been the growth of a contemporary movement known as the "animal rights movement."

The contemporary political movement for animals thus has turned
to the language of rights and to the competing philosophical foundations associated with rights. With this move, many groups working on
behalf of animals have also turned to the legal language of rights. In so
doing, the movement has adopted an indefinite language shaped by
various philosophical, political, and legal meanings.

How has the meaning of rights constituted the attitudes, goals, and
practices of the animal rights movement? Have prevailing definitions
of moral and legal rights been accepted by movement activists? If so,
have animal rights activists been misled by a naive faith in rights to
deploy a counterproductive language?[4] Or have movement activists
sought to challenge prevailing conceptions of rights by re-creating and
redefining the meaning of rights? Do the words and strategies of this
movement foster alternative images of rights that counter dominant
definitions?

This chapter begins to explore how the meaning of rights has constituted this movement and how the turn to rights talk by this movement constitutes meaning. After first offering a brief history of the animal advocacy movement, the chapter then traces the philosophical
foundations of animal rights so that we may begin to understand the
construction of meaning associated with animal rights. As we shall see,
the philosophical debates surrounding animal issues offer various constructions of meaning, many of which develop notions of rights in general and animal rights in particular. By tracing these philosophical
foundations, we can examine: (1) the philosophical extension of rights

language to animals and (2) the concepts and languages that compete with the notion of animal rights.

With the philosophical debates as a backdrop, we can then ask what the extension of rights language to animals does to the overall meaning of rights. In this regard, we will explore several questions. Are critics correct in suggesting that the extension of rights drains the language of its meaning, content, and power? Or, in contrast, can rights be effectively stretched to include animals? Is rights language filled with alternative meaning when expanded beyond humans? Can such an expansion of "the circle" reconstruct the meaning of rights and reinforce the power and content of the language?

Through an investigation of these questions, this chapter lays the groundwork so that we may examine in the following chapters the movement's political appropriation of rights language and the implications for the legal meaning of rights. If the philosophical foundations of animal rights fill rights language with alternative meaning but this meaning is not articulated or accepted by movement activists, then critics may still be correct in saying that the power of rights language has been undermined. In addition, if the general meaning of rights is either drained or reconstructed, we must ask what this does to the legal meaning of rights. Thus, this chapter provides the background that will allow us to proceed with the discussion of how the legal meaning of rights constitutes and is constituted by social movement activism.

The History of the Animal Advocacy Movement

The history of concerted Western activism for animals dates back to the mid–eighteenth century. Prior to that time, activism on behalf of animals was sparse, although a few examples of animal protectionism can be found. For instance, in 1567, Pope Pius V issued a decree condemning bullfighting (Niven 1967, 43). In general, however, most activism for animals prior to the eighteenth century involved individuals who chose to treat animals compassionately. Both Pythagoras of ancient Greece and Leonardo da Vinci of the Renaissance reportedly purchased caged birds in order to set them free (39). These and other animal sympathizers spoke out on behalf of animals and took some individual actions to protect them. Nonetheless, organized efforts to safeguard animals were largely nonexistent.

The animal advocacy movement developed in the 1800s. Since its appearance, the movement has generally been divided into two branches, one calling for humane treatment of animals and the other demanding a complete end to human use and abuse of animals. Advocates pressing primarily for improved treatment of nonhumans fall within what is referred to as the animal welfare movement or the humane movement. Advocates in favor of abolishing animal experimentation, meat consumption, and the like, have referred to their branch of the movement in a number of ways: the animal rights movement, the antivivisection movement, and the animal liberation movement. As we shall see below, through most of the nineteenth and twentieth centuries the call for humane treatment of animals dominated the advocacy movement. It was not until the 1970s that the animal rights movement established itself as a powerful branch of animal advocacy.

The Birth of the Animal Welfare Movement

In the 1800s, a concerted effort took shape in England to advance the well-being of animals. This was preceded by a sixty-year period in which numerous works were published that critiqued the prevalent cruelty to animals. These included publications that condemned cock throwing, denounced cruel treatment of horses and cattle, and promoted the notion that humans have a duty to treat animals with kindness (Niven 1967, 53–54).[5] Although these writings were well beyond the mainstream, Charles Niven's history of the humane movement suggests that

> the literary effort during the years 1740 to 1800 was slowly softening up the resistance of the general public to change. The writers were, so to speak, the artillery bombarding a position from a reasonably safe distance; the brunt of the fighting had to be done by the Members of Parliament. (55)

In 1800, the fight in Parliament commenced and the history of humane legislation was born. Sir W. Pultiney introduced a bill in the English Parliament to stop bullbaiting (57). Although the bill failed to pass, the legislation received much publicity and led to an increase in the debate over animal cruelty. In 1809, a more comprehensive bill aimed at preventing "wanton and malicious cruelty to animals" passed the House of Lords but failed in the House of Commons (Carson 1972, 49). It was not until 1822 that legislation safeguarding animals was enacted into law in England. In that year, the Martin's Act—designed to prevent cruelty to cattle—passed both houses of Parliament.[6]

At about the same time, organized activism in realms beyond the legislature began to grow. The Society for the Prevention of Cruelty to Animals (SPCA) was formed in 1824 as a private organization to enforce the new law (Carson 1972, 53). Widely accepted as the first animal protection organization, the SPCA sparked the initial growth of what became known as the animal welfare movement. Although the SPCA struggled early on, its fortunes changed in 1840 when Queen Victoria decreed that the group become the Royal SPCA. Soon after, additional branches of the newly named RSPCA were established, and similar organizations were formed in several European countries (54).

In the early years, the welfare movement in England focused on cruelty to domesticated animals. However, in the 1860s, a new branch of the animal advocacy movement was born: the antivivisection movement. Led by Frances Power Cobbe, this arm of the movement sought to protect animals used in scientific experimentation. But soon after the antivivisection movement began to split. Some within the movement demanded the total abolition of vivisection while others took the more moderate position of wishing to minimize the suffering of animals used in experiments. This particular split also led to a more general division between antivivisectionists and those on the welfare side.[7] Despite these schisms, the new branch of the animal protection movement achieved some success. In 1876, a bill was passed in Parliament that aimed to safeguard laboratory animals, and by the turn of the century numerous antivivisection groups had sprung up throughout Europe.[8]

Animal welfare activism soon crossed the Atlantic and made its way to the United States. Prior to the mid–nineteenth century, animal protection was as minimal a concern in the United States as it was in other Western countries.[9] But the birth of animal welfare in England sparked the worldwide growth of the movement. Animal welfare was brought to the United States in the 1860s by Henry Bergh, who had been influenced by events in England. Through Bergh's efforts, the New York state legislature passed an anticruelty statute in 1866, which read:

Every person who shall, by his act or neglect, maliciously kill, maim, wound, injure, torture or cruelly beat any horse, mule, cow, cattle, sheep or other animal belonging to himself or another, shall upon conviction be adjudged guilty of a misdemeanor. (Niven 1967, 108)

The legislature also established the first private humane organization in the Western Hemisphere, headed by Henry Bergh and known as the American SPCA. With the law and its delegated powers, Bergh and the ASPCA prosecuted several cases involving mistreatment of horses, calves, and chickens (Carson 1972, 96).

From Welfare to Rights

As the years passed, the ASPCA and other humane organizations moved beyond their concern with farm and work animals to become generally associated with protecting dogs and cats. Many factors contributed to the welfare movement's change of focus (see Niven 1967, 108). Humane organizations were generally located in cities where, after the turn of the century, cats and dogs comprised the majority of animals. City dollars going to fund humane societies were logically allocated to city animal issues such as funding clinics and dealing with stray animals. Moreover, regulating animal use in rural areas would have been an expensive and time-consuming task.

This change of focus combined with the two World Wars and rapid world industrialization to draw attention away from animal concerns. As a result, the humane movements in Britain, the United States, and elsewhere weakened in the first half of this century. At the same time, activism geared toward antivivisection slowed down significantly. The 1960s saw a rise in concern for animals, but it was not until the 1970s that a strong resurgence of the movement, in a new form, took place. With Singer's publication of *Animal Liberation* in 1975, the present-day animal rights movement was conceived. Singer's work inspired many, including the founders of People for the Ethical Treatment of Animals (PETA), the leading animal rights organization in this country. Singer elaborated a utilitarian approach without the intention of making the claim that animals have rights. Nevertheless, his work inspired the move to rights talk.[10] The reborn, reoriented, and renamed movement grew rapidly in the 1980s, establishing itself in popular terms as the *animal rights movement* with the underlying philosophy that animals should be granted rights.

With the emergence of the animal rights movement came conflict with the already established animal welfare movement. Differences in focus, philosophy, language, and tactics promoted this conflict. The welfare movement, with its twentieth-century emphasis on companion animals, generally ignored issues relating to farm animals, experimentation, hunting, and so forth. Indeed, it was not uncommon for board members of humane organizations to support hunting and meat consumption. Animal welfare groups frequently worked with local governments in running animal shelters and maintaining spay and neuter clinics. Moreover, welfare groups held that treatment of animals should be guided by compassion: animals deserve some protection, deserve to be treated humanely, but do not have rights. As such, welfarists have, for the most part, been reform oriented, interested in cooperating with government to increase protection for animals but not seeking a fundamental alteration in the human treatment of animals.

In contrast, the newest branch of the animal protection movement aims to abolish animal exploitation. Like some of the earlier antivivisectionists in England, the present-day animal rights movement is not satisfied with the goal of improving the conditions under which animals are used. Instead, the animal rights movement is seeking a radical change in our treatment of and attitudes toward animals. According to most animal rights activists, animals should not be made to suffer on account of human desires. Hence, our desire for meat, fur and leather clothing, sport, and entertainment does not justify the pain animals experience in the process of fulfilling it.[11] Moreover, our attitudes toward animals must change. Animals should be granted respect, dignity, and equal consideration rather than being treated as inferior beings and objects of human use and abuse. Whether activists make their arguments on the grounds of utilitarianism, rights, or equal consideration, they challenge the "speciesist" view that, like racism and sexism, arbitrarily distinguishes between groups of beings, making one group superior to the other. To achieve changes in treatment and attitude, activists frequently speak not simply of being compassionate and caring but of extending rights to animals.

Although the split between the animal rights and the animal welfare movements remains, greater understanding and cooperation has narrowed the gap between the two camps. Humane societies have

increasingly challenged abuses of animals in fur farming, food production, and experimentation, and they have also promoted vegetarianism. Some humane societies even refer to themselves as animal rights
groups.[12] The result has been greater consolidation and increasing reference to a single animal rights movement.

The Growth and Composition of the Animal
Advocacy Movement

Since its inception in the United States, the animal advocacy movement
has grown significantly. By 1991, there were approximately 900 animal
protection groups in the United States with a total budget estimated at
$50 million.[13] These groups are composed of both national groups and
local grassroots organizations that address various issues concerning
animals. Although there are no definitive numbers detailing which of
these groups are specifically for animal rights and which are for animal
welfare, it is clear that over the past two decades most groups have
increasingly taken up issues associated with animal rights concerns. In
addition to the 900 groups, there are approximately 3,500 private
humane societies, which provide such things as animal shelters and
spay and neuter clinics.[14] Moreover, ad hoc groups are continually
being formed around the country in high schools, on college campuses,
and in response to particular local issues.[15]

The evidence that is available, while imperfect, verifies that the
movement has grown substantially.[16] In the early 1980s, it is estimated
that three million people in this country contributed to animal protection organizations. In 1991, the number increased to ten million, a
growth rate of over 200 percent.[17] In the early 1980s, it is roughly estimated that 150 animal protection organizations were in existence.[18] By
1988, this number had increased to 700, and, as already mentioned, it
jumped to 900 by 1991, reflecting a 28.5 percent increase over a
three-year period (*Newsweek*, December 26, 1988, 51). Another piece of
evidence that illustrates both the growth and influence of the animal
protection movement comes from statistics regarding the number of
animals euthanized each year. In the early 1980s, animal shelters euthanized some twenty million animals each year. By the early 1990s the
annual number of euthanizations was down to six million. This significant decrease suggests the success of education programs aimed at the
problems of animal overpopulation.

Along with the numbers, evidence from group activities demonstrates the expansion in the size and influence of the movement. According to the National Park Service, approximately 24,000 animal supporters turned up in the nation's capital to march on behalf of animals in June 1990, a number "roughly six times larger than any previous pro-animal demonstration held in the U.S." (*Animals' Agenda*, September 1990, 38). Animal advocacy groups have experienced major success in combating the fur industry. The antifur campaign carried out by many groups around the country is widely believed to have contributed to the closing and bankruptcy of fur salons around the nation and, more generally, to the significant decline of the fur industry.[19] Animal advocacy groups have also experienced important successes in halting animal testing by cosmetics companies.[20] Anecdotal observations suggest more of the same: vegetarianism for ethical reasons appears to be on the rise and less laughable; animal protection concerns make more headlines and have been taken up in television shows, comic strips, and even commercials;[21] "cruelty-free" products are increasingly available in stores; and even Burger King offers meatless burgers at some of its locations (*PAWS Action*, March 1992, 2).

While the animal protection movement has grown significantly in recent years, the composition of its membership probably has not changed dramatically. Although documentation of the movement's composition in the 1970s and early 1980s is lacking, it is clear that from its founding days in the 1800s women have made up the majority of the movement's membership. Female dominance in movement membership continues today. According to a 1991 survey, women comprise 78.3 percent of the membership, outnumbering men by almost four to one.[22] However, the gender split in membership is not reflected in the organizational leadership, where men dominate. This gender disparity was apparent at the national March for the Animals, in June 1990, where the majority of marchers were women yet "Fewer than ten female activists were on the roster" (*Animals' Agenda*, September 1990, 39). In addition, my own informal observations at protests, meetings, and other activities demonstrate that women comprise the majority of the movement's constituents. For example, at one 1990 march in Seattle for World Laboratory Animal Liberation Week, approximately 75 people turned out, only about 20 of whom were men. More dramatically, the participants in the day-long PETA 101 seminar in Seattle drew 200 people. More than 90 percent of the participants were women, and one of the PETA instructors confirmed that this high percentage was quite common at PETA seminars around the country.

The age composition of the movement is mixed, although most members are between twenty and fifty years of age, and people in their thirties comprise just over a third of the membership.[23] On the other hand, the racial composition is not mixed. Ninety-seven percent of the movement's membership is white. The urban-rural mix of the movement reflects that of the overall population.[24]

Two of the most significant characteristics of the movement's constituency relate to education and wealth. Respondents in a 1991 survey revealed that movement members are highly educated. Eighty-two percent have attended college; of these, 53 percent have completed a four-year degree, and 33.3 percent hold a master's or Ph.D. In addition to being educated, movement constituents are well off in terms of wealth. Close to 40 percent reported annual incomes of $50,000 or more. An additional 40 percent reported incomes between $20,000 and $50,000. As one would expect with these education and income numbers, the occupations of movement constituents are highly skilled. Near 50 percent work in executive or managerial jobs, close to 30 percent hold technical or sales jobs, and 10 percent are students (Bartlett 1991, 2).

Contradicting the common criticism that proponents of animal protection care more about animals than humans, the Utah State University survey offers the following statistics:

> [T]he vast majority of survey respondents reported involvement or identification with other progressive social movements: 98.4 percent with the environmental movement; 88.8 percent with the civil rights movement; 83.3 percent with feminists; 86.3 percent with the anti-apartheid struggle; 82.4 percent with the anti-nuclear movement; 83 percent with the anti-war movement; 70.9 percent supported student rights; and 58.2 percent were interested in gay liberation (24.9 percent were neutral). On the sensitive subject of abortion, 61.4 seemed to favor abortion rights, 12.5 were neutral, and 26 percent appeared to be against it. (2)

On the issue of rights versus welfare, this survey illustrates a growing consensus among the membership. Only 8.8 percent of respondents referred to themselves as strictly animal rights proponents; similarly, only 5 percent considered themselves animal welfarists. In an apparent demonstration of unity, 80.1 percent considered themselves both. With regard to specific issues, respondents demonstrated expanding support for positions that have been traditionally associated with animal rights concerns.

> Respondents were almost unanimously against hunting, trapping, fur wearing, intensive animal agriculture, and animal experimentation. . . . Respondents were not unanimously opposed to eating meat, racing horses, and keeping animals in zoos, but it was close. (Bartlett 1991, 2)

My own interviews with activists confirmed the general thrust of these statistics. Activists were highly educated, white, middle to upper-middle class, opposed to eating meat, hunting, and fur wearing, and against most animal experimentation. The participants in my interviews also demonstrated strong and committed connections to other progressive causes, especially civil rights, women's rights, and the environmental movement. And, while activists expressed concern over problems resulting from the split between the traditional welfare movement and the newer rights movement, they also suggested that the divide has been narrowed by growing consensus and unity.

As a whole, evidence demonstrating the growth and composition of the movement is promising for animal advocates. The expansion of the movement certainly provides it with greater power to advance its various goals. If growth continues—and there is little evidence to suggest that it won't—the movement will be able to effect greater change. But size itself does not hold the sole promise for movement success. The movement's composition is of particular significance. As the survey of movement constituents concludes,

> Animal rights activists appear to be resource-rich adherents with the income, experience, education, and social positions necessary to capture the political opportunity and financial support required for social movement success. (Bartlett 1991, 2)

Western Thought and Animals

While the animal advocacy movement is a relatively recent phenomenon, philosophical debate surrounding animals is far from new.[25] Indeed, discussion concerning the role, nature, and value of animals dates at least as far back as the sixth century B.C. (Brumbaugh 1978, 7). However, the contemporary debate differs from that of the past in both extent and form. In terms of extent, philosophical discussion regarding animals in the West was sparse prior to the nineteenth century. As Bernard Rollin notes,

> [D]espite the perennial presence of ethical questions, and the perennial writings of those men who articulate these questions for their own age, Western thought has been characterized by a major omission, an omission so pervasive as to have become essentially invisible. (1981, 4)

Moreover, the form of the contemporary dialogue has largely taken shape around the language of rights, with the debate centered around the question: Do animals have rights?

Traditional Western Views of Animals: Irrationality and Inferiority

Although Eastern thought, including the Hindu and Buddhist traditions, demonstrates concern over animal suffering, Western religious and philosophical thought lacks significant concern for animals.[26] Judeo-Christian morality expresses a hierarchy of life in which man, made in the image of God, reigns supreme over all living creatures on earth. The book of Genesis establishes man's preeminence over the world and its animals in the following quote:

> And God created man in his own image, in the image of God created he him; male and female created he them. And God blessed them: and God said unto them, Be fruitful, and multiply, and replenish the earth, and subdue it; and have dominion over the fish of the sea, and over the birds of the heavens, and over every living thing that moveth upon the earth. (Gen. 1:27–28)

While the Old and New Testaments express the Judeo-Christian notion of human control and superiority over animals, the Old Testament does demonstrate some sympathy toward animals. For instance, the Jewish tradition of keeping kosher is in part justified by the requirement that animals be slaughtered with a minimum of pain. In addition, several references in the Old Testament convey compassion, including the statement, "A righteous man regardeth the life of his beast" (Carson

1972, 15). Nevertheless, these references are few and uphold man's dominion over beast. The New Testament lacks even minimal hints of compassion toward animals. Moreover, Christianity devalues animals in holding that they are devoid of immortal souls. Thus, the Western religious heritage has largely ignored concern for our nonhuman counterparts and supported human dominion over the animal world.

Religious philosophers, including St. Augustine and St. Thomas Aquinas, supported and expanded upon the notion of human control over animals. Augustine's *The City of God*, first published in 1467, distinguished animal from human life by virtue of the latter's ability to reason. This distinction, created by God, gives humans the prerogative to use animals as they see fit (1981, 31–32). The thirteenth-century writings of Aquinas similarly focus on rationality. Aquinas argued that nonrational creatures, being devoid of the capacity for freedom, can be employed as instruments to benefit humankind (1928). He further maintained that the only justification for restricting cruelty toward animals is to avoid extending cruel treatment to humans (1964).

Like these religious perspectives, Western philosophy in general depicts animals as irrational (or nonrational) and inferior. Literature from ancient Greece displays the commonly held view that humans reign supreme over the animal world. Aristotle suggested that the human capacity for rationality gives us natural dominion over animals. According to Aristotle, human and nonhuman animals share similar attributes with regard to their senses and capacity for experiencing pain. Nevertheless, he contends that nature creates a hierarchy based upon reason. Humans—creatures with the greatest reasoning capacity—stand at the apex of the hierarchy. Moreover, the natural ladder implies that all inferior creatures exist to serve as instruments for the benefit of superior beings. Aristotle used this hierarchical theory to justify human dominion over both animals and other humans deemed less rational, including slaves and women.[27]

In the seventeenth century, Descartes provided a theory supporting human use and abuse of animals that went beyond the issue of rationality. Descartes equated animals with machines; like machines, animals lack thought, understanding, and consciousness. Descartes rested this view on the grounds that animals are devoid of the capacity to speak, that is, the capacity to form sentences or signs expressing thought. Inability to speak, Descartes asserted, demonstrates total absence of reason, but more than that it displays that animals are "natural automata," machines without thought and soul. As such, humans are justified in using animals for their own purposes (1971).[28]

Although not all philosophers agreed with Descartes's depiction of animal automata, most accepted the view that, because of reasoning deficiencies, animals are distinct from and inferior to humans. In *The Leviathan*, first published in 1651, Hobbes, for instance, suggested that humans have natural rights to dominate irrational creatures (1986). Some philosophers did recommend compassionate treatment of nonhuman creatures despite the acceptance of human dominion. However, this recommendation was based solely on the benefits to humans that would accrue from compassionate treatment of animals. Locke and Kant, two eighteenth-century philosophers, argued that cruelty to animals might result in cruelty toward humankind. Locke stated that "they who delight in the suffering and destruction of inferior creatures, will not be apt to be very compassionate or benign to those of their own kind" (quoted in Clarke and Linzey 1990, 119). Likewise Kant, who argued that animals exist for humankind and can be used as a means to an end, suggested that "we have duties towards animals because thus we cultivate the corresponding duties towards human beings. . . . [F]or he who is cruel to animals becomes hard also in his dealings with men" (1930, 240).

Concern for Animals in the Classical Tradition:
The Move to Rights

Throughout history, Western religious and philosophical thought has put forth the notion of human superiority over animals and nature. Only a handful of philosophers, both religious and secular, challenged this perspective by disputing the presumption of human supremacy. Pythagoras and Plutarch, two of the earliest challengers, questioned human consumption of animals in making a case for vegetarianism.[29] Although such philosophical defense of animals was uncommon before the sixteenth century, concern for animals began to grow as theoretical interest in human freedom expanded. Sir Thomas More's *Utopia*, first published in 1516, included a vision of a world that lacks hunting and animal sacrifice. Montaigne, in 1580, asserted that animals have the ability to communicate and referred to humans as impudent for considering themselves superior.[30] In sharp contrast to the Cartesian image, Voltaire argued that animals hold the capacities to think and understand. Likewise, Hume suggested that animals possess reasoning powers. Even some theologians challenged the traditional views, arguing that animals, like humans, have immortal souls.[31]

One of the most influential thinkers who contributed to the classical and contemporary debates regarding animals was Jeremy Bentham. In the late nineteenth century Bentham applied his utilitarianism to animals, opposing the view that the human capacity to reason justifies dominion over animals. According to Bentham, animals are sentient creatures, which, like humans, experience both pain and pleasure. As such, animals deserve consideration, as do all beings capable of happiness and suffering: "[T]he question is not, Can they *reason?* nor, Can they *talk?* but, Can they *suffer?*" (1879, chap. 17, sec. 1). Although utilitarian calculation of the overall benefit to the community might justify exploitation of animals (as it would humans), Bentham's theory suggests that it is not acceptable to cause unnecessary animal suffering.

Like Bentham, Charles Darwin influenced human conceptions of animals. In asserting that humans evolved from other life forms, Darwin's theory of evolution challenged the religious view that confers human dominion over animals. This theory observed the similarities and relations between human and nonhuman animals in opposition to the generally accepted distinctions and thereby "confirmed the idea of the universal kinship between man and animal . . ." (Niven 1967, 79).[32] Darwin, in pointing to such similarities, suggested that the higher mammals share emotional and intellectual faculties. Moreover, while Darwin recognized distinctions between humans and animals, he stated, "Nevertheless the difference in mind between man and the higher animals, great as it is, certainly is one of degree and not of kind" (1906, 128).

Throughout this philosophical debate, little was said of animal rights.[33] However, the expansion of rights language promoted by Enlightenment theory and natural rights philosophy eventually spread to animals. Herman Daggett, in 1791, spoke of animal rights, stating,

> I know of nothing in nature, in reason, or in revelation, which obliges us to suppose, that the unalienated rights of a beast, are not as sacred, and inviolable, as those of a man: or that the person, who wantonly commits an outrage upon the life, happiness, or security of a bird, is not as really amenable, at the tribunal of eternal justice,

as he, who wantonly destroys the rights and privileges, or injuri-
ously takes away the life of one of his fellow creatures of the
human race. (Quoted in Clarke and Linzey 1990, 132)

John Lawrence and Thomas Young, both defenders of animals, spoke
in terms of animal rights.[34] Bentham, while a utilitarian and critical of
the notion of rights, did state that "The day *may come*, when the rest of
the animal creation may acquire those rights which never could have
been withholden from them but by the hand of tyranny" (1789, chap.
17, sec. 1, emphasis in the original). And Schopenhauer, arguing that
humans have obligations toward animals, notes that the European system of morality crudely denies rights to them (1965).

It was Henry Salt who first extensively used the notion of animal
rights. In an 1892 work entitled *Animals' Rights*, Salt begins by asking
whether the lower animals have rights and proceeds to answer the
question in the affirmative. He speaks explicitly in terms of rights, suggesting that earlier thinking on human rights promoted the extension
of rights to animals.

> A great and far-reaching effect was produced in England . . . by the
> publication of such revolutionary works as Paine's "Rights of
> Man," and Mary Wollstonecraft's "Vindication of the Rights of
> Women;" and looking back now, after the lapse of a hundred
> years, we can see that a still wider extension of the theory of rights
> was thenceforth inevitable. (1980, 4)

Salt goes on to warn that we must move beyond sympathy and compassion to the notion of rights because

> every great liberating movement has proceeded exactly on these
> lines. Oppression and cruelty are invariably founded on a lack of
> imaginative sympathy. . . . When once the sense of affinity is awak-
> ened, the knell of tyranny is sounded, and the ultimate concession
> of "rights" is simply a matter of time. (21)

Contemporary Philosophy and Animals:
Singer versus Regan

Salt's insights into the relationship between human and animal rights,
and what he referred to as the inevitable extension of rights, went

largely unnoticed for years. While Salt and others spoke of animal rights, the concept and terminology did not become widespread in the United States or other Western countries until recent years. The first half of the twentieth century witnessed a lull in both philosophical thought and political activism involving animals. Prior to the 1970s, the language of compassion dominated popular discussion involving animals. This language, promoted by the animal welfare movement, stressed that humans should treat animals with care, kindness, and compassion. Although not based on any specific philosophical foundation, the language of compassion accepts a basic assumption of liberal theory: that inferior, irrational beings can be used to advance the desires of superior, rational beings but should be generally treated with kindness and sympathy.[35]

In the 1960s, philosophical and political activity increased, but it was not until the 1970s that animal rights, as a theoretical and political discourse, gained ground. In the 1980s the discourse made further headway, and by 1990 animal rights had moved beyond the radical fringe and penetrated mainstream philosophical and political debate. As noted at the outset, the recent philosophical analysis dealing with animals is, for the most part, divided between utilitarian and rights-oriented approaches. The former, first elaborated largely by Peter Singer (ironically considered the father of the present day animal *rights* movement), draws on classical utilitarianism. The latter, elucidated in Tom Regan's *The Case for Animal Rights* (1983), extends the notion of rights to animals.

Singer applied the utilitarian approach to animals in his 1975 groundbreaking work, *Animal Liberation*. In that work, Singer begins by defining equality, suggesting that equality does not imply actual sameness between beings. Instead, equality is a principle that prescribes how we should treat one another. Drawing on Bentham's utilitarianism, Singer argues that the guiding moral principle of equality holds that "the interests of every being affected by an action are to be taken into account and given the same weight as the like interests of any other being" (5). In other words, beings must be granted "equal consideration" regardless of the differential abilities held by each being. Thus, intelligence, strength, speed, and other attributes do not imply that any being deserves more equal consideration than others.

Singer disputes the argument that intelligence gives humans the rights to use animals and deny them equal consideration: "If possessing a higher degree of intelligence does not entitle one human to use another for his own ends, how can it entitle humans to exploit nonhumans for the same purpose?" (1975, 7).[36] On this view, intelligence and rationality are arbitrary demarcations that do not give certain beings moral status over others. Distinguishing humans from animals on the basis of rationality therefore creates an unjustifiable moral delineation. Like racism and sexism, which result from arbitrary differences in skin color and sex, "speciesism"—prejudice favoring one's own species over members of other species—stems from arbitrary distinctions based on intelligence.

Alternatively, Singer again draws on Bentham to suggest that the capacity for suffering gives beings interests and the right to equal consideration. Here Singer quotes Bentham's comment, cited above: "[T]he question is not, Can they *reason?* nor, Can they *talk?* but, *Can they suffer?"* (1975, 8). He goes on to assert that

> If a being suffers there can be no moral justification for refusing to take that suffering into consideration. No matter what the nature of the being, the principle of equality requires that its suffering be counted equally with the like suffering—in so far as rough comparisons can be made—of any other being. (8)

With this moral guideline, Singer argues that animals, entities capable of experiencing pleasure and pain, have interests and thus deserve equal consideration.

With regard to rights, Singer observes that the language is convenient in the realms of politics and the media, "but in the argument for a radical change in our attitude to animals, it is in no way necessary" (1990, 8).[37] According to him, the theoretical argument for considering animals does not rest on the question of whether they have rights. Rather, the issue is whether they have interests. Basing interests on suffering avoids the question of rights. If a being deserves equal consideration given its interest in not suffering, then there is no need to raise the issue of rights.

Equal consideration, or extending the notion of equality to animals, forms the basis of Singer's theory. At bottom, Singer seeks to include animals in the moral community and extend our accepted ethical guidelines to them, and he justifies this inclusion on the grounds that there is no nonarbitrary distinction that should keep animals outside the ethical realm. Singer urges us to "extend to other species the basic principle of equality that most of us recognize should be extended to all members of our own species" (1976, 149).

Like Singer, Tom Regan (1983) seeks to extend our notions of justice and morality to animals. Unlike Singer, Regan does see the need to raise the issue of rights. According to Regan, it is rights that must be extended to animals. He thus rejects Singer's utilitarianism despite his recognition of Singer's contribution to awakening concern for animals.[38]

Regan's case for animal rights begins with the view that at least certain animals—mammals—have consciousness. Rejecting Descartes's theory of animal automata, Regan turns to Darwin, who held that humans share with some animals the characteristic of consciousness. Regan contends that mammalian animals have beliefs and desires upon which they act. The notion that these animals have beliefs and desires is supported by common sense, ordinary language, evolutionary theory, and observable behavior. Moreover, Regan suggests that several implications arise from the conclusion that animals have beliefs and desires, including the idea that animals have perception, memory, intention, self-consciousness, a sense of the future, and interests.

From here, Regan elaborates a formal principle of justice, rejecting both perfectionism and utilitarianism.[39] Regan concludes that the way to determine an individual's just deserts is through "the equality of individuals view, which holds that what individuals are due is equal respect for their equal inherent value" (1983, 263). Moreover, "moral patients"—individuals unable to control their own behavior in ways that would make them morally accountable, such as infants, severely retarded humans, and animals—do not have less inherent value than do "moral agents." This conclusion is based on what Regan calls the "subject-of-a-life" criterion, which holds that individuals are subjects of a life and thus have inherent value if they have beliefs, desires, preferences, intentionality, sentience, a sense of their own future, identity over time, and individual experiential welfare. Mammalian animals, Regan asserts, have these characteristics and hence have inherent value and are due equal respect.

The "equality of individuals view" leads Regan to argue that moral rights apply to mammalian animals. Regan defines moral rights by drawing on J. S. Mill who stated that to have a right is "to have something society ought to defend me in the possession of" (Regan

1983, 269). In other words, having a right means having a "valid claim" upon society.

> Since the respect principle sets forth an unacquired duty of justice, calling for the respectful treatment of all who have inherent value, it is argued that those who have this kind of value have a valid claim, and thus a right, to treatment respectful of their value. Because both moral agents and patients have value of this kind, and have it equally, both are shown to have an equal moral right to treatment respectful of their value. (266)

Thus, Regan makes the case for animal rights.

Regan notes the political utility of employing the rights approach by quoting David Lyons, who suggests that rights play the role of arguing for changes in the social order (Regan 1983, 269). However, the thrust of his argument does not rest on the political efficacy of rights. As he notes in "The Struggle for Animal Rights," the rights view "is rationally the most satisfactory moral theory," with "the best reasons, the best arguments, on its side" (1990, 184).

From Regan and Singer we see the debate between utilitarianism and rights take shape over the issue of animals. Despite their differences, Singer and Regan agree that extending our notions of justice and morality to animals is at the heart of contemporary theories concerning animals. Although these two philosophers differ on the particular notions of justice we need to extend, they both discuss this expansion by drawing an analogy to movements to liberate blacks and women. Animals are simply the next part of the "expanding circle" of the moral community.

Alternative Contemporary Approaches

Although the utilitarian versus rights debate dominates recent philosophical discussion concerning animals, other scholarly approaches are on the increase. In particular, feminist approaches, ecofeminist analyses, and more holistic approaches that include broad environmental concerns have made their way into the philosophical conversation regarding animals. These approaches challenge both utilitarian and rights analyses and seek to provide alternative perspectives regarding the moral position of animals.

In the past few years, feminist perspectives have been extended to the animal issue. Josephine Donovan's article "Animal Rights and Feminist Theory" (1990) provides a good example of this application and displays one feminist critique of rights and utilitarianism. Donovan begins by asserting that contemporary animal rights theory contains an inherent, problematic bias toward rationalism that would best be overcome by drawing upon cultural feminism to develop a more sound ethic for animals.[40] The problem with Regan's natural rights approach rests in his argument that animals must have "subjective consciousness" or "complex awareness" for rights to be applied. This, Donovan contends, privileges rationalism over sentiment, thereby repeating the Kantian error that Regan critiques. Singer's utilitarianism, while superior to Regan's rights theory, is also defective since it calls for a quantification of suffering, or "a 'mathematization' of moral beings" (358). Such quantification, Donovan claims, supports a predilection for science and rationalism. In response to Singer and Regan, Donovan recommends a turn to cultural feminism, which suggests that domination of nature and animals is based in Western, male thought. To overcome attitudes that perpetuate domination, we must move away from works like Regan's and Singer's, which draw upon the Western, male tradition, prioritize reason over sentience, and reinforce the views that have long justified control and exploitation of animals.

Like Donovan, scholars in the growing school of ecofeminism maintain that male-dominated society is responsible for numerous forms of oppression, including oppression of women, minorities, animals, and nature. Feminists and ecofeminists contend that nature has been defined by the masculine world as "the other," which must be controlled and subdued.[41] As such, women, animals, and the environment have been objects of male domination.[42] Patriarchy, as one scholar puts it, is a disease, and "The treatment of nature and animals is the vilest manifestation of that disease" (Collard 1988, 1).

Ecofeminism maintains that patriarchy, as the root cause of oppression, must be abolished. In doing so, we must avoid the misguided application of philosophical thought that replicates and privileges patriarchy. We need to develop a new ethic drawn from the perspectives and experiences of those who have been oppressed by the patriarchal system. Feminist theorists frequently recommend an increasing valuation of sentiments and recognition of the importance of responsibility and caring.[43] Applying this recommendation to animals and nature, feminists and ecofeminists stress the need for compassionate, responsible treatment of animals that moves beyond condescension. Some feminists and ecofeminists go further, endorsing animal liberation. Collard, for example, states that "it is a fact that no woman will be free until all animals are free and nature is released from man's ruthless exploitation" (1988, 1). Likewise, Norma Benney states of women, "If we struggle to free ourselves, without realizing that we are also crushing the most oppressed and exploited creatures on the planet, we can only fail" (1983, 151).

In dealing with animal concerns, ecofeminism often expresses the notion of a holistic worldview. Marti Kheel explores the potential application of ecofeminism to both animal and environmental issues and endorses a holistic approach. Kheel argues for a new ethic, to be applied to both animal and environmental concerns, that would overcome the dualism prevalent in the patriarchal world.

> By challenging such dualities, it then becomes possible to conceive of dissolving the divisions that separate the individual and the whole, reason and emotion, the domestic and the wild, animal liberation and environmental ethics. (1988, 17)

In so doing, a holistic ethic can be developed that brings together and interconnects all aspects of life and nature.[44]

The ethic of holism presented by some ecofeminists is shared by others and is a growing part of the philosophical discourse concerning animals. In 1979, Michael W. Fox put forth a holistic view, arguing that human consciousness has developed through stages. Passing through the humanitarian and natural rights stages, human consciousness reaches the final "transpersonal or co-creative" stage, also referred to as "earthmind." In this last stage, humans work in harmony with nature.

> It is the stage of integration and synthesis, of consummate stewardship where man's interests are not in opposition with the rest of creation. Rather man's needs complement those of creation, since through him creation is expressed. It is as though nature is gaining its ultimate expression through man as consciousness completes the evolutionary cycle: the organic ascending to the psychic or conscious realm, the created (man) becoming at one with creation (as co-creator). (53)

Fox, in stressing the unity between humans and the whole of nature, critiques Singer for only addressing sentient beings and ignoring nonsentient creations. Despite this critique, Fox states that "the animal rights issue is an important transition in our efforts to change consensus values and attitudes" (54–55). Rights for both sentient and nonsentient creatures form "stepping stones for the gradual transmutation of society and consciousness . . ." (56).

Overall, the recent philosophical debate surrounding animals has begun to challenge traditional Western paradigms. As such, these alternative approaches to animal issues parallel more general philosophical debates. As feminism, ecofeminism, and postmodernism have gained in stature as alternatives to classical Western thought, so too have alternatives to utilitarianism and rights theory expanded in the debate over animals. Yet, despite the expansion of philosophical debate, and despite the utilitarian challenge to rights theory, the language of animal rights has prevailed in the political realm.

The Philosophical Extension of Rights

The philosophical attempt to extend rights to animals outlined above might be cited by some scholars as a further indication of the trivialization of rights. Several scholars critique rights language on the grounds that its extension to various progressive causes empties the language of its content and power. The multiplication of rights, on this view, trivializes the concept and its underlying values (Glendon 1991, xi; see also Putnam 1976). Hence, to suggest that rights apply not only to humans but also to animals undermines the notion and meaning of human rights. Furthermore, it is argued, putting forward animal rights raises the question of where to draw the line. Do plants have rights? Do future generations have rights? Does the planet have rights? The slippery slope onto which we fall when rights are extended too far diminishes the power and utility of rights, for if we extend rights to everything then rights become meaningless.

While there is reason to suspect that boundless expansion trivializes existing rights, two questions remain. Does the animal rights movement demonstrate that rights can be extended to animals without diminishing rights of content, meaning, and power? And, if so, how far can rights be extended before they lose their meaning? In addressing the first question, I shall argue that both the philosophical and political

activism of the animal rights movement illustrates a powerful extension of rights.[45] Indeed, I shall suggest that it is the very extension of
rights to animals that advances the strength of rights language. Rather
than trivializing the language, the expanding scope of rights promoted
by animal advocacy strengthens the concept of rights, and it does so
through a reconstruction of the meaning of rights. As for the second
question, I will offer some speculations suggesting that if rights are to
be extended to nonsentient, nonliving beings a significantly transformed understanding of rights would have to be advanced. More
likely, increasing respect and protection for nonsentient beings would
be better advanced by an alternative to rights language.

At bottom, animal rights theory suggests that if we attribute rights
to humans and we look at the similarities between humans and animals
there is no logical reason why we should not attribute rights to animals
(at least to those animals whose characteristics are sufficiently similar
to humans). In fact, to deny rights to animals and, at the same time,
accept human rights is to be logically inconsistent. From this perspective, the fundamental characteristic shared by humans and animals is
sentience, the ability to experience pleasure and suffering. Sentience,
not rationality, forms the basis upon which we should attribute rights
because if rational ability were the basis it would be acceptable to deny
rights to irrational human beings. Thus, two underlying assumptions
drive animal rights theory. First, we agree to attribute rights to beings,
and, second, we agree that it would be wrong to deny all rights to irrational human beings.[46]

If this view is accepted, then the slippery slope argument must be
rejected. To deny rights to animals simply because extending rights
may lead to problems further down the slope is not persuasive. Indeed,
applying the slippery slope argument to deny the extension of rights to
animals fosters an arbitrary demarcation at the level of species. The
danger of such a capricious demarcation is clear when we consider that
the same line can be drawn further up the slope, as it has in the past,
within the human species. The slippery slope argument thus is not
unique to animal rights. It was the kind of argument expressed by
many who wished to deny rights to blacks, women, and other marginalized groups. If we agree that the slippery slope argument does not
justify denial of human rights, we similarly have to agree that it does
not, in itself, warrant denial of animal rights.

Nevertheless, it is true that the extension of rights does lead us to consider the slippery slope. That is the very nature of the "expanding circle." While some find this extremely problematic, the slippery slope can be reconstructed in a way that bolsters the meaning of rights. This occurs when the slippery slope is redefined as the expanding circle. The less pejorative expanding circle encourages increasing compassion, caring, and awareness of "the other." The expanding circle makes us aware of who and what have been excluded from moral consideration, thus highlighting mistreatment of the other. Moreover, in this culture, rights language happens to be one of the most common and accepted ways of heightening awareness of marginalization and mistreatment. Rights language thus becomes the means by which the circle expands, and the other is included within the parameters of moral consideration.

By expanding the circle, the application of rights to animals does not necessarily undermine the meaning of rights. I suggest, in contrast to what critics of rights suggest, that the very act of extending moral rights to animals strengthens the meaning of human rights in several ways. First, it reaffirms the rights of humans who lack rational capabilities. By basing the allocation of rights on sentience over rationality, animal rights reaffirm the rights of mentally disabled human beings and children. Second, it reinforces the notion that arbitrary demarcations, including those that justify racism, sexism, and other "isms," are inappropriate. Third, it advances the values of sentience, feeling, and empathy. In doing so, the philosophical expansion of rights to animals does not trivialize rights or empty them of their content. To the contrary, it fills rights with an alternative content—sentience—that reaffirms human rights and concomitantly advances animal rights.

Although stretching rights to animals initially fosters claims of absurdity that may undermine the power of the language, upon more careful inspection, the stretch is hardly absurd. Most of the absurdity claims arise from superficial responses such as "animal rights means pigs in school, driving cars, and voting" and "animal rights activists hate humans and love animals."[47] These types of allegations can be easily dismissed in such a way as to reinvigorate rights with power. All animal rights philosophers and proponents agree that granting rights to animals does not imply granting animals the same rights that humans hold, just as proponents of human rights agree, for instance, that the rights of children can be restricted. In addition, the allegation that animal advocates hate humans is largely exaggerated. In fact, philosophical and movement literature concerning animal interests frequently reaffirms human rights.[48]

In sum, the philosophical extension of rights to animals does not necessarily diminish the power or meaning of rights language. To the contrary, it begins the process of infusing rights with alternative meaning. However, none of this suggests that rights can be unceasingly extended. Indeed, rights language is constrained due to the fact that if we go too far there is a danger that rights will lose their meaning. Even within the notion of animal rights, the problem of where to draw the line is seriously debated. Should insects be granted rights? Should lower-level animals, such as those without central nervous systems, be accorded rights? Given the problems of defining rights within the animal kingdom, philosophical and political activism that aspires to advance rights for plants or future generations may run into problems.

It is, as yet, unclear how far rights can be extended beyond animals before they lose their content. What is clear, though, is that the philosophical basis for extending rights to animals does not necessarily imply a further extension of rights to plants, the unborn, the earth, or future generations. By basing rights on sentience, animal rights theory limits the expansion of rights to those beings that are capable of suffering. In other words, sentience is the barrier that limits further sliding down the slippery slope. Future generations, by definition, are nonsentient because they have yet to come into existence. Although there is evidence that plants react to stimulus, it is generally accepted that plants do not experience suffering. Thus, granting rights to animals does not, by itself, entail awarding rights to future generations, plants, or the earth. Extending rights to animals may logically require a similar extension to unborn fetuses if it could be shown that fetuses experience suffering through abortions.[49] But beyond that, expanding the circle to animal rights does not lead to an unending slide down the slippery slope.

Granting rights to nonsentient beings would, at minimum, require a significantly transformed understanding of rights—one that moves beyond both rationality and sentience. More likely, respect and protection for nonsentient, nonliving beings would be better fostered by an alternative to rights language. For this very reason, advocates of holistic perspectives seek to move beyond rights. Despite this limitation of rights language, attributing rights to animals begins the move away from a human-centric view of the world by highlighting the moral worth of animals. As such, rights theory has already helped pave the way for the elaboration of alternative ideas which are even more inclusive than animal rights.

Conclusion

We should not be surprised by the turn to rights language or by the influence rights analysis has had on animal issues. Given Western theory's emphasis on natural rights and human rights, the extension to animal rights is hardly shocking. Still, there is understandable concern that extending rights too far may diminish the power and content of rights language. However, I have argued that extension of rights to animals as it is promoted in philosophical works has not and does not threaten to undermine the power and meaning of the language. To the contrary, expanding rights to animals reaffirms human rights in a variety of ways and imbues rights language with a content emphasizing sentience.

If it is true that philosophical debate over animal rights has offered alternative meaning to the language and reinforced the power of rights, then it may be said that specific debate over animal rights has constituted the meaning of rights in general. It is certainly true that rights theory in general has constituted the development and meaning of animal rights. But it also appears that the development of animal rights philosophy shapes, or at least has the potential to shape, the meaning of rights. By infusing rights with alternative content, the philosophical meaning of rights is reconstituted. Although this infusion of alternative content has not replaced more traditional notions of rights, it has offered a competing perspective on how rights might be understood.

Still, to say that the philosophical extension of rights to animals maintains the power and meaning of rights language by imbuing rights with alternative content does not, by itself, demonstrate that the meaning of rights, in general, has been significantly altered. Nor does it demonstrate that the more specific meaning of legal rights has been reconstituted. Moreover, even if the power and meaning of rights language is maintained in the philosophical realm, this does not alone answer the concerns of critics of rights. Although philosophical work may, as I have argued, sustain the potency of rights, political activism may yet undermine it or fail to succeed in persuading the public and its officials that rights can have an alternative basis. Thus, we must go beyond the philosophical debate over rights to ask whether the political activism of the animal rights movement demonstrates that rights language can be stretched to include animals without diminishing rights of content, power, and meaning.

This leads us to address further concerns raised in the scholarship on rights language. Are activists captivated by the "hollow hope" of rights led to deploy an ineffective and even harmful language (Rosenberg 1991)? And do the language and meaning of rights shape this movement in detrimental and undermining ways? These questions relate to the larger issue of whether the appropriation of rights language contributes to social movement attempts to advance social change. If recent legal scholarship is correct, there is good reason to be skeptical of the turn to rights language common in modern movements. There is reason to believe that political activists seeking to advance progressive social change are misguided by the empty promise of rights. Whether animal rights activists are misled in this way and, as a result, diminish the effectiveness of their movement and the power of rights are issues that must be addressed.

Chapter 3

The Political Deployment of Rights

Although the language of rights, on its surface, says little of community or convention, those who exercise rights signal and strengthen their relation to a community. Those who claim rights implicitly agree to abide by the community's response and to accord similar regard to the claims of others. In a deeper sense, those claiming rights implicitly invest themselves in a larger community, even in the act of seeking to change it.

—Martha Minow

To examine the implications of the deployment of rights, we now move beyond an inspection of the philosophical and delve into the political. To do so, this chapter begins to explore the political deployment of rights language by examining the use of the language within movement literature and activities and within the popular media. As in the last chapter, I will argue here that the appropriation of rights language by this social movement has not diminished the power or meaning of rights. A review of movement literature, activities, and popular media illustrates that rights are being imbued with new content in the realm of political activism. Specifically, the movement communicates the values of sentience, caring, relationship, responsibility, and community through the deployment of rights. As a result, these values increasingly penetrate rights, thereby challenging and modifying the individualistic assumptions underlying traditional rights talk, and providing the language with new meaning and force.

I will also suggest two primary reasons why the infusion of these alternative values is likely to be successful in altering and reinvigorating rights language. First, as in the previous chapter, I will suggest that it is the very move to animal rights that advances the adjustment in the underlying meaning of rights. Advancing rights for animals has inspired a focus on the relationship between humans and their nonhuman counterparts. Addressing this relationship has highlighted the shared characteristic of sentience and put forth the notion that it is sentience, not rationality, that makes one a member of the moral community. Moreover, since animals cannot claim or secure their rights within the human community, extending rights to animals has enhanced the notions of care and responsibility. Overall, the move to animal rights has promoted a wider sense of community—one that incorporates both human and nonhuman life.

Second, I will suggest that the indeterminate nature of rights contributes to the possibility of incorporating alternative values into rights language. As several scholars have suggested, rights are indeterminate (Tushnet 1986; Dalton 1985; Kennedy 1986; Singer 1984). That is, recognizing a right does not determine the future in any significant manner or provide any certainty. It does not establish, in a specific or determinate way, which beings are rights holders, how rights holders will be protected, or what other related rights will be granted. Although scholars have pointed to the indeterminacy of rights as a critique of the language, I will argue that indeterminacy offers flexibility and the potential to advance new conceptions of rights.

By arguing that rights language, as deployed by this movement and reflected in the media, instills new content into the language and, at the same time, maintains its power, I offer an alternative interpretation of rights. This interpretation suggests that the prevailing and traditional meaning of rights, while important in shaping social movement activism, does not straightjacket a movement into a particular set of predominant values. To the contrary, the open, fluid, and indeterminate nature of rights provides social movements with the opportunity to reshape and reconstruct the meaning of the language. Relatedly, I offer in the following chapter a second alternative perspective of rights, arguing that in this social movement activists are not misled by a naive faith in rights to deploy a counterproductive language. Rather, activists strategically and consciously deploy rights as a result of their critical understanding of the politics of the language. In short, the argument put forth in this and the following chapter suggests that, given the opportunity to redefine the meaning of rights through political and strategic activism, we must reconsider the strategic mobilization of rights in a way that recognizes its potential to advance social change.

Rights in Practice

Philosophical activism surrounding humans and animals, along with political activism promoting human rights issues, contributed to the practical deployment of rights language by the contemporary animal rights movement. A review of the present movement's use of rights language demonstrates four points. First, there has been increasing use of rights terminology by the movement. Second, the media have accepted the terminology and expanded its use. Third, both the media and the movement employ animal rights terminology generally as a label, without extended explanation or justification of the concept. Finally, despite the limited justification of animal rights, within the deployment of the language there are implicit and explicit connections to the concepts of relationship, responsibility, caring, and community.

This last point is most crucial for understanding the way this movement has constituted the meaning of rights and for responding to critics of rights language. Critics of rights contend, among other things, that the language is embedded within traditional liberal ideology that privileges the value of individualism (Medcalf 1978; Bruun 1982). By privileging individualism, rights language fosters separation and conflict and thereby inhibits appreciation for relationship and community (Glendon 1991). In addition, the dominant conception of rights in this culture, critics argue, is a negative one that stresses the right to be free from the interference of others and the state. As such, rights language undermines the values of responsibility and caring within the community.

If, as will be argued here, the deployment of rights language by this social movement effectively supports the concepts of relationship, caring, responsibility, and community, then we may conclude that critics have been inaccurate in their attack against rights. We may further conclude that infusing rights with content that competes with individualism provides the opportunity to reinvigorate the power and meaning of the language. Finally, we may interpret this appropriation of rights not simply as one that seeks to include a marginalized group into the mainstream but as one that challenges and attempts to transform the very conception and understanding of the language. In other words, the deployment of rights by this movement both extends the language and, more importantly, alters the underlying substantive terms of the language itself.

Rights Language in Movement Literature

Content analysis of movement literature illustrates the pervasive deployment of animal rights language.[1] To determine how rights language is presented by the movement, I performed content analysis on four examples of magazine-length movement literature—*PAWS News, PAWS Action, PETA News,* and *Animals' Agenda*.[2] In addition, I reviewed newsletters from several animal protection organizations, including the ASPCA, the Fund for Animals, the National Anti-Vivisection Society (NAVS), the American Anti-Vivisection Society (AAVS), Feminists for Animal Rights (FAR), and the Humane Farming Association (HFA). Along with newsletters, I examined numerous pamphlets and circulars from these and other animal protection organizations.[3]

Movement literature focuses on the existing treatment of animals. Unlike philosophical writings, movement literature is not devoted to justifying the notion that animals have or should be given rights. Although articles in newsletters and magazines sometimes present philosophical arguments related to animal rights, for the most part the notion is taken for granted and accepted without question. Moreover, only rarely are discussions of specific animal rights included.

Instead of focusing on theoretical arguments, newsletters describe different forms of animal experimentation, critique particular experiments, review animal treatment in food and clothing production, and so forth. Movement literature is therefore primarily descriptive with little high theoretical content. This descriptive tack makes sense given the commonly held view among activists that their most important task involves educating people about how humans treat animals. Displaying animal treatment, according to activists, itself attracts support. The assumption is that, once people see how our culture handles dogs, cats, monkeys, cows, pigs, and even rats, they will be prompted to reevaluate their own views and uses of animals.

Education and information put forth to encourage a transformation in popular attitudes constitutes the first step in gaining support. The movement then seeks to inspire involvement in changing the common treatment of animals. Thus, along with description, movement literature includes advice and recommendations for action.

PETA uses this approach in most of its literature. For instance, the May/June 1989 issue of *PETA News* focuses on fur. Most of the issue depicts the treatment (or mistreatment) of minks and foxes raised on fur farms and captured through trapping, as the following excerpt demonstrates.

> Animals confined on fur farms, mostly minks and foxes, are born in spring. Their mothers are kept as breeders for several years, and must give birth in tiny cold metal cages, about one foot wide by two feet long. They are kept outdoors in rows, usually under a metal overhang. After just a few weeks the infants are separated from their mothers and put two, three or four to a cage. Due to confinement they often go insane; fighting is common, and even cannibalization occurs because of stress. (*PETA News*, May/June 1989, 8)

The following pages go on to describe the trapping and killing of minks and foxes and the fur industry's response to animal advocacy. Finally, PETA provides a list, always entitled "What You Can Do." In this instance, the recommendations include distributing antifur material, donating furs for protest activities, boycotting American Express and other supporters of fur, and supporting PETA (9).

Within this 19-page issue, PETA makes little mention of animal rights: five references in all. These references take the form of labels. There is mention of "animal rights activities" and "animal rights groups" in Europe and one comment by a PETA intern that refers to the group as an "animal rights organization." The newsletter omits the philosophical argument that extends rights to animals such as minks and foxes. The newsletter likewise neglects specific arguments suggesting that animal suffering is unacceptable, relying on the description to make this case.

This approach typifies most movement literature on the subject. In 5 randomly selected issues of *PETA News*,[4] 64 references were made to the term *rights*. Only 4 of the 64 related to the philosophical justification for animal rights. In 5 issues of *PAWS News* and 5 issues of *PAWS Action*, a total of 124 rights references appear.[5] Of these, 12 were associated with the theoretical argument for animal rights, and 8 of these 12 appeared in one article. In 5 issues of *Animals' Agenda*, a total of 309 rights references were made. Only 8 of these were related to the philosophical justification of animal rights.[6]

As these numbers indicate, the predominant use of rights terminology comes in the form of a label, and this label is pervasive. Moreover, movement literature contains only limited references to or discussions of animal rights theory. There are, of course, exceptions. For instance, in the January/February 1992 issue of *Animals' Agenda*, a Point/Counterpoint article covers the animal welfare versus rights debate. This six-page article presents the views of philosopher Tom Regan and law professor Gary Francione, who defend the concept of animal rights. On the counterpoint side, Ingrid Newkirk, national director of PETA, suggests that animal rightists should not cast out welfarists and should be grateful for the reforms achieved by the welfare movement.

Another exception appears in the October 1987 issue of *PAWS News* in an article entitled "Snakes Alive! Animal Rights Over Exploitation." In the article, reprinted from the *Seattle Times*, PAWS explains the concept of animal rights within the context of protesting a rattlesnake roundup.

> The alien concept of animal rights approaches animals from a completely different angle. Animals have inherent rights apart from our uses of them. These include freedom from pain, protection from harm, the ability to move about and socialize naturally, an appropriate habitat, and so forth. (15)

The article goes on to suggest that since "human rights philosophy is blind to intelligence, race, appeal, and appearance," demarcation at the level of animals is "selective and whimsical" (15).

The presentation of philosophical arguments in the rattlesnake article and the Point/Counterpoint debate is the exception within movement literature. More common are articles such as "Urban Wildlife: Reclaim Their Birthright," "Animals and Islam," "Wolves and Dogs: Canine Cousins," "Dog Lab Cancelled," "Pet Theft Bill Becomes Law," "Nordstrom to Close Fur Salons," and so forth.[7] These articles, as the titles suggest, are mostly descriptive. In addition, newsletters contain information on upcoming activities, descriptions of past activities, and advertisements for such things as cruelty-free products. Each volume of *Animals' Agenda* contains reviews of organizational activities and special events concerning animals under the headings of News Shorts, International Briefs, and Animal Newsline.

Like newsletters and magazines, pamphlets published by animal rights organizations are generally descriptive and apply rights terminology as a label with little justification of the concept. PETA publishes pamphlets and "factsheets" covering a range of issues. A short pamphlet entitled *Cosmetics Testing* briefly describes painful animal testing, suggests that these tests are not necessary, and provides alternatives to animal testing. Similarly, a factsheet entitled *Traveling Animal Acts* describes abuses that wrestling bears, diving mules, and other animals experience in the entertainment industry: "Confined to tiny transport cages animals must endure constant stress. They often suffer from temperature extremes and irregular feeding and watering." Like these PETA circulars, other organizations publish pamphlets that describe animal abuse. For instance, in one Fund for Animals pamphlet entitled *Furs: Who Really Pays?* descriptions of painful leg traps and the caging of minks and foxes combine with gruesome pictures of these activities to dissuade people from buying fur.

Within these pamphlets, there may or may not be mention of animal rights. In the fur pamphlet published by the Fund for Animals, the only mention of rights is on the back page, where, set alone on the bottom of the page, there is the exclamation "Animals Have Rights Too!" The PETA factsheet on traveling acts says nothing of animal rights, and the cosmetics testing pamphlet only mentions the term on the back page in describing PETA. PETA, as the pamphlet reads, "is a national nonprofit animal protection organization dedicated to establishing and defending the rights of all species."

There are, again, exceptions to be found in the occasional pamphlet that provides more extensive analysis of animal rights. In a PETA Kids circular entitled *Let's Talk about ANIMAL RIGHTS*, the introduction states the following:

Many animals share our world. All of us—including human beings—think and act differently, but we have the same basic needs and feelings. When you support animal rights, you support the right of *all* individuals to live without fear, pain and suffering.

Similarly, in a PETA pamphlet entitled *Animal Rights: Why Should It Concern Me?* the following argument is made in defense of animal rights:

Animals are valuable in and of themselves, not merely as com-
modities to feed or clothe or entertain us, or to be our "tasters."
Each animal is an individual whose life is as dear to him or her as
yours is to you. We have no right to take the life of a fox for her
coat, or a pig for his flesh, simply because we desire those products. Just as we would balk at testing drugs on the mentally
retarded, the disabled or the elderly, we must protest the use of
rats, rabbits and chimpanzees for similar purposes. These animals
are as capable of suffering physical pain and psychological
anguish as a human being. Our exploitation of other species for
our own profit is as reprehensible as the exploitation of people of
another race or sex for pleasure or profit.

Along with these two PETA circulars, several other organizations publish leaflets and brochures that articulate justifications for increasing
our consideration of animals.[8]

Despite the fact that rights terminology is, for the most part,
employed as a label, the underlying and implicit point made in the
newsletters and pamphlets is that abuse of animals is unacceptable
because it is unjust. The appropriation of rights terminology by itself
connotes and signifies notions of justice. In our culture, in which rights
are deployed continually to express ethical judgments about right and
wrong, extending the language to animals does the same. Applying
rights to animals signals that animals are a part of the moral community, and, as such, it implies that human relations to our nonhuman
counterparts must be governed by moral guidelines.

It is therefore not at all surprising that movement literature generally takes as given the ethical argument that justifies bringing animals
into the moral community. It is also not surprising that the movement
relies on rights terminology to do this. Rights language carries within it
the notions of fairness and equity. Rights are recognized and accepted
within our culture as a primary symbol of justice. As such, rights language possesses a power that invokes images of right and wrong.

Relying on rights language is also important for a movement that
has been traditionally associated with emotionalism and sentimental-
ity. Rights language provides the power of reason in contrast to an
appeal to the emotions. Although the animal rights movement combines the emotional appeal with an appeal to reason in order to increase

its persuasiveness, it is the balance between these appeals, using rights as the balancing mechanism, that is significant. Thus, movement literature works on human feelings by showing pictures of horribly abused cats, dogs, and monkeys—"cute" animals—that outrage our emotional sensibilities. At the same time, movement literature works on human rational abilities by invoking rights terminology and explaining that oppression of animals is akin to oppression of humans.[9]

Rights Language in Movement Activities

Like movement literature, the activities of animal rights groups involve mention of the language without much analysis or support of it. The marches, protests, meetings, panels, and seminars I have attended employ the phrase *animal rights* with minimal self-conscious elaboration. The June 1990 national March for the Animals provides a clear example. At this march of approximately 24,000 people, a countless number of participants carried signs, wore T-shirts, and sold merchandise that made reference to animal rights, whether it was in the name of an organization, such as the Aspen Society for Animal Rights or the Georgia Lesbian Ecofeminists for Animal Rights, or more general statements like "Animals Have Rights!" and "Animal Rights Now!" As the march proceeded from the Washington Monument to the steps of the Capitol, the most common chant was the following:

What do we want?
Animal Rights.
When do we want it?
Now.

During the speeches (which individually lasted only a few minutes), numerous references were made to animal rights. Lawrence Carter, director of the Health Care Consumer Network, stated, "There was a time when someone would mention the word *animal rights* and they were laughed at. But no more." Alex Pacheco, chairperson of PETA, said, "We've got to get animal rights back into the White House where animal rights belongs." Law professor and movement activist Gary Francione made a somewhat more extended reference to animal rights in his brief speech.

Today we are here to affirm our commitment to an idea: the idea of
animal rights. Today is a turning point. Animal welfare is dead.
We are animal rights activists. That's why it is particularly appropriate that Tom Regan is the cochair of this march. It is Tom Regan
who gave us a theory of animal rights, and it is now up to us to
make sure that that marvelous theory is integrated into our legal
system.

Although many others referred to animal rights and the animal
rights movement in their short speeches, only a few spoke in detail
about the subject. Of course, there was little opportunity for lengthy
discourse on rights or anything else given the time limits on each
speech. But, despite the lack of detailed elaboration of the concept, the
perception that this gathering expressed support for animal rights, uni-
fying the movement behind the label, was evident. Along with the
many references to animal rights, several speeches referred to the
attempt to unify the welfare and rights components of the animal protection movement into the animal rights movement. Peggy McCabe,
director of the National Anti-Vivisection Society, proclaimed, "It is our
belief that all animals, human and nonhuman, possess the right to be
treated with respect, with compassion and with justice." McCabe went
on to say that a draft of a formal "Declaration of the Rights of Animals"
had been endorsed by more than forty national organizations, and two
members of Congress, Charles Bennett and Tom Lantos, proceeded by
reading the Declaration aloud.

> Whereas it is self-evident that we share the earth with other crea-
> tures, great and small, that many of these animals experience plea-
> sure and pain, that these animals deserve our just treatment, and
> that these animals are unable to speak for themselves, we do there-
> fore declare that these animals have the right to live free from
> human exploitation, whether in the name of science or sport, exhi-
> bition or service, food or fashion; have the right to live in harmony
> with their nature rather than according to human desires; and
> have the right to live on a healthy planet. Adopted and proclaimed
> on the tenth day of June, 1990, Washington, D.C.

Two more speakers called for unification under the title of animal
rights. One was John Kullberg, then president of the ASPCA, a tradi-

tional welfare group, who asserted, "This movement has always been an animal rights movement." The second was Tom Regan, the philosopher of animal rights. Regan spoke last, concluding the day-long series of speeches with a song. Regan led as thousands of people sang the following words on the Capitol lawn: "We speak for the animals, their pain and ours is one. We'll fight for the animals, until their rights are won." The song lasted for several minutes, and when it finally ended the crowd spontaneously began chanting the phrase *animal rights*.

Other marches, protests, meetings, and panels sponsored by groups within the movement demonstrate similar deployment of rights language. I experienced one of the more insightful examples of this deployment at PETA's Animal Rights 101 Seminar. PETA sponsors this day-long seminar in order to provide basic skills for the "beginning animal rights activist."[10] Although the seminar is entitled "animal rights," the focus is on movement strategies such as investigating cruelty cases, writing news releases, dealing with the media, organizing a new group, promoting letter-writing campaigns, and so on. The seminar did begin with a discussion of how to respond to challenging questions like the common one asked about the choice between experimenting on a dog versus a baby. After much input from the class, the leader of the discussion explained that the ethical issue has to be the bottom line in everything, and she recommended reading Regan's *The Case for Animal Rights*. However, before and after that comment, little was said about ethical issues or the concept of animal rights.[11] The bottom line was taken as a given; after all, the room was filled with 200 committed animal advocates.

The many group meetings, marches, protests, panels, and talks I have attended demonstrate a particular use of rights language, one that refers to rights without significant philosophical justification of the concept. That animals should be granted rights is taken as evident, given that animals experience pleasure and pain and are not sufficiently different from humans to justify their exploitation. Thus, the detailed philosophical discussion of animal rights that forms the backdrop for activism remains largely within the philosopher's realm rather than within activist literature or tactics, where it resides in most other social movements.

Nonetheless, the connection between the label *animal rights* and the various actions taken on behalf of animals maintains the implication that the goal of the movement is to secure justice for animals. Just treatment of animals, it is implied, is secured through recognition of rights. When Peter Linck proclaimed at the March for the Animals that "the animal rights movement has arrived" and immediately connected that proclamation with the statement "the time has come for the hallowed halls of Congress to become imbued with moral and ethical concern for all who are alive and living," the implication was clear. And when activists marched down the street in front of people and news cameras chanting "animal rights" and carrying signs showing chimps in shackles, cats with electrodes in their brains, and dogs in cages, they were suggesting not just that animals should be treated more kindly when in their cages but that keeping animals in cages unjustly violates their rights.

Infusing Rights with Alternative Values

In both movement literature and activities, the deployment of rights language implicitly and explicitly connects our treatment of animals with the notions of relationship, responsibility, caring, and community. In contrast to the more standard, individualistic emphasis of rights, the language used by this movement stresses: (1) human relations to the animal world, often expressed by relating various forms of human oppression with animal oppression; (2) the responsibility humans have toward animals that, in the face of human oppression, cannot protect or speak for themselves; (3) the values of caring, compassion, and empathy toward our nonhuman counterparts which, like us, are sentient beings capable of experiencing pain and suffering; and (4) an overarching notion of community that extends beyond humans, nationality, religion, and ethnicity to include animals and frequently the planet as a whole.

Examples of these implicit and explicit connections within movement literature and activities are seemingly endless. In one article in *PAWS News* entitled "Rescued!" the following question is raised: "What do you do about abused lions, bears, sheep, goats, and monkeys in need of help?" The answer: "Rescue them, and find them permanent sanctuary homes" (February 1989, 1). Without mentioning rights, this article suggests that humans have a responsibility to rescue and defend animals in need. Similarly, in a PETA factsheet on the abuses of dissection, the statement of a biology teacher invokes the values of responsibility, caring, and community: "[A]s educators we have a major responsibility to help young people awaken respect for life and to develop love and admiration for all living things."

The push for responsibility and caring toward animals is also made explicitly in connection to rights. In one PAWS handout—simply entitled *PAWS*—the group defines itself in the following manner:

> The Progressive Animal Welfare Society (PAWS) advocates kindness and responsibility towards *all* animal life. Through community education efforts, PAWS works to enhance the public's awareness that animals have the right to protection from suffering, pain, and abuse.

In this quote, rights language is deployed in direct connection to the notions of responsibility and caring. Not only are the terms *kindness* and *responsibility* used, but the right of animals suggested in this statement is the right to protection. Such a right clearly implies a reciprocal responsibility on the part of humans to ensure that animals are accorded protection.

In a similar vein, a ten-page pamphlet, *Objecting to Dissection: A Student Handbook,* published by the Animal Legal Defense Fund (ALDF), encourages students to act on behalf of animals.

> There are relatively few legal restraints today on human exploitation of animals; anti-cruelty laws that protect some animals against the worst kinds of abuse are often not enforced. It ultimately falls to individuals like you and me to promote rights for animals and ensure them the protection they cannot give themselves. (3)

Like the PAWS circular, this pamphlet promotes the notion of responsibility. Since animals cannot defend themselves, humans are responsible for protecting the rights of animals.

Newsletters and circulars also make continued references to the relationship between human and nonhuman animals when arguing for animal rights. In doing so, the movement both implicitly and explicitly puts forward a view of an extended community. This community encompasses all life, human and nonhuman alike. For instance, pointing to our relationship to animals, a NAVS information circular on chimpanzees begins by stating "Chimpanzees are humans' closest relatives." An antifur pamphlet published by the Humane Society of the

United States, *Fur Shame,* points to this relationship by stating "Millions of sentient mammals—who have highly evolved central nervous systems and thus suffer and feel pain just as humans do—are brutally raised or trapped and killed each year for fur garments." Connecting our relations to animals with a notion of a broad community, one NAVS circular, bearing the title *National Anti-Vivisection Society,* exhorts readers to "Support the NAVS and THE CAMPAIGN FOR LIFE and add your voice to those of caring people whose reverence for life extends to all creatures." Another circular published by Trans-Species Unlimited, called *Animal Rights: What's it all About?* elaborates at length the notion of animal rights and the need to extend rights to animals. It goes on to say:

> The reciprocal goals of human and animal liberation point to the necessity of a global ethic of sharing the earth, a move away from man-centered, technological exploitation towards holistic naturalism—a reverence for the earth and its inhabitants as a single, finite, organic system.

Most frequently, the association between rights and relationship is made by connecting speciesism with racism and sexism and by pointing to the expanding circle. The Trans-Species Unlimited pamphlet makes this point clearly.

> Only when we come to recognize that the liberation of non-human animals is demanded by the same ethical principles which prohibit racism and sexism, will we be prepared to extend to animals those legitimate rights which heretofore have been reserved for humans alone.

Put another way, a *NAVS Bulletin* article entitled "Speciesism/Sexism: Exploitation in the 20th century" states:

> Animals are an extraordinary and often beautiful part of the chain of life, and if life is at all cherished and respected in us, it should also be in them.
> The real plea of all rights movements, civil rights, women's rights, children's rights, is that each individual be allowed to fulfill

whatever potential is possible, without interference from others whose interests are too often self-centered. "Possible potential" is an enormous concept for exploration when applied to animals. But the animal rights movement asks, "Have we really the right to deny it?" (no. 2, 1988, 22)

As this quote suggests, once we consider the relationship between humans and animals as "part of the chain of life," we must extend respect to the latter. But more than respect, this quote contends that recognizing the link to animals requires an extension of rights.

Another way in which rights have been employed by this movement to emphasize alternative values is through the language of human rights. First, by pointing to specific human rights that allow individuals to act on behalf of animals, rights are connected to responsibility and relationship. For instance, in *Objecting to Dissection*, published by the ALDF, both animal rights and a student's right to refuse dissection are raised. In discussing the latter, the following point is made:

Every time a student exercises his or her right not to dissect animals, the consciousness of the entire academic community— including teachers, administrators and classmates—is raised. By exercising your rights as a student, you can help build a bridge between human and non-human animals. (2)

A second way human rights are deployed in a manner that stresses alternative values is by suggesting that human rights are not absolute. Rather, human rights are constrained by the rights of others and by our duties toward others. For instance, a pamphlet on vivisection published by NAVS, entitled *National Anti-Vivisection Society*, suggests that "Vivisection is accurately called 'speciesism.' Like racism and sexism, it is rooted in traditional elitist attitudes. Those with influence claim for themselves additional rights of which they deprive others." Similarly, in *Animal Rights: What's It All About?* Trans-Species Unlimited states:

In short, animals, like humans, have an intrinsic moral right to exemption from the infliction upon them of unnecessary suffering and death. To deny them these rights—to treat animals differently simply and solely because they belong to a different species—is *speciesism:* precisely parallel to, and objectionable on the same grounds as, racism and sexism.

Like movement literature, movement activities connect rights language to alternative values that move beyond individualism. The March for the Animals provided an opportunity for speakers to make these connections, and many did. Gary Francione referred to animals as "our nonhuman sisters and brothers" and immediately proceeded to affirm the movement's commitment to the "idea of animal rights." Pointing to the relationship between speciesism and violations of human rights, California Congressman Tom Lantos stated:

> This is the last great movement of compassion in the U.S. And as all other movements of compassion that have triumphed, we shall triumph, too. It wasn't so long ago historically that men and women were sold like cattle. It was not so long ago historically that our struggle to create human rights here and abroad was ridiculed and denounced.

Similarly, Peter Singer made the connection between speciesism, racism, and sexism, as he does in his philosophical work. And Carol Adams, author of *The Sexual Politics of Meat* (1990), expressed the common oppression experienced by women and animals.

Other activists at this gathering associated rights with a broad notion of community. Peggy McCabe invoked the image of an overarching community that encompasses more than just the human species.

> We are simply people who are aware of our link to what has been called the web of life; and who have extended our compassion to all who are capable of suffering. We share a common credo: all animals without regard to species are entitled to certain fundamental rights.

Similarly, Michael W. Fox pointed to the relationship and referred explicitly to the need to grant rights to animals: "All humans are animals. And since animals are our relations, their personhood and right to equal and fair consideration needs to be acknowledged by all people."

In short, rights language as deployed in movement literature and activities has been associated with the values of relationship, responsibility, caring, and community. Constant reference to the label *animal rights* is combined with the facts of mistreatment, the proposition that animals are related to humans and part of the community of life, and the suggestion that we have a responsibility to act on behalf of animals. As a result, the deployment of animal rights within movement literature conveys values that contrast with the traditional individualistic underpinnings of rights.

Rights Language in Media

The movement's advancement of animal rights issues and debates has had a profound influence on popular media. Over the past decade, the media have responded to the growth in animal advocacy by increasingly taking up the concerns expressed in this activism.[12] Moreover, media attention to animal rights issues and advocacy has become more respectful.[13] In seriously acknowledging animal concerns, the media have allowed animal rights to penetrate the realm of mainstream public debate.

Rights language in the media parallels the use of the language within movement literature and activities. The media have come to refer to groups seeking animal protection as "animal rights groups" and to define the movement as the "animal rights movement" except in clear cases in which the group involved is a humane organization or when making a distinction between animal rights and animal welfare. In addition, the deployment of the language is generally in terms of the label rather than in terms of defining what is meant by rights or how the notion is justified. Nevertheless, the association between the term *animal rights* and movement activities has advanced the notion that animal rights advocacy seeks to deliver justice and fair treatment to animals.

There is significant evidence demonstrating that the media have accepted animal rights terminology. Most articles mention animal rights in reference to groups, activists, and the movement. "Perhaps most telling is the fact that newspapers no longer use quotation marks when discussing animal rights" (ASPCA 1990, 95). Moreover, articles and radio and television coverage increasingly note the expanding legitimacy of animal rights. For instance, a 1988 *New York Times* article

states: "Rights advocates say public attitudes have changed significantly in recent years, at least to the extent that the notion of animal
rights is no longer ridiculed" (Johnson 1988, 40).

On the other hand, letters to the editor against animal rights
demonstrate continued attempts to delegitimize the movement and
raise questions about the comment that the notion of animal rights is no
longer ridiculed. For instance, numerous letters to the editor attacked a
New York magazine article covering the battle between furriers and animal rights groups. These letters referred to animal rights activists as
"fanatics," "extremists," and "ding-dongs" and included such comments as "You have a group of nuts that care only about killing mink
and raccoons" and "Most of the animal-rights/anti-fur lunatics I have
met seem to be extremely unhappy, misanthropic people" (*New York*,
January 9, 1990, 6–7; February 5, 1990, 9). Yet, despite continued
attempts by the opposition to undermine animal rights concerns,
media reports have developed an increasingly respectful attitude
toward the movement.

Like movement newsletters, the large majority of news articles that
cover animal issues provide factual information about events and
activities in which the movement is involved. This majority makes
mention of rights solely as a referent to the movement and its activists.
Articles focusing on the use of animals in research, clothing production, and food consumption speak of the "animal rights movement,"
"animal rights groups," and "animal rights activists," but they do not
go much further than that. The titles of these articles demonstrate the
references: "Fur's a-Flying: Furriers Defend their Industry's Practices
as Animal-rights Activists Continue Protests," "Animal-Rights Activists Target Gillette," and "Animal Rights Activists' Day in the Sun"
(Kirkby 1989; Hunt 1990; Harriston and Thomas-Lester 1990). Of
course, not all titles make note of animal rights. Many have a more specific focus such as "Stricter Regulation Sought over Labs Using Animals in Research," "Referendum Would Toughen Massachusetts Farm
Rules," and "As the Image of Furs Suffers, So Does Profit" (Knobelsdorff 1987; Ross 1988; and Hochswender 1989). But even these articles
mention animal rights.

Many news stories that cover the movement at length begin by
making the distinction between the animal rights and welfare movements. These articles generally point to the growth of the former in the

1980s, and sometimes note the conflict between the two. A *New York Daily News* article demonstrates the split between rights and welfare by pointing to the former's desire to abolish animal exploitation and the latter's call for greater humanity and the minimizing of pain during animal use (Hackett 1989). Numerous articles make this distinction, some separating rights and welfare groups as different movements but most considering them to be at different ends of a single movement's spectrum. Regardless, nearly every article makes reference to the "animal rights movement."

Although most articles devote little space to justifying the view that animals have rights or stating what this really means, many include a few sentences that provide some background on the concept. In doing so, articles frequently quote animal rights activists as they attempt to support and justify their case. For instance,

> Alex Pacheco, chairman of People for the Ethical Treatment of Animals, said his group believes that all animals have the same right as humans to life and freedom from being subjected to experiments. "We feel that animals have the same rights as a retarded human child, because they are equal mentally in terms of dependence on others," he said. (Bishop 1989, 7)

In another, activist George Cave is quoted as saying "The issue is clear cut. To kill an animal to wear its skin is a violation of basic principles of decency and civilization" (Hirsch 1988, 11). In a *Newsweek* piece, naturalist Roger Caras endorses the notion of animal rights "which, although different from our own, are just as inalienable" (1988, 57)[14]

There are exceptions to this minimal justification and explanation of rights. Two are often found in Op-Ed pieces and letters to the editor. In these, supporters and opponents of animal protection bring out the philosophical arguments relating to rights. Colman McCarthy, a noted syndicated columnist and supporter of animal protection, has written Op-Ed pieces pointing to the philosophical underpinnings of the movement. In one such article, entitled "Philosopher of Animal Rights," he succinctly summarizes Singer's explanation of speciesism, stating that Singer "put forth persuasive ethical reasons for change" (1990, 23). In another, McCarthy states that the movement has a new understanding, the strength of which "can be judged by the intellectual depth of its philosophers, who are making the moral case that the animals being eaten, hunted and experimented on by man are individuals with rights that demand respect" (1984, 8).

In other Op-Ed pieces, supporters of the movement connect animal rights to human rights. Spence Carlsen wrote that the concept of animal rights is misunderstood and will be appropriately understood only when people begin to see the arbitrary distinctions that separate human and nonhuman animals. He states: "What we don't realize, until we really examine our beliefs about animals, is that these rights cannot belong exclusively to human beings. There is no non-arbitrary way to exclude such things as the right to life from non-human animals" (1987, 5). Others link human and animal rights in a different way, making the argument that promoting better treatment and caring for humans will inspire concern for animals. Curtis Sitomer writes: "But we are still a far cry from giving animals the rights and dignity we theoretically afford humans. Perhaps when people do a better job of respecting one another, they will then learn to extend that outreach to other species" (1989, 13).

A second exception to the limited philosophical discussion is the rare, lengthy article that deals with animal concerns. One such article explains how the author, after interviewing several animal rights activists, found himself questioning his own views and being "drawn into the logic of animal rights" (Wright 1990, 21). This logic stems from "the core of the case for animal rights: the modest claim . . . that animals are sentient beings, capable of pleasure and pain" (21). The author goes on to discuss the problems of limiting rights to humans and of resting that limitation on the fact that humans have greater linguistic and rational capacities than animals do. This article does what has so far been unusual in the media, connecting in detail the term *animal rights* to the philosophy of animal rights.

In general, philosophical support for animal rights can only be brief in media reporting. It is not surprising, then, that such support is minimal. But when people do seek to raise the justification, they frequently turn to the notion of sentience. For instance, in a two-paragraph letter to the editor, Sandra Peterson writes:

The animal rights groups with which I am familiar do not suggest that animal rights are equatable with human rights. They do maintain that conscious, feeling creatures have the right to life free from gratuitously imposed suffering. They raise the question of whether this right is violated by the routine harvesting of animals in order that people might wear their skins and eat their bodies. (1989, 20)

Similarly, Rob Kader, in a letter to the editor responding to an animal rights group's rescue of chickens from an overturned truck, states:

You must realize that these animals are not just machines, but living things that do experience pain. Just because their physical attributes don't relate to ours, or because they aren't as "cute" as Spot, the pet dog, doesn't make their life any less valuable. (1990, 21)

Overall, the animal rights movement has had a strong impact on the media. The media, in seriously acknowledging animal rights concerns, have, in turn, advanced animal rights language. As a result, the media have extended a measure of legitimacy to the animal rights debate. Even in reports on the opposition, the fact that the debate generally occurs on the terrain of rights contributes to the shaping of the notion of animal rights.

Furthermore, just as in movement literature, the use of the rights label by the media connotes the underlying issue of justice. In penetrating the media, animal rights terminology helps advance the proposal that animals should be recognized as part of the moral community. Most justifications of animal rights within the media make two related points: first, animals are sentient beings capable of experiencing pain and suffering; second, and following from the first, animals are related to humans with respect to sentience and therefore must be accorded rights. Making these two points helps push rights language beyond its common meaning by stressing sentience over reason and by expressing the relationship and connection between species.

Conclusion

In the realm of political activism, animal rights has become the dominant language of the contemporary movement. To be sure, animal rights language continues to compete with the welfare movement's language of compassion. Nevertheless, popular debates and discussion regarding animals are now dominated by the language of rights. Moreover, the movement increasingly combines the language of compassion with the language of rights, arguing that humans should provide compassionate, kind, and caring treatment to animals because animals have a right to such treatment.

Just as we should not be surprised by the turn to rights language in the philosophical realm, we should not wonder at the political deployment of the language. In a culture such as ours, in which the powerful and accepted language of rights permeates all levels of political action and discussion, and in light of the rights-oriented movements of the 1960s and 1970s, it makes considerable sense that the animal advocacy movement appropriated rights. In addition, we should not be surprised by the limited philosophical analysis of animal rights within organizational literature, movement activities, and media reports. The familiarity of rights language in general makes it easy to appropriate without extended justification. As Singer perceptively noted, "the language of rights is a convenient political shorthand . . . more valuable in the era of thirty-second TV news clips than it was in Bentham's day" (1990, 8).

What may be surprising is that this movement deploys rights in a way that stresses the values of relationship, responsibility, caring, and community. Unlike the traditional, liberal conception of rights, which emphasizes individualism, separation, and freedom from interference, the implicit and explicit association of these alternative values with the terminology of animal rights has helped to imbue the language with new content. As a result, the construction of animal rights based on the associated notions of sentience, reciprocal responsibility, and relationship to a broad community begins to challenge the liberal, individualistic underpinnings of rights and fosters a reconceptualization of the language.

Of course, it is impossible to say at this early stage whether the infusion of these alternative values will alter the language of rights in the long run or result in the extension of rights to animals. Nevertheless, five points can be made. First, the animal rights movement provides evidence to counter the claim of critics who argue that rights language is inherently individualistic and cannot be made compatible with values of responsibility and community. We must at least admit that the potential exists to cultivate alternative values upon which rights can be founded. In this way, the animal rights experience supports the work of some scholars who have sought to advance a "collective" understanding of rights (Campbell 1983; Lynd 1984).

Second, this potential for countering the individualism of rights demonstrates that extending rights to animals does not necessarily undermine the power and meaning of the language. On first glance, it might appear that such an extension would rob rights of their meaning. But upon reflection we see the possibility for reinvigorating the language. Third, the very fact that advocates have attempted to extend rights to animals has helped highlight these alternative values. Since most animals do not have the same intellectual and rational abilities as humans, philosophers and activists have had to look for other common characteristics that unite humans with animals. This has resulted in the emphasis on sentience, relationship, and responsibility for beings who cannot stand up for themselves. In turn, such a focus moves us away from a human-centric view of community to a wider, more inclusive understanding of the collectivity.

This third point does not suggest that it is only when rights language is extended to animals that it moves beyond individualism. The point is that the recent expansion of rights to animals has fostered reconsideration of the meaning of rights. To a greater degree than past attempts to extend rights to blacks, women, workers, and other human minority groups, the extension to animals has encouraged scholars and activists—and potentially the broader community—to rethink our conceptions of rights. In the future, this reevaluation of the meaning of rights language may inspire useful reconsideration of human rights issues.

Fourth, the chances of successfully advancing an altered conception of rights are enhanced by this movement's constituency and leadership. As noted in chapter 2, the membership and leadership of this movement appear to be highly educated. In addition, the connection between philosophical and political activism is strong. Activists cite philosophical works frequently.[15] They speak the philosophical language, talking of Singer's equal consideration and referring continually to rights based on sentience rather than rationality. In addition, philosophers who now write on animal issues are also activists within the movement. Singer and Regan are prominent animal advocates. Feminist and ecofeminist scholars, including Carol Adams and Marti Kheel, play a role as animal advocates. Other scholars, including

Michael W. Fox and Steven Sapontzis, are activists as well. This combination of philosophical activism and the political practice of extending
rights to animals is likely to play well to the educated supporters that
comprise this movement. As one animal advocate stated in a letter to
the editor published in *Animals' Agenda*,

> In 1987 I was not an animal rights advocate. Then I met Tom
> Regan. The correctness of his position and the clarity of his
> thought were unassailable. Tom Regan turned a non-active, dis-
> tant sympathizer into a hands-on activist. My story is not unique. I
> have . . . met countless people whom Tom Regan has converted to
> the animal rights movement. (March 1992, 7)[16]

Thus, we have a distinct type of movement led by activists involved in
debating, developing, and articulating its philosophical underpinnings
and supported by a constituency receptive to this philosophical conversation.

Finally, all of the previous points about the movement's deployment of rights language suggest that rights are indeterminate. This in
itself is not a novel observation, but most scholars point to the indeterminacy of rights as a critique of the language, asserting that indeterminacy means that rights cannot be relied upon by movements seeking
social change. In contrast, the experiences of the animal rights movement offer a different perspective on indeterminacy. Although admit-
tedly indeterminacy poses a problem, it also offers flexibility. As
McCann contends,

> it is important to understand that these inherited legal symbols
> and discourses provide relatively malleable resources that are rou-
> tinely reconstructed as citizens seek to advance their interests and
> designs in everyday life. In particular, legal discourses offer a
> potentially plastic medium both for refiguring the terms of past
> settlements over legitimate expectations and for expressing aspira-
> tions for new terms of entitlement. (1994, 7)

For the animal rights movement, the indeterminacy and resulting malleability of the language has provided the opportunity for meaningful
reconstruction.

In short, there is good reason to believe that philosophical and political attempts to extend rights to animals maintain the power of the language while at the same time infusing the language with alternative meaning. Still, this extension of rights is significantly constrained. It is constrained by the fact that not all animal advocates are proponents of rights talk. Even for those advocates who use rights, there is not complete clarity on what the language means or how it ought to be applied. The indeterminacy of rights, while offering flexibility, does create some degree of ambiguity and incoherence. If, for instance, animals have the right to be free from suffering, is it acceptable to kill and eat them if the killing is done painlessly?

Even if these constraints could be overcome, it is too early to tell whether the adjustment of rights language will penetrate popular consciousness and practical usage of rights. Successful penetration will depend upon how well the altered formulation of rights resonates for the public. And, given the historical context of rights language generally and the fact that it has been traditionally associated with individualism and rationality, there is good reason to believe that success, if it is ever achieved, is a long way off.

Nevertheless, the point to be stressed is the following. The ability to extend rights language, alter its content, and maintain its power is clearly constrained, but the constraints do not stem from anything intrinsic in or absolute about rights language. Nor are critics correct to suggest that rights are always constrained because only those in power control the meaning and potency of the language. Instead, the primary constraint stems from the philosophical and practical context within which rights have been deployed. On the other hand, this constraint also provides opportunity: the opportunity to find in the historical practice of rights the foundations for alternative meanings and power and the opportunity to alter the present practical context in which rights are deployed. This is what the animal rights movement has sought to do.

Chapter 4

Rights Strategically Understood

> [T]he very indeterminacy, instability, and relative autonomy of legal norms generally fortify as much as undermine their constitutive power. The flexibility and plurality of our rights traditions allow for adaptation to changing circumstances, for new types of claims by new groups over time, and for continued contests over the legitimacy of prevailing arrangements. . . . To say that rights provide only "momentary" advantages correctly implies that rights offer no timeless assurances. But this observation also implicitly acknowledges that rights discourses can be valuable tools for those with few other cultural resources at their disposal.
> —Michael W. McCann

The ability to transform the notion of rights language while maintaining its power will depend to a large degree on how activists perceive the language. As recent legal scholarship has suggested, political activists may be overly optimistic in their beliefs about rights. This optimism about rights, some contend, may encourage activists to deploy a counterproductive language that undermines movement goals. As a result, an uncritical and naive embrace of rights can inhibit social change.

Whereas chapter 3 reviewed the broad movement's turn to animal rights, this chapter will more specifically explore animal advocates' perspectives on rights language. The following question, drawn from critical legal scholarship, will guide the analysis: Are advocates mistakenly led by what Scheingold calls "the myth of rights" to employ a counterproductive language? With regard to the constitutive character of meaning, we can consider this question in the following terms: Does the prevailing meaning of rights influence movement advocates in a way that detrimentally encourages the use of a problematic language? Or, in contrast, are movement advocates conscious of the problematic nature associated with the prevailing meaning and effects of rights, and do advocates reconstitute the meaning of rights in a manner productive to movement goals?

Exploring these questions, this chapter begins with an overview of critical legal scholarship on rights and some responses to that scholarship. The chapter then evaluates the evidence gathered from in-depth interviews with animal advocates, conducted between 1990 and 1991, on the subject of rights. In doing so, we shall see that, as a whole, animal rights activists are not misled by the myth of rights. Rather, activists maintain a sophisticated and strategic consciousness regarding the deployment of rights. Moreover, the argument suggests generally that a strategic approach to the deployment of rights combined with the fact that the flexible language of rights can emphasize values of responsibility and community offer social movements a productive tool to challenge existing relations of power. Although the weapon provided by rights is constrained and by no means assures success, the potential benefits of rights and the lack of alternative languages suggest that those who would discard rights go too far.

Rights Language and Legal Scholarship

The strongest critique of law and rights leveled by critical scholars contends that use of the legal system is harmful to those seeking social change. According to this critique, asserted predominantly by scholars within the school of thought known as Critical Legal Studies (CLS), the harm stems from the hegemonic character of the legal system, that is, from the fact that the law encompasses a particular ideology beneficial to the status quo (Gabel 1984; Tushnet 1984; Klare 1982; Freeman 1982). In a capitalist society, the underlying hegemonic ideology is founded upon notions of individualism and autonomy. These ideological biases underlying the law impede community and egalitarian values and support existing power structures. Those who think they are advancing change through use of the law are instead replicating and legitimating the dominant values, structures, and ideology of the system. Rather than making real strides, this replication strengthens those in power to the detriment of the marginalized (Abel 1982; Kairys 1982; Kelman 1987).

Like the overall hegemonic nature of the legal system, rights also lead to reinforcement of dominance. For those who seek change, the problem with asserting rights is that it results in co-optation.

People don't realize that what they're doing is recasting the real existential feelings that led them to become political people into an ideological framework that coopts them into adopting the very consciousness they want to transform. (Gabel and Kennedy 1984, 26)

On this view, seeking and attaining new rights can hardly be considered beneficial. Indeed, the attainment of a right may even be more harmful than failure since "winning" a right creates an illusion of success. Such an illusion leads the members of a movement to feel that the battle has been won and results in the diffusion of the movement.

In part, use of rights language reinforces dominance because it "deceives" the powerless who deploy it. According to some within CLS, this deception arises partly from the indeterminate nature of rights, that is, from the fact that the existence of rights does not determine future outcomes or determine how those in power will act (Tushnet 1986, 1984; Dalton 1985). Hence, those in power can interpret rights any way they want and manipulate the language to their benefit. On the other hand, groups challenging the status quo often become mystified by rights. Instead of manipulating rights, the marginalized can become mesmerized and captivated by the ideals of the language. Groups begin to focus solely on achieving specific rights and, in turn, lose sight of their larger, broader goals.

Rights language, according to some within CLS, is deceptive in another way. Given its foundation in liberalism and individualism, rights language minimizes our social and communitarian character and therefore contributes to a false and misleading image of human beings. "[T]he actual capturing of what it means to be human, and in relation to other people, is falsified by the image of people as rights-bearing citizens. It's a falsification of human sociability" (Gabel and Kennedy 1984, 37). And "The concept of rights falsely converts into an empty abstraction (reifies) real experiences that we ought to value for their own sake" (Tushnet 1984, 1364). Rights language thus conceals and falsifies a more complete understanding of ourselves.

The assertion that rights language deceives is not leveled by CLS scholars alone. The deceptive aspect of rights language is related to the notion of the "myth of rights" elaborated by Stuart Scheingold (1974).[1] The myth of rights, according to Scheingold, instills naive faith in the utility of rights and the legal system. Many citizens and social movements attracted by the myth of rights turn somewhat blindly to the law in search of social change. However, this naive and hopeful appeal to rights does little to foster change and instead reproduces existing power distributions.

In addition to these allegations, other scholars critique what'they view as the deceptive side of rights. Some suggest that movements mistakenly equate the formal granting of a right with the substantive attainment of it. Achieving a formal right, some argue, does not necessarily imply substantive change. To the contrary, winning a formal right can mislead groups into believing that they have succeeded by giving the appearance that justice is being served. The appearance of justice provided by the attainment of a formal right frequently conceals the fact that, in substantive terms, the right continues to be violated. Moreover, if the formal recognition of a right gives the false appearance that the battle has been won, this may lead to the dissipation of movement efforts (Bell 1985; Bumiller 1987).

Kristin Bumiller (1988) offers another reason for the mistaken belief that formal rights imply substantive change. Bumiller points to the fact that rights are generally bound up with the notion of individual responsibility. As such, rights may not be protected unless an individual acts to ensure the right. Hence, substantive change is frequently elusive despite the formal recognition of rights. Bumiller finds evidence for this within the realm of formal laws that seek to advance racial equality. Antidiscrimination law, according to Bumiller, has had limited success in achieving substantive change because individuals experiencing discrimination must bear the costs and burdens of applying the law.

The critique, elaborated by CLS and others, that rights language deceives is one that implicitly, and sometimes explicitly, suggests false consciousness.[2] The holders of power do not necessarily have false consciousness, but for the marginalized rights language acts as a "filter" (Tushnet 1984, 1383–84). The marginalized buy into the view that rights protect them from interference without realizing that this belief perpetuates their own oppression.

In fact an excessive preoccupation with "rights-consciousness" tends in the long run to reinforce alienation and powerlessness, because the appeal to rights inherently affirms that the source of social power resides in the State rather than in the people themselves. (Gabel and Harris 1983, 375)

There have been numerous responses to these critical assessments of rights. Some scholars have elaborated what has been called the "minority critique" of CLS. This critique suggests that the CLS indictment of rights is unrealistic, overlooks the context and experiences of discrimination, and ignores the importance of rights for marginal and oppressed groups. By neglecting the experiences and perspectives of oppressed groups, CLS underestimates the need for rights (Delgado 1987; Crenshaw 1988; Williams 1987). In a related fashion, other analyses argue that CLS assessments of legal ideology are overly simplistic. Use of rights language is not all bad or all good but a complex mixture of both (McCann 1989; Minow 1990; Merry 1986). Moreover, the indeterminate nature of rights language not only means that the powerful can impose their views but that opportunity exists for flexible interpretation of rights by the oppressed. Oppressed groups can therefore employ rights as a weapon against the dominant (McCann 1994).

Scheingold provides an example of this latter response to CLS, referring to this mixed and complex story of law as "soft hegemony" (1989). While Scheingold on the one hand agrees that the dominant tendency of rights is to reinforce the status quo, he suggests that through "a politics of rights" the language can be a useful political resource for the goals of movement mobilization. On this view, rights "offer considerable cultural space for liberating activism" (86). Like Scheingold, other scholars argue that rights may contribute to the goals of movement building, organization, and solidarity. While rights may impose a variety of constraints, the deployment of rights can be a radical and liberating experience within certain contexts (Schneider 1986; Crenshaw 1988; McCann 1994).

The debate outlined above points to the varied limits and possibilities of rights language.[3] Yet the following question remains open: Are movement activists, particularly those seeking to advance the values of community and responsibility, mistakenly led by the myth of rights to employ a problematic language? To further examine this question, the remainder of this chapter explores the deployment of rights language by the present-day animal rights movement.

Strategic Consciousness of Rights

To discover whether the animal rights movement's appropriation of rights confirms or contrasts with critical perspectives of the language, I conducted in-depth interviews with animal advocates. These inter-

views sought to ascertain how activists view and deploy rights language.[4] Although activists' perspectives on rights were mixed, three
overwhelming points emerged from these interviews. First, activists
did not demonstrate a false, unrealistic, or naive hope in rights. Their
views were critical, cautious, and balanced. Activists recognized the
potential benefits of rights language but at the same time articulated
the problematic side of rights. Second, activists revealed a strategic
understanding of the meaning of rights. While they expressed strong
and committed ethical views regarding the role and value of animals,
activists also maintained a strategic approach to advancing their ethics.
Third, the critical and strategic approach taken by activists suggested
that these key movement players are not simply shaped by prevailing
and traditional conceptions of rights; instead, the activists offer reconstructions of rights that challenge predominant views and seek to
recast the meaning of rights. Overall, the interviews indicated that
activists are not captured by the myth of rights. To the contrary,
activists' views and uses of the language seek to promote what Scheingold calls "a politics of rights" (1974). In so doing, activists strategically
constitute the meaning of rights.

The Benefits of Rights Language

Although not all activists agreed on the benefits of rights talk, and not
all mentioned each of the benefits to be discussed below, on the whole,
the interviews demonstrated that activists are aware of various advantages to be gained from deploying rights. Furthermore, activists'
depictions of these advantages were generally couched in strategic
terms. That is, activists spoke of rights not just in moral and philosophical terms but in terms that related to strategic practices and
movement goals. Finally, the benefits articulated by activists were not
expressed as anything intrinsic to rights. Instead, activists recognized
the contextually specific nature of rights in this culture and at this
point in time.

Rights as a Popular and Accepted Language

Legal scholars have frequently suggested that rights talk is a central
part of American culture and thought (Haskell 1987; Glendon 1991;
Minow 1990; Scheingold 1974). As such, deployment of rights allows

people to key into a familiar and accepted concept. Recognizing the prevalence of rights, animal advocates have deployed the concept to advance their cause.[5] In doing so, they deploy both the accepted notion of human rights and the more controversial concept of animal rights. By turning to human rights guarantees, activists attempt to make an analogous case for animals. Of course, drawing such an analogy and attaching a popular concept to a new issue does not ensure acceptance of a new idea. Indeed, it can even foster claims of senseless absurdity, as it did and often still does in the case of animal rights. Yet, with time and persuasive efforts to justify the new concept, the popularity of rights can contribute to the advancement of new ideas.

In interviews, activists pointed to the importance of raising the popular notion of human rights in making the case for protecting the interests of animals. Activists did so in two ways. First, they used human rights in making the connection to animal rights. Activists continually drew the analogy between the rights of humans and nonhuman animals in order to justify the notion of animal rights, under the assumption that the large majority of people accept the concept of human rights. As one activist put it, "When we look to see why we think humans have rights, I think the reason is that humans have particular interests. And there's every reason to believe . . . that animals have a lot of those same interests."[6] More generally, activists frequently spoke of "extending" the accepted notion of rights.

> Our system is totally organized around the concept of rights. I think that it's like fitting a slot into the system. People can relate to it easily. "Oh yeah, rights." We talked about women's rights and rights for blacks, and now we're talking about rights for animals. So people conceive of it as an extended circle.

Similarly, another activist stated, "All I know is that there needs to be a further move of extending out of rights. I don't know where it will ultimately end, but I know it's not far enough at this point."[7]

Second, activists employed the popularity of human rights in an inverted manner, questioning the assumption that humans have the right to use animals. As one activist put it,

> I'm more apt to use rights language to challenge people about their own conceptual frameworks. Like, "What gives you the right to do

such and such?" If you say to them, "What gives you the right to
do this?" they have to start thinking about it. . . . [It's] kind of a consciousness raising exercise.

Other activists echoed this point.

> The burden is on the users and exploiters [of animals] to establish
> what gives *them* the right to do what they do. Unless it can be
> shown to me that we have some inherent right from somewhere to
> use and kill and torture other beings of any species, I don't think
> the burden of proof has been met.

Although animal rights talk has by no means gained the acceptance of human rights talk, we saw in chapter 3 that its popularity has
increased dramatically over the past two decades. In interviews,
activists pointed to the increasing prevalence and acceptance of animal
rights talk. One activist suggested that the movement has become more
comfortable with speaking in terms of rights because the media and the
public have increased their acceptance of the notion.[8] According to
another activist, who expressed many criticisms of rights language,

> People still think more of the animal rights movement than animal
> liberation. It's become a more popular term in people's minds. It's
> an easy thing to hook into. People know immediately what things
> you're about.

A third advocate stressed the media's role in popularizing the concept
of animal rights, arguing that the media has regularized and normal-
ized animal rights language.[9]

    In invoking human rights and connecting them to animals, advo-
cates resort to an authoritative language. To be sure, such a resort does
not guarantee acceptance of animal rights. Yet, from the perspective of
the marginalized, rights language is a powerful tool because it provides
a means of entering popular discourse. It gives a voice to the silenced
and a language with which to articulate demands for change (Matsuda
1987; Delgado 1987). The language is particularly useful due to its
recognition and common usage throughout society. Activists, aware of
the ubiquity of rights, appropriate the language in an implicit attempt

"to turn society's 'institutional logic' against itself" (Crenshaw 1988, 1366).

The Power of Rights

Along with its familiarity, rights language is a powerful medium for a variety of reasons. First, rights language is persuasive talk that provides a solid normative foundation from which to wage social struggles.[10] The search for normative grounding is a method rooted in our society, and the "persistence of rights talk implies an aspiration to base moral arguments on the basis of reason" (Appleby 1987, 812). Rights talk is therefore significant not only due to its acceptance and common usage but because its very usage provides "invigorating words with the power to explain" (Minow 1987, 1881).[11] Second, rights talk generates discussion, debate, and education, thereby rousing thought and dialogue. The very battles and disagreements prompted by rights talk can be beneficial because they promote analysis and dialogue (Schneider 1986; Minow 1990; McCann 1994; Matsuda 1987). And, third, rights may contribute to a sense of self-worth and definition for movement activists. As Elizabeth Schneider concludes in her study of the women's movement, rights can enhance self-worth and empowerment: "The articulation of women's rights provides a sense of self and distinction for individual women. . . . Claims of equal rights and reproductive choice, for example, empowered women" (1986, 625).

Animal advocates articulated the various benefits that stem from the deployment of rights language. One advocate indicated the persuasive nature of rights by stating: "Within the human consciousness we try to create structure out of chaos. The concept of rights is part of that, trying to categorize and make structure out of things." Another activist explained how rights, when applied to animals, could potentially persuade people to change their attitudes.

Five years ago there were very few people who were abolitionists. Now there are a lot more of those people. And I believe that that has come about as a result of rights language. . . . Once you accept that an animal has a right, it's sort of hard to eat them. Because if an animal doesn't have a right not to be eaten, then it's sort of silly thinking about it having rights. Whereas in the pre-rights talk, when you talked about humane treatment of animals, it always made sense to talk about it being all right to eat animals as long as they were humanely treated and killed.

Some activists further highlighted the power of the language by suggesting that it generates discussion, debate, and education. Rights claims, as these activists noted, spark debate and thought about the prevalent position of animals in our society. Unlike animal protection and animal welfare, which are more easily accepted, mention of animal rights activates discussion and analysis. According to one activist,

> More than anything, [animal rights] provokes discussion because it seems so outrageous as opposed to humane treatment. . . . Even people making fun of it promotes discussion of it, and I think that's very, very helpful. It frightens a lot of people, but I believe that's an obligation. If you tell people things they accept, then why bother?

Similarly, attorney Gary Francione related the following:

> When I first started talking about animal rights . . . people would say "why talk about rights, why not talk about welfare? It will upset people." Who gives a shit about upsetting people! One of the ways you educate people is to shock them. When I teach law, some of the things I say are totally outrageous, because I do that to stimulate them, to challenge them.

A third activist, more in favor of the language of liberation, suggested that the current prevalence and persuasiveness of rights is useful to spark the move to other ways of speaking. According to this activist, we should

> learn to trust our instincts and feelings; we don't need to rely on the terminology of obligations and rights. And yet I think so many of us are socialized to not trust our instincts and it takes that springboard of [rights] terminology to push us in that direction, to realize that we should have been trusting our instincts all along.

Some activists further articulated the contribution that rights language makes to advancing a sense of self-worth and definition for activists. Ingrid Newkirk, cofounder and national director of PETA, succinctly made this point in the following fashion. According to Newkirk, talking about rights has

> allowed people to come out of the closet, which is always important. People who felt in their hearts that animals weren't things, that felt that they would be called an animal nut. . . . It's allowed people to strengthen their positions and to feel fortified at being part of a movement that is going for something they feel is important to them.

Overall, activists stated that, while the future may hold something different, the present power of rights language should not be ignored. As one activist put it,

> If society ever gets rid of the notion of rights and just starts talking about fair treatment, or what is just, or whatever, that's fine. . . . I just think that as political discourse it has a meaning and to not use that discourse when you're talking about animals and to use it when you're talking about other oppressed groups I think is . . . to say, well, my issue is not as important as those issues.

The Drawbacks of Rights Talk: Activist Perspectives

Some of the most significant evidence supporting the argument that animal rights activists are not duped into using rights comes from their critical assessments of the language. Activists repeatedly advanced various critiques of rights, thereby illustrating their thoughtful and serious consideration of the concept. Although, again, not all activists mentioned each of the following drawbacks, taken together their views suggested an awareness of the problematic aspects of rights.

The Association with Radicalism

Probably the most common criticism leveled by activists pointed to the continued association between animal rights and extremism. Despite the popularity of rights in general and the increasing acceptance of the term *animal rights*, activists suggested that, in the minds of many, animal rights remains a radical concept. According to one activist, the lan-

guage "really alienates a lot of people. I think they think that's too radical. . . . Animal rights is a kind of buzzword." A second activist suggested that speaking of animal rights "sets a lot of people off." Likewise, a third noted that "it almost seems to be a red flag to some people.
When you think of rights it brings up very strong emotions in people."

Illustrating the association between animal rights and extremism,
and the strategic response to this association, one activist related the
following story. The leaders of a well-known humane organization

> made a conscious decision to not focus on the term *animal rights*
> but focus on the term *animal protection*. They think it will help
> embrace those who see animal rights as an extremely radical phi-
> losophy and, rather, would be more comfortable with animal pro-
> tection as a description. But in the same breath that [they were]
> sharing with me the decision to do this, [they were] saying "we do
> not deny animal rights."

Many animal rights organizations continue deploying rights in
spite of, and sometimes because of, its connections to radicalism. Moreover, while many express wariness regarding the radical connotations
of animal rights, they also note that this connection is not peculiar to
animal rights or to rights language alone. Earlier rights movements
were similarly associated with extremism. One activist made this point
in the following manner:

> It's like people who say I'm not a feminist, but I'm in favor of equal
> pay for equal work. . . . People are ready to concede they agree
> with you on lots of things, but they're not ready to make that jump
> and label it that thing they've heard has been so fringey for so long.

Association of Rights with Humans

Activists indicated a further drawback to animal rights language, suggesting that rights are commonly viewed as applying only to humans.
As a result, the application of rights to animals often elicits dismissive
reactions. As Francione stated, "people that aren't used to thinking
about animals as rights holders may dismiss you more easily." Attorney-activist Steve Ann Chambers suggested that connecting the language of rights to animals is a big problem: "Most people see animals

as a different status than humans. Humans have a much higher status than animals; the 'they are here for us' kind of mentality. It's pretty difficult to turn that around." On a somewhat different note, one activist noted a further dismissive response generated when rights are applied to animals: If animals have rights then where does the extension of rights end? "One of the problems of giving rights to animals is, well, where are we going to draw the line? That's an argument that's very effective against extending rights at all."[12]

Activists frequently mentioned the dismissive attitudes elicited when people associate specific human rights with animal rights. In particular, activists pointed to common rebuffs that suggest the absurdity of giving animals the right to vote, drive, speak freely, or obtain an education. For instance, one activist stated that when talking about animal rights, "you'll get back, 'Well, do you think they should vote?' which is not what we're after."[13]

An additional problem arising from the association with human rights stems from the specific connection between the language and the movements for civil rights and women's rights. Many activists suggested the difficulty of arguing that the move to animal rights is the next logical extension following civil and women's rights. The difficulty is that claiming such an extension may alienate minorities and women who interpret the extension as bringing them down to the level of animals.

The Divisive Nature of Rights

A number of activists echoed a common criticism of rights leveled by legal scholars who suggest that rights are inherently divisive. According to this critique, rights language encourages conflict and competition because rights imply corresponding obligations. For instance, when the claim is made that children have a right to education, there is an implication that someone has the corresponding obligation and burden to provide for that education. In addition, rights frequently foster conflict as a result of the competition between rights and the need to balance one right against another. Thus, for example, when women claim the right to choose whether or not to have an abortion, the opposition asserts the competing rights of the fetus. In some such situations, the conflict between rights is zero-sum.

Marti Kheel, ecofeminist scholar and activist in Feminists for Animal Rights (FAR), voiced this common critique, arguing that rights are "dualistic."[14] Rights are "part of the competitive world view. You have a right to something against somebody." Likewise, Lauren Smedley, another activist in FAR, elaborated this critique in clear terms. According to Smedley, rights are

> very limiting because they're dualistic, and they assume a competition-based type of arena for resolving the issues and for meting out justice. You have the problem just like you did with civil rights and any type of minority rights, and what are called women's rights: every right is considered [to be] conflicting with another right. A women's right not to be harassed on the street is conflicting with the man's right of freedom of speech and to harass women. It's one right against another. In that sense rights are very limiting and they're inadequate.

In a more general sense, activists pointed to the way rights language creates cleavages within the overall animal protection movement and divides it from other social movements. As Lucy Kaplan, staff attorney for PETA, stated, the terminology of rights

> has certainly divided some compassionate people from other compassionate people, because there are still compassionate people who think that our duties are limited to keeping animals comfortable while they're being exploited. So it has been divisive.

Relating the animal rights movement to other social movements, Kheel critiqued rights language.

> I just think it has a whole host of problems, including the fact that it alienates us from the environmental movement. There is a division between the animal liberation and environmental movement[s] and I think that rights terminology is one of the things that perpetuates that. Because it's not very easy to talk about rights for rivers, streams, air, and so on. . . . Rights terminology neglects the environment. I think it's very problematic with the terminology of rights because it is traditionally associated with an atomistic worldview. You have to be an individual entity to have a right. At

least up until now it hasn't been successfully assigned to more than an individual entity.

Rights and Paternalism

In addition to the above criticisms, three activists suggested a feminist critique of rights. Rights, according to these activists, are inherently paternalistic due to the fact that they are assigned by those in power to those without power. As one advocate put it, "Using the language of rights you have the dominators giving something to the dominated, giving this language of rights to the dominated. And that is disgusting in that way." According to Kheel,

> I see obligations and rights as coming out of the patriarchal frame-
> work. . . . [They] feed into that kind of worldview that says there
> are subjects and objects. Subjects are the rights givers and they're
> given to objects. . . . Who are we to be giving rights to animals? Is it
> just a matter of power? . . . Humans may have assigned that role to
> themselves, the powerful rights givers. But I think that's where a
> lot of the problems stem from, seeing our species as somehow
> unique in the universe that has been given these powers of stew-
> ardship.

As these comments imply, the act of granting rights to animals replicates the hierarchy of power. It perpetuates the prevailing attitude of human superiority over inferior animals. As such, animal rights language or even the attainment of animal rights does not necessarily foster significant social transformation. Instead, it reinforces the paternalistic and hierarchical system characteristic of the status quo.

Rights as a Philosophical Construct

A final critique offered by activists points to problems with the philosophical nature of rights language. Several activists asserted that rights language as a philosophical construct is vague, insufficiently defined, and therefore misunderstood. As Tim Greyhavens, executive director of PAWS, summed it up, "it is such a vague philosophical term that it's very confusing to people." Similarly, Dr. Elliot Katz, director of In

Defense of Animals, stated: "I think it has not still been defined. What rights are you trying to achieve? What exactly are rights? I think it's still somewhat vague. . . . The concept of rights still needs to be refined and figured out." And, as Ingrid Newkirk succinctly put it, "I think a lot of people misunderstand [rights language]."

Marti Kheel and Lauren Smedley addressed the vagueness of rights language by suggesting the general problem of finding the source of rights. According to Kheel, rights language "assumes that humans have rights. So right from the start you're starting with a problematic situation. You can't prove why humans should have rights." In a similar vein, Smedley stated,

> there still is an inherent assumption that there are these inalienable rights. And that assumption includes within it the notion that the inalienable right derived from somewhere. And if you can't agree where that right has arisen from, then you have to get back to who says that living things have a right. . . . [We assume that the rights] come from God, so it's just religious by its very nature.

On a rather different note, one activist critiqued the philosophical nature of rights by pointing to the separation between theory and praxis. According to this activist, rights language is "philosophical; it's not action oriented. People need to see something to focus on as opposed to just a general concept of rights." The activist maintained that philosophers should continue to define and clarify the concept of rights. However, he recommended that animal protection organizations focus on practical rather than theoretical activity and stress direct action to halt animal abuse.

Lack of Alternatives

In deciding whether and when to deploy rights, activists sought to weigh the costs and benefits of the language. In doing so, activists repeatedly returned to one crucial question: If not rights, what else? By asking this question, activists articulated the view that rights language remains important partly due to the lack of alternative languages. Without persuasive, alternative ways of speaking, the turn to rights is understandable.

Many activists who recognize the problematic nature of rights continue to employ the language due to the lack of options. As Virginia Knouse, president of PAWS, stated, the phrase *animal rights* is sometimes associated with animosity. "But how do you put it? I haven't come up with a better way." Likewise, a second activist stated: "The term *animal rights* has developed almost a negative connotation, but I can't think of a better way to describe it. They do have a right to live and a right not to be used by us."

Other advocates indicated the need to use rights language given that we live in a rights-oriented culture.

> I think [rights terminology] is effective if you're working with the given system. You're going to have to use that kind of terminology if you want to draft any kind of legislation to protect animals right now. I don't see how [animal organizations] could really accomplish anything without saying that animals in, say, meat production have rights.

A number of activists who were explicitly concerned about the drawbacks of rights admitted that within this cultural context rights play an important role. According to one,

> In a sense I think rights are nonsense. . . . [But] as long as we keep talking about rights, as long as we are living in a society where the language is a language of rights, then I think it's important that we talk about rights. As long as we're talking about humans having rights, to the extent that we're not talking about animals having rights we denigrate their position in the moral status.

On a more specific note, some activists expressed the power of rights language relative to others. Attorney-activist Kaplan argued that in comparison to the alternative notion of animal interests, rights are quite useful: "Rights in our culture are readily enforced. Interests don't often have the forum where they can be enforced." Francione, comparing rights to welfare, stated:

> I think the language of rights is very, very important, and it has made the movement progress a lot more than the movement would have progressed if we were talking about animal welfare because we had to get out of the rut of thinking that it was OK to

exploit animals as long as we did so in a particular way. That's the
welfare mentality. That's what had to go. That went when we
started talking about rights.

Activists, in making these points, echoed the views of scholars
who critique CLS. Several scholars, particularly those who have offered
what has been called the minority critique of CLS, argue that many are
too quick to dismiss rights. Without alternative ways of speaking, the
dismissal of rights may do more harm than good, especially for the
marginalized. Indeed, some scholars evaluating rights suggest that
powerless groups seeking social change must employ prevailing languages. "Demands for change that do not reflect the institutional
logic—that is, demands that do not engage and subsequently reinforce
the dominant ideology—will probably be ineffective" (Crenshaw 1988,
1367; see also Piven and Cloward 1977). Hence, there is a sense in
which we can understand the turn to rights generally, and the turn to
animal rights specifically, as acts of self-defense in the struggle for
change (Crenshaw 1988, 1382).

Countering the Myth of Rights: A Strategic and
Critical Reconstruction of Rights

In the interviews, activists revealed a strategic understanding of rights.
By referring to the popularity of rights, by suggesting the persuasive
and activating nature of the language, and by recognizing the lack of
alternatives, activists demonstrated an awareness of the purposeful
method in which rights can be deployed. Moreover, by articulating the
various drawbacks of rights, activists presented a critical and cautious
approach to the language out of which they offered a reconstruction of
rights.

Activists also revealed a strategic approach to rights by referring to
the strategic nondeployment of rights. Activists suggested that in certain situations it makes sense to avoid the terminology. One activist
who commonly uses the language suggested that he avoids the term "if
I'm in a group of old fogies . . . and I do not want to be threatening."
Another activist more generally made the point in this way: "I swing
between animal rights organization and animal advocacy organization,
depending on . . . [the] particular context."

One of the most significant areas in which activists strategically
avoid rights language is within the courtroom. As we will see in the fol-

lowing chapters, several animal protection organizations employ a litigative strategy in attempts to advance their goals. Many of these are self-declared "animal rights" groups. Moreover, many lawyers involved in legal activity speak of animal rights and express the goal of extending legal rights to animals. Yet, there is an irony regarding animal rights and litigative activity: within the courtroom, lawyers tend to avoid the "legal" language of animal rights.

Lawyers and nonlawyers indicated the movement's strategic aim to extend legal rights to animals and to reconstruct the legal meaning of rights. "We want to endow animals with rights so that they'll be part of the legal system so that you can address their problems with law." Activists suggested that, within the judicial arena, it makes sense to seek rights. According to one attorney-activist who spoke critically of rights language, there is good reason to seek legal rights for animals.

I'm sensitive to the fact that that's really all we've got right now. Obviously right now rights are a very useful way of trying to gain some protection for animals. And in the legal arena there has been no move at all away from rights and interests as a way of distinguishing amongst the haves and have-nots, and allocating resources and respect. . . . I think it's going to be many, many years before a judge would say "in the interest of justice I recognize that every person deserves care" or something besides just having a right.

Similarly, nonlawyer Kheel, who also expressed strong criticism of rights language, suggested a role for rights.

I think that if I were going into courtrooms, it might not sway the judge too much to talk about my having this sense of interconnection with all of life. . . . It might be to my advantage to talk about rights in that kind of context. . . . Within the legal tradition there's almost no way to talk about things outside of a rights context. The legal tradition is based on that whole notion.

Despite the expressed need to pursue rights within the judicial arena, lawyer activists noted that, when actually in the courtroom, speaking of animal rights is off limits. When asked whether lawyers use the term *animal rights* in court, one lawyer stated, "I haven't, because they don't have rights, so people would laugh at me. I would if they had them, but not until they have them." Likewise, another lawyer stated,

> I never mention it. I talk about interests. I think interests is com-
> pletely accurate, and why put up a red flag if you can get the same
> exact thing [another way]. . . . I just can't take the chance in court
> that I'm going to get some flaming conservative who doesn't even
> believe that gay people should have rights.

Although animal rights talk has not found an explicit place within the courtroom, another version of rights talk has: human rights talk. As Kheel noted, "Of course, there are ways to use rights to protect animals without assigning animals rights, in terms of doing violation to some human law. [And] I know that you can sue somebody for property damage." Likewise, Francione pointed to the effectiveness of deploy-ing, in litigation, a student's right not to dissect as a means of implicitly suggesting animal rights. Thus, while attorney-activists strategically avoid animal rights talk in court, they deploy human rights talk in a strategic bid to advance the ideals of animal rights.[15]

The strategic attitude toward animal rights displayed by activists supports the contention that activists have not wholeheartedly bought into the language of rights. They did not express a faith in rights that might be interpreted as depicting the myth of rights in action. Instead, activists articulated a critical perspective combined with a strategic approach: activists weighed various drawbacks of rights language against its potential benefits.

Further evidence supporting the claim that activists are not capti-vated by the myth of rights comes from their comments regarding the philosophical basis of rights. Several suggested that the notion of rights is a philosophical and human construct not a natural right handed down from on high. In so doing, activists distinguished their use of rights from traditional natural rights theory. As Dr. Neal Barnard, director of the Physicians Committee for Responsible Medicine, put it, "[R]ights are things that no one possesses. . . . You don't have a rights gland in your body. Rights are things that other people say you pos-sess. It's a mental construct. . . . Animals have rights if humans accept that they have rights." Another activist reiterated this point.

> Some people use the idea of rights as God-given rights. . . . I believe
> that human society has created the concept of rights, that rights are

given to protect vulnerable individuals and to try and have some sort of balance and fairness, and so forth.

A third activist expressed how rights are constructed.

> The whole concept of rights is a human-assigned, philosophical, ethical term anyway. Inherently rights is something we make up. As our species we have decided to use this term because it's a philosophical concept we've decided to apply. . . . If we assign rights to this type of life, then there's a carryover on some philosophical reasons on why we assigned those to humans or to upper-level mammals, or whatever. . . . I think that it really does come down to a matter of philosophy and looking at why we assign rights to any particular species, item, person, whatever.

These perspectives on rights counter the argument put forth by critics that the deployment of rights leads to "reification," that is, to abstraction, illusion, and mystification. Rather than getting caught up in abstractions or buying into the notion of objective rights, activists recognize the practical construction of rights and their ability to take part in this construction. By suggesting that logic necessitates the granting of rights to animals as long as we live in a world where we choose to assign rights to humans, activists rely on practical construction to extend rights claims to animals.

In sum, the interviews with animal rights activists indicate that the turn to rights does not imply the overwhelming lure of the myth of rights. By consciously, critically, and strategically deploying rights, activists appear to be overcoming the myth of rights and purposefully engaging in the politics of rights. In so doing, activists reconstruct the meaning of rights as a persuasive, powerful, albeit limited, tool that is useful especially in the face of weaker alternatives. Thus, even if it turns out that the use of rights is counterproductive, this study establishes an important point: that activists strategically and critically turn to rights without being misguided by false consciousness.

Countering Counterproductivity: The Reconstruction of Rights

Most scholars critical of rights do not deny that the language has some potential benefits. Nevertheless, many maintain that the liberal and individualistic underpinnings of rights conflict with the values of community, relationship, and responsibility. Rights language, it is alleged, privileges individualism and undermines the social and collective aspects of humanity (Gabel 1984; Tushnet 1984; Medcalf 1978; Glendon 1991). Moreover, the competitive nature of rights language pits one right against another. This competition separates individuals and groups that might be better served as a united force. Competition also inspires counterrights claims that are used to challenge and rebuff new rights demands (Medcalf 1978; Bruun 1982; Scheingold, 1989; McCann 1986). As a result, several critical scholars assert that, given the prevailing meaning and foundations of rights, the language is counterproductive for movements seeking egalitarian social change. Progressive movements should therefore avoid rights and turn toward languages more supportive of collective ideals (Gabel 1984; Tushnet 1984; Medcalf 1978).

Although the animal rights movement provides some evidence suggesting the competitive and individualistic nature of rights, it also demonstrates that the meaning of rights language can be reconstructed to support more egalitarian values. In addition, this movement's experiences pose a question for those critical of rights talk: If not rights, then what? Despite the liberal foundations of rights and the potential conflicts fostered by collisions between rights, a reconstituted language of rights can be deployed to advance notions of responsibility, relationship, and community, and they can do so more effectively than the available alternatives.

Responsibility, Relationship, and Community

Several scholars contend that rights capture a devotion to the individual and liberty but fail to provide grounding for the community. One such scholar, Joseph Raz, offers a critique of rights based on his conclusion that the individualistic nature of right-based theories denies the intrinsic value of collective goods. Raz comes to this conclusion from his duty-based definition of rights: "'X has a right' if and only if X can have rights, and, other things being equal, an aspect of X's well-being (his interest) is a sufficient reason for holding some other person(s) to be under a duty" (1986, 166). Understood in this way, Raz argues that right-based moralities are likely to be only individualistic. Because collective goods affect the lives of large segments of the population rather than one individual, it is "difficult to imagine a successful argument imposing a duty to provide a collective good on the ground that it will serve the interests of one individual" (203). Hence, the rights that will be protected are individual rights founded on individual interests and guaranteed by the duties of others. Collective goods will, in turn, be generally neglected.

On different grounds, Mary Ann Glendon (1991) advances a critical analysis of the individualism of rights. For Glendon, rights language in this culture promotes "hyperindividualism" to the detriment of the community. The American rights bearer is solitary, separate, and disconnected. A distinctive feature of American rights talk is "its extraordinary homage to independence and self-sufficiency, based on an image of the rights-bearer as a self-determining, unencumbered, individual, a being connected to others only by choice" (48). In conjunction with the lone rights bearer, rights talk advances an "exaggerated absoluteness" that makes individuals believe they have a right to do whatever they wish. This illusion of absoluteness creates false expectations and promotes social conflict. The combination of exaggerated absoluteness and hyperindividualism problematically excludes concern for responsibility, relationship, and community. As a remedy, Glendon recommends that we adopt the language of relationship, responsibility, and community in order to refine the language of rights (xii).[16]

Glendon and Raz are not alone in pointing to the individualism of rights and the seeming neglect of community (see Medcalf 1978; Bruun 1982; Rose 1985; and Bumiller 1988). It has commonly been noted that the individualistic component of rights arises, in part, from the view that rights attach to individuals *as* individuals and are owned by individuals as property (Scheingold 1989). As Staughton Lynd (1984) describes the critique of traditional rights rhetoric, "[I]ndividuals are imagined to *possess* rights in the same way that they possess more tangible kinds of property" (1419). Jeremy Waldron describes the individualistic nature of rights theory, noting that

> with rights the link between interest and duty is individualistic. Though X, Y and Z all share an interest in bodily security, still the interest in X's case must be of sufficient importance to warrant imposing all the duties necessary to protect *his* (X's) bodily security, the interest in Y's case must be of sufficient importance to

warrant imposing all the duties that are necessary to protect *his* (Y's) bodily security, and so on. Even when we apply rights through universalization rather than on the basis of attention to individual detail, we do so because we are convinced more or less a priori of the importance of the interest in the case of each individual who may fall under the scope of universalization. (1987, 185–86)

As a result, rights language appears to privilege the autonomous individual over, and often at the expense of, the community.[17]

Does the use of rights by animal advocates maintain a devotion to individualism and neglect for the community? To consider this question, I will first suggest that the individualistic nature of rights language does not necessarily undermine community and collective relationships. I will then speak specifically to animal rights language, pointing to the ways in which activists stress relationship, responsibility, and community in their constructions of rights.

As Waldron persuasively argues, it is easy to exaggerate the objection that the individualism of rights neglects collective values. Not all rights, Waldron notes, are solely oriented toward individual concerns. Some, even though they protect individual interests, are prerequisites for communal life.

We cannot participate in discussion if *I* am gagged and bound; *they* cannot live and thrive as a polity if *she* is under a banning order, and so on. Without wanting to be at all reductivist about communal life, one can insist that there are certain things *individuals* can suffer which may make communal life impossible and which therefore anyone with a concern for community will want to prevent. (1987, 185)

Waldron's point suggests that, despite their individualistic form, rights need not preclude communal concerns.

Tom Campbell comes to a similar conclusion in making the case for socialist rights. Like Waldron, Campbell notes the individualistic configuration of rights. However, he asserts that this individualism does not necessarily imply selfishness or possessiveness. In capitalist society rights are likely to be correlated with self-centered attitudes. But this correlation may be contingent and

does not establish that possessive and selfish attitudes are presup-
posed by the institution of rights. . . . Nevertheless, it is clear that
rights do have a close connection with individualism if only
because they characteristically belong to individuals and all relate
in some way to those aspects of rule-governed behavior which cen-
tre on benefiting specific persons. What needs to be argued by the
reformist is that this does not necessarily embroil rights in the sort
of individualism which accepts or glorifies conflict between selfish
and self-sufficient persons. (1983, 84)

It is this argument that Campbell and animal rights proponents
advance.

As we have seen, the animal rights movement certainly does not
discard rights talk. It does, I suggest, begin to redefine the meaning of
rights in ways that minimize selfishness and stress relationship,
responsibility, and community. In so doing, animal rights may help to
provide an alternative to an individualistically oriented notion of
rights.

The language of animal rights refers to a general ideal and value
concerning proper care and treatment of animals. It does not simply
refer to the particular, individual rights of animals. It implies a broader
ethic, suggesting that animals deserve consideration because they, like
humans, experience pain and pleasure. The ethic further holds that animals should be treated with dignity rather than as objects of human
enjoyment. Thus, the meaning of animal rights embodies an ethic that
reorients our perceptions of animals, our perceptions of human relations and responsibility toward animals, and our perceptions of the
value of life.

To make this case, activists make evident the relationship between
humans and animals and connect animal rights with human rights. As
suggested earlier, philosophers and activists alike relate animals to
humans by pointing to their similar experiences and characteristics. As
such, animal rights talk emphasizes relationships and connections, and
it is upon the basis of this connectedness and continuity that humans
have responsibilities toward animals.

To be sure, there is considerable reinforcement of individualism
within animal rights language. This stems largely from the negative
concept of freedom often associated with animal rights. For instance, it
is argued that animals should be free from exploitation and abuse, and

should be left in their natural settings. Yet, animal advocates also promote more positive conceptions of liberty, suggesting that animals be free to exist in safe and thriving environments. This positive conception of liberty counters individualism because it does not rest on the self-centered individual. It rests on an image of a community of thriving beings, a community that could not thrive and would indeed suffer without the protection of certain individual rights.

Moreover, this positive liberty implies an affirmative responsibility on the part of humans to maintain and promote viable ecological habitats and wilderness areas. Responsibility is embedded within the notion of rights because rights imply duties. Raz, as noted above, sees duties as central to the definition of rights. Simply put, "Rights ground duties" (1986, 186). By grounding duties, rights impose responsibilities upon others. This is the way animal rights activists construct the meaning of rights. As attorney-activist Kaplan observed during an interview, "[R]ights connote reciprocal duties. . . . Our realization that we have duties to animals . . . is so overdue that I prefer any analysis that imposes some duty on us." Such an imposition of responsibility and duty is particularly important in the case of animals, which cannot speak on their own behalf.

The above discussion provides some reason to believe that the individualism of rights is not in all cases incompatible with responsibility toward the community. There remain, however, some potential problems arising from the reciprocal duties contained within common interpretations of rights language. One significant problem, asserted by Glendon (1991), is that the duties imposed by rights take the form of absolutes. That is, when activists assert animal rights, they imply an absolute entitlement for a particular class—animals—and they do so even if such an entitlement interferes with community interests and needs. Rights absolutes thus impede compromise and cooperation that benefit the entire community.

A second problem relates to the problematic competition fostered by duties. Richard Flathman (1976) argues that for A, the rights bearer, to have a right to X, X must be advantageous to A and disadvantageous to B, the person with the correlated duty. Because of this disadvantage, B will generally wish to avoid the obligation to A even though B may believe that A is justified in having a right to X (80–81). On this definition, problematic competition is an inherent component of rights. Med-

calf, who also holds that the duties associated with rights foster competition, suggests that this may inhibit collective approaches to solving
problems.

> Relationships conducted in terms of "my rights and your responsi-
> bilities" can eliminate vast creative possibilities. Thinking in "I"
> units and accepting one's self as a definable assortment of rights
> and responsibilities can destroy collective forms of action and
> human interrelationships. (1978, 114)

The competition fostered by rights may lead to a practical limitation of the language. Because reciprocal obligations emphasize the
competitiveness of rights, rights talk may encourage counterrights
claims. These counterrights claims challenge new calls for rights and
mobilize the opposition. Thus, critics of rights suggest that using the
language is politically and practically limiting because it fuels the
opposition in ways that undermine social reform efforts.

A third problem suggested by Raz (1986) is that duties, and therefore right-based theories, do not do enough to provide for morality.
Countering Ronald M. Dworkin's (1977) view that political morality is
right-based, Raz attempts to demonstrate that right-based moralities
are "impoverished." Even if rights impose duties, this imposition
remains within the realm of individualism and does little to provide
the foundation for collective goods.

These potential problems are certainly important to consider.
However, none is fatal to reconstructing rights in a way that emphasizes responsibility and community. To demonstrate this point, let us
consider each problem in turn.

Exaggerated Absoluteness

The critique of rights offered by Glendon (1991) is a persuasive one and
it demonstrates a significant constraint of rights language. In animal
rights, this problem becomes particularly apparent in the issue of animal experimentation. Ardent animal rights activists argue that recognizing the rights of animals implies that experimenting on animals is
unacceptable. Even experiments that seek to find cures for fatal dis-
eases like cancer and AIDS are deemed incompatible with animal

rights. The absoluteness of animal rights, demonstrated in this issue, clearly inhibits compromise, and furthermore it undermines support for the movement.[18]

On the other hand, in response to exaggerated absoluteness, two points can be made in defense of rights. First, the exaggerated absoluteness of rights is itself exaggerated. While there is no doubt that rights are frequently articulated in absolute terms, there is nothing inherent about rights that makes them absolute.[19] Although people in this country, for instance, claim an absolute right to free speech, most would, when pressed, admit that this right is limited if such speech endangers life. Similarly, while most people refer to the inviolability of freedom of religion, most would also agree that this freedom does not permit human sacrifice. Hence, rights, while often articulated in absolute terms, are generally admitted to be qualified.

Second, while it may be true that rights promote an exaggerated absoluteness, there are at least two instances in which such absoluteness is desirable. One instance is during the early stages of activism on behalf of oppressed groups. In this culture, the stark demand for rights is extremely useful for groups denied fair treatment in the community. It is all too easy for those who have already been accorded rights to argue that additional rights claims interfere with compromise. For groups excluded from fair treatment, their initial goal is not to compromise but to be heard and granted respect. In fact, compromise at early stages of movement activism is likely to lead to co-optation and dispersion of movement energies.

The other instance in which absoluteness may be desirable is when there is good reason to promote absoluteness. Consider, for example, the case of experimentation. Most people in this country would agree that experimenting on humans against their will is unjustifiable.[20] This absolute perspective is almost certainly desirable,[21] despite the fact that the community as a whole might benefit from experiments on humans.[22]

Exaggerated absoluteness, while somewhat problematic, does not fully undermine rights language. It does highlight the often competitive and conflictual nature of rights. However, in some instances, conflict should be highlighted. Highlighting conflict brings to the fore interests that have been excluded and obligations that need to be fulfilled. Hence, the exaggerated absoluteness of rights, with its downside, has the advantage of emphasizing the obligations that are a part of relationships and communities.

Counterrights Claims

But what about the practical problems of highlighting the conflict of rights? What about the counterrights claims that are inspired by a turn to rights language? Critics suggest that a significant problem with rights language rests in the fact that it promotes continual conflict between differing rights. Glendon (1991) and others speak of the stand-off of one right against another and the increasing collisions between rights (Bruun 1982; Scheingold 1989; Medcalf 1978). Claims to rights imply corresponding duties to ensure those rights, and conflict between competing rights is quite common. As such, the maintenance or creation of a right is often possible only at the expense of other rights. This leads to the deployment of counterrights claims by the opposition, which serves to stunt and rebuff new calls for rights.

The animal rights experience lends credence to this depiction of rights. The argument that the rights of animals should be recognized has inspired many countervailing rights claims. Two examples clearly demonstrate such counterclaims: the fur battle and the battle over animal experimentation.

In the 1980s and early 1990s, animal rights groups, both separately and in cooperation, launched a powerful antifur campaign. This campaign raised public consciousness regarding the conditions under which animals are trapped and reared. The media focused significant attention on this antifur battle, publishing some lengthy articles covering the debate and examining the decline in fur sales (see, e.g., Kasindorf 1990). This antifur campaign contributed considerably to the growing public awareness of animal rights, and it achieved some success in reducing sales and contributing to the decline of the fur industry. At the same time, this campaign provoked many counterrights claims.

In particular, consumers and producers attacked by animal rights activists articulated the counterclaim of "freedom of choice." As many articles demonstrate, this claim is commonplace in profur reactions. One woman, responding to antifur activism asked, "Whatever happened to freedom of choice?" (Williams 1989, 8). Challenging the attempt to ban fur sales in Aspen, Colorado, Mark Kirkland, president of Aspen's Concerned Citizens Coalition and manager of a fur store, stated: "What the fur vote really boils down to is an infringement of our civil liberties. . . . We really deplore the attempt to legislate away people's freedom of choice" (Kasindorf 1990, 32). Likewise, Jeanie Kasindorf's lengthy article in the magazine *New York* entitled "The Fur Flies: The Cold War Over Animal Rights" (1990) prompted what the magazine editors referred to as "an extraordinary response" in terms of letters to the editor, many of which spoke of freedom of choice.[23] One furrier asserted that antifur activists are "interfering with people's freedom of choice of how to live, what to eat, and what to wear." Another furrier stated: "Lest you forget, allow me to remind you that freedom of choice is the cornerstone of our society." And another writer commented: "What distinguishes human beings from other animals is our ability and right to make personal choices" (*New York*, January 29, 1990).

In addition to invoking the right of free choice, profur people also speak of the rights of furriers and the right to work, albeit less frequently than they mention the right to choose. One letter to the editor asked, "Incidentally, have any of these ding-dongs given thought to the thousands of people who would be without work if the fur industry were outlawed? I guess their right to make a living just doesn't count" (*New York*, January 29, 1990). This counterrights claim is a common one that goes well beyond the issue of fur. In the battles over protecting wildlife habitat from logging and development, in the challenges to factory farming, and in several other conflicts, business and labor interests frequently invoke the right to work.

Like the antifur campaign, the attack against vivisection has provoked counterrights claims. Animal advocates calling for protection of animals in research laboratories have been rebuffed by two types of counterclaims. The first advances the common academic freedom argument. Scientific researchers assert that animal rights activists are interfering with the freedom to pursue knowledge. Researchers support their right to academic freedom by calling upon the Constitution's First Amendment guarantees. The second counterrights claim asserts the human right to health care and the right to be free from disease. As one editorial sums it up,

Modern medicine is one of our civilization's great engines of practical liberation. Pain and disease are forms of oppression. Millions of our fellow human beings have been freed of their burden by medical research. The arrogant cant of unthinking zealots must not obstruct this selfless enterprise. (*Los Angeles Times*, April 27, 1990)

Putting forward this counterclaim, the medical and scientific community has waged a campaign that asks the question "Your child or your dog?" This question starkly pits the rights of animals against the rights of humans. Using an advertisement showing a little girl in bed with her stuffed animals, the research community tells us "It's the animals you don't see that really helped her recover" (Stevenson 1989, 5). In doing so, the medical community implicitly and effectively promotes human rights to counter animal rights.

It is beyond contention that the antifur and antivivisection campaigns, along with others, have generated counterrights claims. Thus, critics of rights language are correct to point out the potential conflicts elicited by rights claims. But what critics do not recognize is that it is not the rights assertion itself that creates the conflict. Other languages besides rights would provoke the same types of counterclaims. Indeed, any language advancing the assertion that humans should give up using animals for food, clothing, entertainment, and research would prompt significant conflict and many counterclaims. Thus, as Minow puts it, "To believe that rights, when claimed and recognized, create conflict and adversarial relations . . . is to presume that there would otherwise be community and shared interests. I suggest instead that legal language translates but does not initiate conflict" (1990, 291). Whether the language be liberation, compassion, or consideration, the interests of humans would be challenged, competition would ensue, and the response would take shape in terms of counterclaims.

Moreover, while we can admit that problematic collisions and conflicts are increased by the deployment of rights language, we can also look at these collisions in another way. The deployment of animal rights challenges the exaggerated absoluteness of rights critiqued by Glendon and others. Indeed, animal rights challenges such exaggeration by the very act of promoting the counterrights claims. When humans respond to animal rights by saying "I have a right to choose to wear fur," "I have a right to eat meat," and "I have a right to hunt for recreation," they point to the exaggeration of thinking that rights imply the privilege of doing whatever we want. Certainly, it would be agreed that there is no right to hunt humans because we recognize that the countervailing right to life prevails over the right to hunt. What animal rights suggest is no different. Animal rights hold that "we don't have a right to arbitrarily kill and exploit" (Kaplan, interview). The notion of animal rights thus contends that the exaggerated absoluteness of human rights is misinformed and must be refined to take into consideration the responsibilities humans have toward others.

Of course, it might be said that while animal rights challenge the exaggerated absoluteness of human rights, it simply replaces it with an animal rights absolute. To be sure, the problem of absoluteness does not disappear with animal rights, just as it continues to exist with human rights. Nonetheless, as discussed above, the notion of exaggerated absoluteness is itself overstated, and there are times when absoluteness (or something close to it) is desirable. What's more, if the notion of animal rights were ever to be incorporated into prevailing consciousness and law, the opportunity might arise to work out the conflict and effect some compromise. But, until then, expecting animal advocates to push for compromise in a system they view as grossly unequal and unfair might be expecting too much.

Right-Based Moralities

The final problem to consider revolves around Raz's contention that right-based moralities are "impoverished." At bottom, Raz argues that there is more to morality than rights and duties. Right-based moralities do not account for situations in which we "ought" to do something but have no real "duty" to do it. Moralities grounded upon rights also do not extend moral significance to acts of supererogation (i.e., acts that are praiseworthy but not morally required). Finally, right-based moralities do not allow for recognition of the intrinsic moral value related to virtuous acts and the pursuit of excellence (Raz 1986, 195–96).

To respond directly to the substance of Raz's arguments, we could elaborate a theory of rights. Alternatively, we could look to the works of Dworkin and others, who defend right-based moralities. These options would, however, take us beyond the scope of this work. Fortunately, for our purposes, there is a way to answer Raz without directly addressing the substance of his concerns.

The response to Raz can be found in the defense of rights elaborated by Waldron. Waldron takes a modest approach to a theory of rights, an approach I shall accept for the current analysis. This approach suggests that we need not argue for a comprehensive right-based theory. We need not hold that all political or moral values are right-based. We need only make the more modest claim that some values, albeit important ones, are accounted for on a right-based foundation. On this view we may grant, for the sake of the argument, that Raz's points might be correct. However, we do not have to give up rights to make this concession.

Waldron employs this logic to counter the communitarian objection to rights. He argues that, while there may be important collective interests that cannot be captured by the individualistic form of rights, rights are still essential to protect certain individual interests.

> The modest function of a theory of rights is not to claim completeness but to draw attention to these important individual interests. One is not guilty of any crass or misguided individualism simply for expressing moral concern about certain of the ills that may befall individual men and women, or the harm and neglect that individuals may inflict on one another. It is *awful* to be locked up or silenced, *terrifying* to be beaten and tortured, and *appalling* to be left to starve or vegetate when resources are available for food and education; and one may think these ills so bad that their avoidance should be an overriding aim of any decent society. (1987, 187)

Waldron then suggests that protecting individual interests via rights is not debilitating to communitarian interests. Protecting individual interests, he argues, will not occupy all our resources and energies.

> That leaves the possibility for other goods to be pursued. And certainly one who accords priority to the protection of these basic individual interests is not committed to the view that, once this basic task is taken care of, all the *other* goods to be pursued in society have to be individual in character. (187–88)

In sum, we need not make the argument that all moral and political values are right-based (although some may want to do so). Leaving that argument aside does not imply that rights and duties are unimportant. Furthermore, rights do not preclude concern for communitarian goods. Indeed, some rights may be preconditions for certain communal goods. And even with their individualistic orientation, rights may be constructed in ways that stress the values of community, responsibility, and relationship.

Animal Rights versus Alternative Languages

I have argued to this point that animal rights language as deployed by this movement begins to refine the meaning of rights. The ethic captured by animal rights supports the relationship and continuity between human and nonhuman life and thereby advances a broad notion of community. Moreover, it has been argued that the ethic of animal rights is at least as supportive of mutual responsibility as of individualism. Indeed, the advancement of animal rights moves us away from the stark, simplistic hyperindividualism suggested by some scholars by countering the prevailing view that individual humans have a right to do whatever they want to animals and nature. The responsibility and implication of relationship underlying animal rights thus suggest that rights language can be infused with values of caring and community, where the notion of community includes more than just the community of humans. Furthermore, while it may be true that animal rights talk perpetuates a type of absoluteness, the exaggerated nature of this absoluteness is itself exaggerated. At times, absoluteness may be desirable and may heighten awareness of responsibility.

But might there be other ways of speaking and advancing the cause of animals that do not inspire some of the drawbacks associated with rights? Might critics of rights be correct in advising a turn to alternative modes of speaking? I shall argue here that when we compare the various choices it becomes clear that, at least in the present, rights language is the most productive for those interested in advancing the cause of animals.

As we have seen, the traditional animal welfare movement employed the language of compassion rather than rights. The welfare movement maintained that humans ought to be compassionate to animals. This language was, and continues to be, associated with the language of protection. If we are to be compassionate and if compassion is an ideal to be fostered, animals deserve at least some protection against humans who lack compassion.

From the perspective of animal advocates, the primary problem with the language of compassion and its associated language of protection rests in the emphasis on humans. Humans, in fulfilling their proper role in humanity, should treat animals with compassion and concern. If not, the important result is not so much that animals will be harmed but that humans will be acting cruelly. The reflection, then, is upon human activity and character rather than on animals. Moreover, the notion of protection tends to inspire paternalistic attitudes toward animals. Animals need protection because they cannot help themselves. This paternalistic perspective does two things. First, it suggests human superiority over the nonhuman world, with humans acting as the defenders of animals. Second, the paternalism stemming from protectionism clouds the fact that the protection animals require is protection against humans. As such, protectionism, again, is human-centered. The concept of human protection of animals both includes the notion of hierarchy and suggests that animals need protection from something besides humans.

Another problem with the language of compassion stems from its limited nature. As it is traditionally understood, the notion suggests that humans should be compassionate in our use of animals. In other words, humans can use animals for whatever ends we desire, but in doing so we should strive for compassionate treatment. Thus, when raising animals for clothing, meat, entertainment, and so forth, the conditions should be tolerable. As long as our treatment of animals is not characterized by wanton and gratuitous cruelty, then compassion is being achieved. From this perspective, animals are still viewed as objects for human pleasure and disposal, and the assumption of animal inferiority is reinforced.

To critique the language of compassion is not to say that the notion of compassion should be discarded. Animal rightists would not suggest that we avoid speaking in terms of compassion. Indeed, references to compassion and caring endure within the animal rights movement. However, these references are combined with the notion of rights. And the need to join the concepts is apparent as long as compassion, when it is used alone, is associated with kindness to inferiors, as it still is within the notion of animal welfare.

In addition to the language of compassion, activists increasingly employ animal liberation in contrast to animal rights. As noted previously, the book that inspired the animal rights movement and is often cited as its bible is entitled *Animal Liberation*. Despite the title, the language of liberation never gained the prominence now associated with animal rights.

The language of liberation lacks the power of rights, probably because it is not a common language. Certainly the concept of liberty plays an important role in Western thought and ideology. Nonetheless, liberation does not bring with it the same kind of familiarity and popularity as does the language of rights, especially in the United States. This may well change as people move more and more to the concept of animal liberation. Utilitarians, uncomfortable with the notion of rights, feel more at ease with the language of liberation. Likewise, feminists concerned with the drawbacks of rights talk have moved toward the concept of liberation. But animal liberation as a general language for the movement is not likely to attain much power in the near future given that it is only recently that the notion of animal rights has begun to be taken seriously.[24]

The language of equal consideration, like liberation, has expanded. Singer lays out the concept of equal consideration in *Animal Liberation*,[25] and, as a concept, it is quite useful. But as a movement label it does not work well. The "animal equal consideration movement," the "equal consideration movement," and the "animal consideration movement" are all awkward. But, more than awkwardness, the problem with equal consideration is that it lacks the history, background, and recognition that make animal rights powerful.

Along with considering animal rights in comparison to the specific languages of compassion, liberation, and equal consideration, we should consider another general alternative to rights talk. That is, we should consider whether it might make sense to speak not of animals having rights but of humans lacking the right to harm animals. Wesley Hohfeld's jurisprudential analysis of rights, privileges, duties, and powers is useful for this consideration (1919). Using his analysis of these terms, one might want to argue that even if animals do not have rights we can still prevent harm to animals by arguing that humans have neither the right nor the privilege to harm them. If we can make the case that humans lack the right and the privilege to mistreat animals, this might be a more easily accepted and effective route to the protection of animal interests.

To some extent and in certain contexts this case has already been accepted. Animal welfare laws regulate and forbid certain abuses of animals. These laws are not based on any notion of animal rights. They are based essentially on the notion that humans do not have the right to, for instance, torture kittens simply for the sake of torture. In addition, the argument that humans lack the right to abuse animals is one that is often made by animal rights activists.

However, to base protection of animals in all cases on the grounds that humans lack the right and privilege to use animals in certain ways will likely not be persuasive unless animals have some sort of counterclaim against humans. Without such a counterclaim, animal advocates will be hard pressed to restrain human uses and abuses of animals. If animals are viewed as beings without rights or interests worthy of protection, then there is little to counter the contention that humans have at least the privilege, if not the right, to use animals as they see fit.

Furthermore, the focus on the lack of human rights raises one of the same problems that arises with the language of compassion: the emphasis again is on humans. For animal advocates who wish to increase respect for nonhumans, an argument based largely on a lack of human rights does not place enough emphasis on nonhumans. To put it another way, such an argument does not bring animals into the moral community; it only restricts human action regarding those beings beyond the moral community. This is not to say that animal advocates should avoid arguing that humans have no right to harm animals. Indeed, such an argument, in conjunction with animal rights, is likely to be effective. But, by itself, such an argument does not do what the language of animal rights has the potential to do: bring animals into the moral community.

This brings us to the strength of animal rights in comparison to the alternatives. Rights talk certainly has its general drawbacks as well as drawbacks connected to its particular usage with animals. For instance, it can be argued that animal rights talk, like the language of compassion, still places humans at the center of analysis. Human rights may still outweigh animal rights, it might be argued. Humans remain superior to animals because of rationality, and therefore they have more guarantees of rights.

Despite these and other drawbacks, rights language carries a great deal of weight. As Salt said,

A great and far-reaching effect was produced in England . . . by the publication of such revolutionary works as Paine's "Rights of Man," and Mary Wollstonecraft's "Vindication of the Rights of

Women;" and looking back now, after the lapse of a hundred years, we can see that a still wider extension of the theory of rights was thenceforth inevitable. (1980, 4)

Rights language has a strong history in this country. Grounded in the Bill of Rights and our natural law heritage, the language has been deployed by numerous social movements in struggles to gain political, social, and economic acceptance. Workers' rights, civil rights, women's rights, and gay and lesbian rights are some of the many precursors of the contemporary animal rights movement. Thus, unlike liberation and equal consideration, animal rights has a history to draw upon and a ready language that is both familiar and accepted.

As the interviews suggest, this power is recognized by many advocates of animals. Brigid Brophy demonstrates this recognition in an article entitled "The Darwinist's Dilemma" (1979). Commenting on a 1965 article she wrote for the *New York Times*, Brophy stated that she chose the title "The Rights of Animals" intentionally to associate it with Thomas Paine's *The Rights of Man*.

> I was deliberately associating the case for non-human animals with that clutch of egalitarian or libertarian ideas which have sporadically, though quite often with impressive actual political results, come to the rescue of other oppressed classes, such as slaves or homosexuals or women. . . . I invoked *rights*, because rights are a matter of respect and justice, which are constant and can be required of you by force of argument; they are not matters of love, which is capricious and quite involuntary. (63–65)

In addition to the persuasiveness and popularity of animal rights language, there is a further strategic reason to continue using it in preference to the alternatives. For years, animal rights supporters were labeled derogatorily as animal lovers, human haters, extremists, little old ladies with twelve cats and tennis shoes, and so on. While these stereotypes still persist, they have decreased significantly. Moreover, the reference to animal rights has become quite mainstream. To change the reference now, at the moment when it has achieved prominence, might do the movement more harm than good.

The argument that animal rights remains more effective than the alternative languages does not imply that simply applying rights to anything automatically creates acceptance. Indeed, various rights-oriented movements have struggled, and continue to struggle, to attain and maintain acceptance and power. The animal rights movement has been similarly engaged in a struggle for acceptance and credibility.

It should also be stressed that none of the above suggests that movements are certain to fail if they avoid rights. The animal welfare movement historically attained success in achieving reforms aimed at restricting cruelty to animals. Over a century ago, the welfare movement gained power, and the movement increased its momentum in the 1960s and 1970s. Thus, we cannot say that the welfare movement has been unsuccessful or blame the movement for not having used rights language.

What is being suggested in this discussion is that the recent practical application of rights language to animal issues makes sense when we consider the context in which the movement developed and the available alternative languages. The animal rights movement grew at a time when other rights-oriented movements had begun to make gains in politics. Rights, as a central and popular language in this culture, were easily extended and appropriated by activists concerned about animals. Moreover, the alternative languages did not have the power, familiarity, and persuasiveness of rights. Hence, when evaluating the productivity of animal rights language, and rights more generally, we must consider contextual factors and the viability of alternative modes of speaking.

Conclusion

There is good reason to be critical of rights language. Within American culture, rights language is founded upon liberalism's hyperindividualism, rights are often thought of in absolute terms, and the deployment of rights frequently exacerbates conflict. Moreover, evidence from past social movements suggests that an overly optimistic faith in rights is misinformed and can improperly guide those seeking progressive social change (Rosenberg 1991; Bell 1985; Bumiller 1988). However, to conclude that most political activists who draw on rights are blinded by false consciousness, that rights must necessarily support hyperindividualism and an exaggerated absoluteness, that all of these drawbacks reinforce hegemony and impede social change, and that rights should therefore be avoided or abandoned assumes an overdetermined view regarding the power of our languages over our actions.

Rights language, like any other language, is indeterminate. Critics point to this indeterminacy in arguing that rights are unreliable. Yet, the indeterminacy of rights does not mean only that the powerful can manipulate the language to their benefit; it also means that the power-less can do the same. Indeterminacy implies a certain amount of flexi-bility for both the powerful and the powerless. Of course, the deploy-ment of an indeterminate language by the powerless is constrained by traditional understandings and practices. Nevertheless, indeterminacy and the associated flexibility allows the powerless to challenge the sta-tus quo using the very language that is deployed by those in power (McCann 1994; Minow 1991; Haskell 1987; Appleby 1987). Moreover, rights are not so indeterminate that they are arbitrary and meaningless. Those in power must, at least to a certain degree, conform to estab-lished rights, and are therefore themselves constrained. If the powerful manipulate rights in too arbitrary or inconsistent a fashion, their manipulation can be called into question.

> At the very least, the fact that dominant groups and officials voice fidelity to legal symbols, norms, and practices creates practical obligations and standards of accountability that constrain their actions. (McCann 1994, 297–98)

Thus, rights become a constraint on those in power and a tool the mar-ginalized can appropriate to check and challenge oppressive forces.[26]

One way that the meaning of rights can be manipulated is to alter the underlying liberal foundations upon which the language is based. While it is true that rights language is founded upon liberalism, it is also true that liberalism contains within it various competing ideals. On the one hand, liberalism stresses Lockean individualism, autonomy, and self-interest. On the other hand, various proponents of liberalism emphasize community, responsibility, and concern for the common good.[27] Rights, likewise, can be infused with these alternative, and often conflictual, ideals. And, while it is true that American culture's Lockean tradition with its individualistic emphasis generally prevails, this prevalence is neither absolute nor incontrovertible. Using rights in a way that emphasizes the values of responsibility, relationship, and community can challenge the prevailing Lockean liberalism and thereby confront the ideology of the status quo.[28]

This is what the animal rights movement has sought to do in reconstructing the meaning of rights. They have employed the indeterminate, flexible language of the status quo and attempted to reconstruct this language in ways that fit within the context of nonhumans. This reconstruction has involved a move away from individualism and toward relationship, responsibility, and community. Moreover, this reconstruction has proceeded in a strategic and cautious manner. Activists can and do think of rights in both critical and strategic terms. Although we must recognize that some activists may be naively misled by a strong faith in rights, at least a significant portion of activists have taken the disadvantages of invoking rights into consideration. Furthermore, many activists maintain a strategic understanding of rights, weighing the political benefits and costs of rights deployment in the context of particular movement struggles.

All of this suggests that rights can be reconstituted and infused with alternative notions and values. Rights need not be discarded, as some critics recommend. A thoughtful, critical, and strategic awareness of rights language provides the opportunity to challenge existing attitudes and power structures. Indeed, infusing rights with the values of community and responsibility provides an opportunity to challenge and refine the meaning of the language. Certainly, there is no guarantee that such challenges will be successful, nor is change likely to be achieved quickly. Yet, when we consider the history of rights, the persuasiveness of the language, and the available alternatives, it seems untenable to discard such an important and useful tool.

It should be stressed that this conclusion is reached largely by recognizing the significance of the context within which meaning is constructed. Within the animal rights movement, four central contextual variables suggest the importance of deploying a reconstituted version of rights. First, the growth of the movement in the wake of other rights-oriented movements helps explain the turn to rights. Second, the lack of viable alternative languages supports the appropriation of rights language. Third, the pervasiveness of rights talk within this culture makes the deployment of rights logical and sensible, at least at the present time. Fourth, and most important for the reconstruction of rights, is the fact that this movement focuses its concern on nonhumans. Placing rights within the context of nonhumans offers the opportunity to re-create the foundational meaning of the language.

Analyzing rights language solely in the abstract, without recognizing such contextual variables, may lead us to misunderstand its strategic and practical importance. In addition, without contextual analysis, our assessment may neglect crucial comparisons with the practical applicability of other languages. Without these comparisons, it is easy to dismiss rights language, as many critics on the left and right do. But such a dismissal ignores the fact that rights language, unlike the alternatives, provides an entry into popular debate. Rights language offers a respected language to the silenced and an ability to communicate demands for social change (Matsuda 1987; Delgado 1987). And a malleable rights language affords the possibility of reconstitution. Thus, it makes practical sense for the marginalized, in seeking to enter and challenge the mainstream, to appeal to a language that is itself mainstream and to at the same time reconstruct this language.

In sum, an assessment of rights language by the animal rights movement specifically and by other movements more generally must consider the complexity of deploying rights language. Recognizing the complexity of any political language means that we must address its diverse and flexible meanings, its potential benefits and costs, its strategic components, and its variations within differing social contexts. When we do so in the case of the animal rights movement, it becomes clear that the practice of reconstructing and deploying rights language plays a significant part in the overall scheme of advancing social change.

Chapter 5

Animals in the Courtroom:
The Direct Effects of Litigation

We've [the Animal Legal Defense Fund] mainly used litigation as a
reaction to harm that's already happened or is about to happen. We
. . . want to go beyond that, with litigation geared towards making
fundamental changes in the legal system.
—Joyce Tischler

We are trying to pound a square peg in a round legal hole. . . . We
are trying to get the courts to consider questions that the legal system was never designed for.
—Stephen M. Wise

Just as the animal rights movement has adopted the language of rights,
so too has it adopted the practice of litigation. With the embrace of
rights language, the movement has been influenced by prevailing conceptions of rights. At the same time, I have argued, the movement has
challenged and sought to reconceptualize the prevailing meaning of
rights. With the embrace of litigation, the movement has been shaped
and constrained by the predominant practices, structures, and meanings associated with this form of legal activity. Concomitantly, as I will
argue in this and subsequent chapters, the movement has constructed
litigation and legal meaning in ways that seek to advance the movement's agenda. In so doing, the deployment of both litigation and
rights language has been implicated in the constitution of meaning.

Using litigation in conjunction with other strategies, animal rights
groups seek to change official law to include recognition and protection
of animal rights. With such a change, the movement hopes to alter prevailing attitudes toward nonhumans. However, this attempt to modify
the existing legal system faces serious constraints. At the heart of these
constraints lies a fundamental challenge: "getting a legal system

designed for humans to take up the problem of animal rights" (Stille 1990, 1).

The constitutional text of the United States says nothing about animals.[1] It provides no explicit equal protection for nonhumans. Judicial interpretation of the constitutional rights to life and liberty has not protected animals from unnecessary pain and suffering. Few written laws in this country provide safeguards for animals. The federal Animal Welfare Act (AWA) establishes some basic standards regarding the care and housing of animals used in research, but it allows many exclusions.[2] Legal standards regulating the raising of farm animals are minimal, and those that do exist are generally concerned with the condition of the meat of those animals. The Endangered Species Act (1973) and the Marine Mammal Protection Act (1975) protect certain species of animals and state anticruelty statutes embody safeguards for domestic animals, but these laws are extremely limited and provide no security for animals as a whole.

The limited extent of formal laws makes the task of protecting animals difficult. In addition, there is only minimal enforcement of laws that do exist. Most legislation involving nonhumans grants enforcement power to a specific government agency. The U.S. Department of Agriculture (USDA), for instance, has the authority to administer the AWA. However, the USDA and other authorized agencies have shown little interest in enforcing animal protection laws (Thomas 1986). At the local and state levels, prosecutors and law enforcement officers display considerable reluctance to enforce compliance with anticruelty statutes (Kasindorf 1990; Zak 1990).[3] Responding to this situation, animal advocacy groups have sought to fill the enforcement vacuum. In doing so, they have encountered the obstacle of legal standing, which frequently acts as a barrier to advocacy groups seeking relief in the courtroom.

The current status of laws concerning nonhumans frames the attitudes, expectations, and practices of the animal rights movement. However, unlike other rights-oriented movements that employ such existing legal resources as the Fourteenth Amendment's Equal Protection Clause and various statutory laws,[4] the animal rights movement has a weak legal foundation upon which to build in the courtroom. Indeed, talking of animal rights in the courtroom is essentially off-limits. Thus, the minimal number of laws, the limited extent of those laws, the obstacles surrounding enforcement, and the prevailing meaning of existing laws constrain the extent to which advocates can advance their goals.

Despite these formidable constraints, movement practices in the realm of litigation are significant in that they have reconstructed the law and its meaning in a variety of ways. From an instrumental perspective, legal challenges brought through lawsuits can directly overturn or modify the prevailing meaning of specific laws and legal procedures. The turn to litigation directly influences the definitions of such things as when groups have standing or when a scientist might be found guilty of cruelty to animals. Litigation can also impact how animals are treated in food production, laboratories, clothing manufacturing, and so forth. Thus, from an instrumentalist standpoint, we look to several questions revolving around the effectiveness of litigation. In what ways and under what circumstances can litigation on behalf of animals be effective? Does this litigation promote changes in the law? Are these changes implemented in practice? What does the use of litigation by this movement tell us about the general effectiveness of litigation?

Along with its important instrumental effects, the turn to litigation as seen from a constitutive angle is equally important. Litigation indirectly constructs meaning beyond the realm of official legal rules. The activities leading up to, surrounding, and stemming from litigation construct the meanings of vocabularies, conventions, and practices relating to animal rights. Thus, from a constitutive view, we focus on questions surrounding the constitution of thought and meaning. How does rights-oriented litigation shape the understandings and consciousness of movement players? How does litigation influence movement activities? How do the attitudes, definitions, and expectations of movement activists shape litigation and, in turn, the meaning of rights?

Viewing litigation efforts from both the instrumental and constitutive perspectives underscores the relationship between the legal practices embedded within litigation and the broad construction of legal meaning. Such an approach also offers insight into a number of instrumental and constitutive concerns. However, we must do more than simply examine litigation from an instrumental and then a constitutive perspective. Instead, we need to move beyond a purely instrumental or constitutive view to one that joins instrumentalism with constitutivism in a way that revises both approaches.

Neither instrumentalism nor constitutivism alone offers a well rounded picture of litigation and legal meaning. The instrumentalist view, taken by itself, neglects broad and significant effects of legal rules and practices. It ignores how things like litigation can shape social consciousness and construct meaning. The constitutive view, as it is generally understood, suggests an overly determined and top-down view of law in which the law, descending from above, invisibly molds people's thoughts and makes social practices, values, and norms appear natural and necessary.[5] This hegemonic understanding of the law discounts the individual's ability to critically see through this hegemony, to consciously resist, manipulate, and challenge the law, and to deploy the law in a strategically instrumental fashion. The constitutive perspective thus emphasizes only one side of law's constitutive character—the side that permeates and structures social practice. It neglects the fact that social practice can reshape and reconstruct the law and that it is often through instrumental activity that such reconstruction occurs.

Exploring instrumentalist concerns with an eye toward the constitutive character of legal meaning and litigation will lead us to an alternative method of evaluating instrumental effectiveness. This alternative, more comprehensive method takes notice of the many subtle and indirect ways in which litigation affects social interaction. At the same time, investigating constitutive issues with an eye toward the instrumental effects of litigation highlights the importance of strategic action, thereby enhancing our understanding of how legal meaning is constructed. In the end, the conjunction of constitutive and instrumental slants will help bring into focus the interaction between the judicial and nonjudicial arenas in which battles over the meaning of law occur and, in turn, illuminate the complex construction of meaning correlated with legal strategy.

As we shall see, exploring the animal rights movement's litigative practices in this way illustrates several important points. For one thing, this exploration highlights the use of litigation as a strategic tool and the important place of litigation as only one of many components within the complex web of social movement strategy. Relatedly, such an examination indicates the significant direct uses and effects of litigation as well as the more indirect relationship between litigation and legal meaning. Furthermore, this exploration provides additional evidence to support the claim that movement activists advocating a litigative strategy are not beguiled by the myth of rights. Taken together, these points shed light not only on the animal rights movement's deployment of litigation but more generally on the litigation efforts and legal practices of other social movements.

To proceed with this analysis of litigative practice, this chapter will focus on the direct, instrumental effects of animal rights litigation. In doing so, I first draw on public law scholarship to define the components of effective litigation. I then go on to assess the instrumental effectiveness of animal rights litigation in light of this mainstream definition. In chapter 6, I further develop this assessment by viewing instrumentalism through a constitutive lens. After suggesting that it is important to recognize not only direct consequences but also the indirect influences of litigation, chapter 6 goes beyond the direct effects of the process to examine the indirect and multiple ramifications of litigative activity. With that foundation, chapter 7 elaborates a constitutive assessment of litigation informed by instrumentalism. The overall assessment of the relationship between litigation and the constitution of legal meaning must therefore be postponed until chapter 7.

Assessing the Effectiveness of Litigation

Most analyses of the relationship between litigation and social change focus on the institutional settings in which law is played out. Mainstream analyses and critical examinations stress case law, the courtroom, judges, lawyers, and the process of litigation. This focus generally leads scholars to assess the utility of litigation in terms of what can be gained within judicial settings.

The first dimension of this assessment rests on whether people and organizations can gain access to judicial institutions.[6] Many examinations of the law suggest that in recent years the tide seems to be turning on accessibility (Casper 1976; McCann 1986; Olson 1984; Richardson and Vines 1970). Some studies conclude optimistically that increased accessibility implies expanded use of the courts by the population. Responding to the growth in organizational litigation, Clement Vose states: "Considering the importance of the issues resolved by American courts, the entrance of organizations into cases . . . seems in order" (1986, 209). Some scholars go further, asserting that increased access translates into greater democratization of the judicial realm. As one scholar asserts, the legal system "provides a uniquely democratic . . . mechanism for individual citizens to invoke public authority on their own and for their benefit" (Zemans 1983, 692).[7]

Other studies associate expanding judicial access with numerous problems. For one thing, scholars questioning judicial capacity argue that a rise in case loads diminishes the court's capacity to perform effectively (Horowitz 1977). Growth in access has also been declared an inappropriate use of the judicial system for policy-making (Rabkin 1989; Bork 1986; Berger 1977; Glazer 1975). According to Donald L. Horowitz, increased access means that the courts must expand judicial capacity. But for Horowitz, the danger "is that courts, in developing a capacity to improve on the work of other institutions, may become altogether too much like them" (1977, 298).

Recent critical scholarship provides an alternative view of judicial access. In contrast to the suggestion that expanding access has opened the courts to more democratic participation, critical scholarship points to the many barriers that inhibit entry. These include financial obstacles, difficulties in obtaining legal counsel, lack of a social organization that encourages the use of law, and local norms that inhibit a turn to legal avenues (Galanter 1974; Handler 1978; Engel 1984). Such entry obstacles, these studies suggest, make litigation an ineffective avenue for many groups within the population, particularly those marginalized groups in greatest need of judicial remedies.

The second component for evaluating litigation, after access, focuses on whether specific cases are lost or won through judicial decisions. The work of Paul Burstein provides an example of this component of evaluation.[8] In several articles, Burstein assesses the successful mobilization of law in terms of whether particular parties involved in litigation win or lose in court (Burstein 1991; Burstein and Monaghan 1986). Burstein suggests that social change is not likely to occur simply as a result of passing laws. The laws must be enforced, and this frequently results from litigation. To enforce the law, litigation must be successful, that is, it must result in direct judicial victories for plaintiffs pursuing lawsuits. In other words, Burstein assumes that legal success is measured by courtroom victory. As he suggests, "One advantage of studying court cases is that it is relatively clear who has won and who has lost" (1991, 1212).

Legal analyses frequently go beyond assessment of litigation in terms of victory for specific parties in lawsuits. Many scholars note the rise in litigation by public interest groups and, with it, attempts to use the courts not simply to win individual cases but to establish broad policy goals (Chayes 1976).[9] Such examinations point to the third component of assessing litigation: the establishment of legal precedent. This aspect of assessment moves beyond direct judicial victory for plaintiffs and advocates and focuses on the broader policy implications that may arise out of legal precedent. In short, evaluations place less importance on the narrow, particular interests of parties and give greater emphasis to the general policy issues that emerge from litigation. For instance, analyses of the civil rights movement stress not only the victory and defeat of the parties in *Brown v. Board of Education* (347 U.S. 484 [1954]) but the far-reaching policy changes associated with the Supreme Court's establishment of precedent (Tushnet 1987; Bell 1985).

This third dimension of assessment is especially important in analyses of social movements that seek far-reaching reforms. Several scholars explore this third dimension by examining how movements employ a litigative strategy with the goal of changing social policy.[10] In doing so, some have addressed the conflict between the short-term aim of victory in the immediate adjudication and the long-term objective of creating policy precedent. Stephen Wasby, for instance, expresses these dual goals, noting that while they may both be sought at the same time conflict often arises between the two: "Obligation to client rather than to group strategy may require accepting a settlement offered the client, thus ending a case in which doctrine favorable to the group might have been developed and requiring the group to seek another case through which to carry out its strategy" (1983, 257).

The final component of evaluating litigation is strongly related to setting precedent and establishing broad policy implications. This component involves whether court decisions are translated into results by effective implementation, thereby influencing society. As Johnson and Canon state, "[J]udicial decisions are not self-implementing; courts must frequently rely on other courts or on nonjudicial actors in the political system to turn law into action" (1984, 25). Assessing the effectiveness of litigation thus requires that we evaluate whether decisions are in fact implemented. Murphy and Pritchett explain:

> In the usual kind of civil litigation, compliance with a decision is routine. . . . It is when the controversy concerns broad public policy, when interest groups or governmental officials are the liti-

gants, and when a court's final decree and opinion relate directly
to future conduct of persons not actually parties to the litigation,
that the matter of compliance becomes complex and interesting.
(1986, 320)

Two components of implementation can be distinguished: legal
compliance and social impact. Judicial decisions are implemented
when relevant parties comply with the specific terms of decisions. Judicial implementation studies examine various constituents of the compliance process: courts, administrative agencies, federal and state legislatures and executives, other public officials, and the public at large.[11]
Implementation studies explore numerous factors that foster and
inhibit compliance with judicial decisions, including communication of
decisions, clarity of opinions, perceived legitimacy and authority of
communicators, and sanctions for disobedience (Baum 1989; see also
Johnson and Canon 1984; Bullock and Lamb 1982; and Brown and
Stover 1989).

In addition to compliance, implementation studies are concerned
with the broader issue of impact. Do judicial decisions have an impact
beyond the direct participants in the litigation? What are the consequences of these impacts? Are there unintended consequences? Do the
consequences advance social reform or do the consequences of judicial
decisions lead to co-optation? (See, for instance, Scheingold 1989; Freeman 1982; Bumiller 1988; Medcalf 1978; and Bruun 1982.)

In light of the diverse constituents and influences on implementation, several scholars have advanced judicial implementation theories
(Johnson and Canon 1984; Bullock and Lamb 1982; Brown and Stover
1989). Scholarly examinations of judicial impact and implementation
generally conclude by recognizing the varied, mixed, and frequently
unclear consequences of judicial decision making. For example, Johnson and Canon conclude that Supreme Court decisions

broadened the scope of freedom of expression in recent years, but
it is not clear to what extent this freedom is more widely exercised
nowadays. In the realm of sexually oriented material, court decisions may well have followed social changes as much as they have
initiated them. (1984, 268)

Likewise, Baum explains that, in the area of school desegregation decisions, the implementation record "is a mixed one" (1989, 208).

It is in the realm of implementation that many scholars criticize litigation strategies, arguing that while victory in court may be attained and precedent established the actual impact on society often is minimal. For instance, the works of Stuart Scheingold, Derrick Bell, Gerald Rosenberg, Alan Freeman, and Kristin Bumiller all address the lack of judicial implementation in antidiscrimination law, thus attesting to the limited effectiveness of litigation.[12] Scheingold (1974) and Bell (1985) maintain that litigative victories in this realm have largely been hollow since they create the appearance of formal equality but in fact result in minimal implementation. Rosenberg (1991) contends that *Brown v. Board of Education* had no impact at all. Freeman (1982) and Bumiller (1987) argue that judicial victory often places the responsibility for enforcement and implementation on the victims of discrimination. For them, litigation in antidiscrimination law has been largely ineffective since the victim must bear the costs of enforcing equal protection laws.

Evaluating litigation in terms of these four components—access to courts, judicial victory for parties, establishment of policy precedent, and implementation of decisions—provides much information and insight into the utility of litigation. The four components focus attention on specific cases, judgments, and particular legal outcomes. Success, from this instrumentalist view, rests in judicial authority and power. Effectiveness requires victory on the way to court, in the courtroom, and in the aftermath of judicial decisions.

By assessing instrumental effectiveness, scholars seek to determine whether litigation contributes to significant social change. Many scholars find hope in the legal strategy, arguing that litigation opens the door for participation and provides the opportunity for social change (Friedman 1985; Casper 1976). In contrast, many critical scholars are skeptical about the opportunities provided by litigation. For them, litigative success at best fosters piecemeal and incremental change and is thus reform-oriented rather than transformative (Bell 1985; Bumiller 1987; Scheingold 1989; McCann 1986). At worst, litigation appropriates the institutions and discourses of those in power, thereby replicating and reinforcing the status quo (Gabel 1982; Medcalf 1978; Bruun 1982). In either of the latter cases, litigation is a limited and limiting strategy for social transformation.

The extent to which litigation is an effective weapon for reform thus remains the subject of considerable debate. On the other hand, the terms of this debate, that is, the categories for evaluating instrumental effectiveness, are generally not the subject of significant disagreement.[13] In light of this agreement, the remainder of this chapter speaks within the terms of the debate by exploring the litigation experiences of the animal rights movement through a focus on the four categories discussed above.[14] A preliminary assessment of the direct effects of litigation will emerge from this exploration. However, as noted earlier, chapter 6 will question the terms of the debate and explore whether this narrow instrumentalism provides a sufficient basis for evaluating the practice of litigation.

Animals in Case Law

In examining litigation on behalf of animals, we can distinguish four basic areas of case law.[15] The first area involves enforcement of laws directly related to the treatment and interests of animals. I refer to this area as animal law. This realm includes litigation that seeks to enforce the federal Animal Welfare Act, state anticruelty statutes, and laws that regulate the treatment of animals in food production, clothing, cosmetics, research, entertainment, and so forth.

The second area of case law is related to yet distinct from the first. This area encompasses numerous environmental laws that directly and indirectly involve animals. Those that directly relate to animals include such things as the Endangered Species Act (ESA) and the Marine Mammal Protection Act (MMPA), which protect certain groups of animals in the name of perpetuating species. The indirect laws include straightforward environmental laws such as the National Environmental Policy Act (NEPA) and various hunting regulations. These laws often refer to animals but only in an incidental fashion, generally requiring the submission of environmental impact statements before actions can be taken that might harm animals. Environmental law is distinct from animal law because the intent of these realms of law differ. While anticruelty statutes protect individual animals, laws like ESA and MMPA are concerned with the perpetuation of entire species. The primary intent of the latter two laws concerns keeping the environment in balance. Hence, ESA and MMPA are more appropriately categorized as environmental laws. Likewise, NEPA and hunting regulations are designed to protect the environment rather than animals. In environmental law, consideration of animals is important only insofar as animals constitute a part of the environment.

The third realm of law associated with litigation for animals I call human law. This area includes laws intended for humans that have no direct relation to nonhumans. The texts of these laws say nothing about animals. Yet litigation involving these laws indirectly can and does affect animals. Animal rights activists indirectly raise animal issues via litigation of First Amendment rights of free speech and thought, freedom of information act cases, open meetings cases, libel suits, tort and small claims cases, and more. These secondary battles are used by activists as a legal alternative in light of the lack of animal laws and the limitations of environmental laws.[16] Activists have found that the domain of human law supplies fertile ground for creative cases and, according to one activist, provides "untapped potential" for litigative strategies (Gary Francione, interview). This realm is especially interesting since it demonstrates the use of human rights claims and litigation in response to constraints in the deployment of animal rights claims in the courtroom.

The fourth area of case law includes cases associated with attempts to obtain legal standing. Animal rights groups, like other advocacy groups, have frequently been barred from bringing legal action as a result of standing rules—rules that govern who may bring lawsuits.[17] In response, animal advocacy groups have challenged standing regulations in order to obtain access to the courts and seek judicial remedies. As will be shown below, lawsuits involving standing do not comprise a distinct realm of case law. Rather, these cases are associated with litigation surrounding animal and environmental law. Nevertheless, for the purposes of analysis, it is helpful to distinguish standing from the other areas of case law.

To begin the assessment of litigation's instrumental effects, I explore the contribution and significance of each area using the four evaluative components outlined earlier. I first address the issue of standing and then move on to examine animal, environmental, and human law.

Standing for Animals

The limited implementation of laws protecting nonhumans has inspired animal advocacy groups to seek enforcement through judicial avenues. Most laws concerning the treatment of animals come under the general heading of anticruelty statutes. These laws exist at both the federal and state levels,[18] with the former contained in the federal Animal Welfare Act. In addition to anticruelty statutes, environmental laws such as the Endangered Species Act provide formal protection for certain animal species. The power to enforce federal laws concerning animals rests generally in the hands of the USDA. At the state level, similar agencies have been delegated the authority to enforce anticruelty statutes.[19] However, at both the state and federal levels, enforcement agents do not have the power to arrest violators, and most of their activities involve bureaucratic administration of licensing procedures (Thomas 1986). Moreover, past actions and nonactions on the part of enforcement agencies demonstrate a general lack of commitment to implement anticruelty statutes. As one article reports,

> local prosecutors rarely enforce those [anticruelty] laws unless someone mistreats a domestic pet or farm horses and cows. "I've been studying this issue for ten years," says David Favre, a professor at the Detroit College of Law. "And I can't remember a time that a prosecutor brought a case against a fur farmer." (Kasindorf 1990, 32)

Another instance of lack of implementation is documented in a 1985 report by the General Accounting Office. The report testified that the USDA failed in its role as inspector of research facilities that experiment on animals. The report found that many facilities had never been inspected, that others had not been inspected with appropriate frequency, and that when deficiencies were found little was done to impose remedies (Thomas 1986; McDonald 1986). Thus, despite institutionalized mechanisms, enforcement power is used sparingly and ineffectively.

In response to this lack of implementation, animal advocacy groups have sought to become the legal guardians of nonhuman animals. In doing so, advocates have come up against the standing obstacle. To gain a judicial hearing on the merits of a case, individuals and groups must meet the standing requirements. At issue is whether the party bringing the suit is the appropriate plaintiff. For the courts this means deciding whether the party

> alleged such a personal stake in the outcome of the controversy as to assure that concrete adverseness which sharpens the presentation of issues upon which the court so largely depends for illumi-

nation of difficult constitutional questions. (*Baker v. Carr*, 369 U.S. 186 [1962], 204)

Demonstrating a "personal stake" is not always an easy task. In 1969, the U.S. Supreme Court stated that standing requires the demonstration that a legal right has been infringed (*Association of Data Processing Serv. Org., Inc., v. Camp*, 397 U.S. 150 [1969]). Federal cases involving standing are bound by the case or controversy limitation of Article III of the Constitution. Under this limitation, a party claiming standing must

> "show that he personally has suffered some actual or threatened injury as a result of the putatively illegal conduct of the defendant," and that the injury "fairly can be traced to the challenged action" and is "likely to be redressed by a favorable decision." (*Humane Society of the U.S. v. Hodel*, 840 F.2d 45 [1988], 51)

While it has been held that the case and controversy requirements do not bind state courts, courts in general have remained hesitant to grant standing to public interest groups, including animal advocacy groups.[20]

The courts have on numerous occasions restricted access to animal advocacy groups by denying standing. The courts generally base this restriction on the holding that in cases concerning the treatment of animals advocacy groups cannot show a direct personal stake or demonstrate a direct injury. For instance, an individual owner of a cat could bring charges against someone who harmed that cat on property rights grounds. However, courts restrict animal protection organizations from initiating such charges, holding that they have no direct stake in the harm inflicted upon that cat. Attorney Joyce Tischler explains the standing barrier in a similar fashion:

> [I]t may upset me that Farmer Jones is raising veal calves under conditions I consider cruel; however, I don't have an economic interest in his calves or a direct enough relationship to them that a court would say I have the right or "standing" to sue the farmer on behalf of myself, my organization, or the calves.
>
> This is a problem in trying to help any animals in whom we have no direct "ownership." (Bring 1991, 43)

The standing obstacle confronted by animal activists is significant. Courts have expressed their hesitancy to extend standing, noting the fear that "utter chaos" would ensue if private parties obtained standing to sue on behalf of animals (*Parker v. Lowery*, 446 S.W. 2d 593 [1969], 595–96). Law review articles on animal law stress the obstacle imposed by standing (Messett 1987; McDonald 1986; Thomas 1986). And animal advocates involved in litigation quickly point out the constraints of standing.[21]

Despite the strong barrier imposed by standing, at least some courts have demonstrated willingness to confer standing to animal advocacy groups.[22] This growing willingness originated not in litigation on behalf of animals but in environmental litigation.[23] The well-known Supreme Court case *Sierra Club v. Morton* (405 U.S. 727 [1972]) gave credence to the idea that guardians of nonhuman entities should be granted standing.[24] In that famous case, the Sierra Club argued that representatives of the public interest should be awarded standing to obtain an injunction against the construction of a recreational resort in the Sierra Nevada Mountains. Despite the majority denial of standing, an important dissenting opinion by Justice William O. Douglas conferred some measure of legitimacy on the idea of giving nonhuman entities standing through representatives. Noting that suits have been brought on behalf of such inanimate objects as ships and corporations, Douglas extended the logic to other nonhuman entities.

Douglas's dissent drew on a famous law review article written by Christopher Stone (1972).[25] Stone's article justifies the granting of standing to nonhumans and recommends that courts confer legal rights to "natural objects" in the environment, including rivers, forests, and animals. He argues that legal rights should be extended despite the fact that natural objects cannot speak for themselves. Incompetent humans, Stone notes, are incapable of speaking on their own behalf, yet they have been granted rights that are protected by legal guardians. The guardianship concept should likewise be extended to natural objects. Expanding on this view in his later work, Stone suggests that suits could be brought "in the name of the nonhuman *alone*. That is to say, a river or valley may be denominated the lead plaintiff, so that the case bears in the official law reports a title such as *Byram River v. Village of Port Chester*" (Stone 1987, 7). In this way, nature would gain standing.

Mainstream legal thought has not adopted the logic of Douglas and Stone, nor have the courts. Nonetheless, the logic provided a foundation for people and groups seeking protection of nonhumans within the legal system. Moreover, in the wake of *Sierra Club v. Morton*, the courts have liberalized standing regulations, stretching "the conventional notions of when a human was being harmed to provide environmental lawyers with an alternate and, in most situations, equally satisfactory route to the courthouse door" (Stone 1987, 6).

Throughout the 1970s and 1980s, this liberalization of standing has led to greater acceptance of suits on behalf of nonhuman entities. Animal advocates have capitalized on this liberalization. Following in the footsteps of environmental groups and drawing on their litigative experiences, animal advocates have challenged the limits on standing. In doing so, they have experienced success—success in gaining judicial access and success in setting important policy precedents on the standing issue. In addition, lower courts are increasingly implementing the newer standing opinions. These successes have led, in turn, to important judicial victories on the merits of particular cases, victories that could not have occurred without standing.

In *Animal Welfare Institute v. Kreps* (561 F.2d 1002 [1977]), the Washington, D.C., Circuit Court of Appeals granted animal advocacy and environmental groups organizational standing. The case involved a government decision to waive a moratorium on sealskin importation from South Africa. The plaintiff, a coalition of animal and environmental groups, challenged the action, claiming standing on the grounds that they had "a personal stake in the maintenance of a safe, healthful and productive environment and in the protection of marine mammals" and an interest in avoiding "injury to the recreational, aesthetic, scientific, and educational interests of their members" (*Animal Welfare Institute v. Kreps*, 561 F.2d 1002 [1977], 1007). The suit was dismissed in district court on the grounds that the organizations lacked standing. On appeal, the higher court reversed the decision. The appeals court stated that, although Congress had not explicitly conferred standing on these groups on the issue of the waiver, Congress had specifically granted the groups standing on the proceedings for permit application, implicitly granting them standing on the waiver regulations. Thus, the court found a statutory basis for standing. Furthermore, the court stated that the "appellants also satisfy the three prerequisites for standing in the absence of a statutory grant" (1006). The court held that (1) an injury in fact had occurred, (2) a causal connection between the injury and the defendant's action had been proven, and (3) the interest to which injury is claimed is within the "zone of interests" protected by the statute. Justice Wright's decision stated:

> Where an act is expressly motivated by considerations of humaneness toward animals, who are uniquely incapable of defending their own interests in court, it strikes us as eminently logical to allow groups specifically concerned with animal welfare to invoke the aid of the courts in enforcing the statute. (1007)

Although not as expansive as Stone or Douglas might have liked, the decision in *Kreps* clearly liberalized standing and set an important precedent. As Stone noted in response to the case,

> The reviewing court impressed an expansive interpretation upon the post-*Morton* law, gave a friendly reading to the facts (one of the groups' members had filed an affidavit expressing a plan to go to South Africa in the future), and proceeded to invalidate the permits on the grounds that South Africa was allowing nursing seals to be clubbed and skinned. (1987, 8)[26]

In addition, the judicial decision was a direct victory for the plaintiffs involved in the suit. While illegal importation of sealskins may have occurred after the decision, the legal ruling was implemented by appropriate government agencies. More broadly, the opinion established a significant precedent that allows increased access to the courts.

In a 1985 case, the Ninth Circuit Court of Appeals denied standing to an animal advocacy group attempting to stop the navy from shooting feral goats (*Animal Lovers Volunteer Assoc., Inc., v. Weinberger,* 765 F.2d 937 [1985]). The court held that the group had not shown an "injury in fact" and could not rest injury on emotional and psychological distress. Even though the denial of standing resulted in a court loss for the plaintiffs, the judicial opinion generated optimism for others seeking standing. The court indicated that organizations demonstrating "longevity and indicia of commitment to preventing inhumane behavior" would be in a better position to obtain standing (939). According to the court, such characteristics are "highly relevant" factors to consider in standing cases (939). Thus, despite the denial of standing, the case displays further liberalization of standing regulations. It sets a precedent for groups demonstrating longevity and commitment, and increases the opportunity for future access to the courts.

In *Humane Society of the U.S. v. Hodel* (840 F.2d 45 [1988]), a prominent animal advocacy group challenged the extension of hunting to wildlife refuges. The district court denied standing but the Washington, D.C., Circuit Court of Appeals reversed and granted standing to the Humane Society of the United States (HSUS). The court repeated the precedent that emotional distress does not constitute a cognizable injury and that a "strong interest" in enforcing environmental laws does not provide an adequate foundation for standing. Nevertheless, the court held that danger to the recreational and aesthetic interests of HSUS members provided a sufficient basis for standing.

In *Hodel*, the court further ruled on the issue of HSUS's organizational standing, providing an expansive and liberal reading of the "germaneness test."

[A]n association has standing to bring suit on behalf of its members when: (a) its members would otherwise have standing to sue in their own right; (b) the interests it seeks to protect are germane to the organization's purpose; and (c) neither the claim asserted nor the relief requested requires the participation of individual members in the lawsuit. (53)

The court easily found that HSUS met the first and third conditions of this test and then expanded upon the issue of germaneness. Since the explicit goals of HSUS speak of protecting all living things and say nothing about protecting recreational and aesthetic interests, the district court found that HSUS had not satisfied the germaneness issue. The federal court reversed this decision, stating that the germaneness condition was not meant to be read narrowly: "Too restrictive a reading of the requirement would undercut the interest of members who join an organization in order to effectuate 'an effective vehicle for vindicating interests that they share with others'" (56). Thus, the court found that the germaneness test requires "only that an organization's litigation goals be pertinent to its special expertise and the grounds that bring its membership together" and that HSUS met this requirement (56). This interpretation set a precedent that widened the door to the courts for groups previously excluded by the standing requirements.[27]

Three more cases in the early 1990s illustrate moments of judicial success on the standing issue and implementation of earlier rulings. In 1991, the Fund for Animals, an organization that frequently sues to halt hunts, was granted standing in federal court to stop the killing of bison that wander outside of Yellowstone National Park. Although the court ruled against the organization in allowing the hunt to continue, the grant of standing furnished entry to the court and established a precedent for future litigation activities. In April 1991, animal protection groups gained a further precedent from the U.S. District Court for Washington, D.C. In that case the court conferred standing upon two animal advocacy groups—HSUS and the Animal Legal Defense Fund (ALDF)—in their suit seeking USDA enforcement of the Animal Welfare Act for rats, mice, and birds (Animals' Agenda, July/August 1991, 37). The grant of standing turned out to be significant in terms of creating a direct judicial victory on the merits of the case and establishing an important precedent: in January 1992, U.S. District Court judge Charles Richey ruled that mice, rats, and birds must be protected by the USDA under the AWA (Animals' Agenda, March 1992, 33).[28] In a third case, the U.S. Supreme Court reversed a 1988 lower court ruling and granted standing to People for the Ethical Treatment of Animals and the International Primate Protection League. The Court held that the groups had a right to sue the National Institute of Health in Louisiana state court over custody of the remaining Silver Spring monkeys. According to Animals' Agenda, this ruling set "an apparent precedent for enforcing state anti-cruelty laws against federal agencies" (September 1991, 35).

In spite of these successes, standing remains a significant obstacle to litigation on behalf of animals. The changing judicial standards make it difficult for lawyers to determine whether groups will be granted standing. Moreover, the courts continue to restrict access by denying standing. For instance, Oregon Circuit Court judge George Woodrich denied standing to PETA and Students for the Ethical Treatment of Animals in a suit that sought to open the University of Oregon's Animal Care and Use Committee meetings to the public (Animals' Agenda, July/August 1991, 37). More importantly, the 1992 grant of standing conferred on HSUS and ALDF in their legal battle to extend the AWA to mice, rats, and birds was later overturned. In January 1994, on appeal in federal court, the grant of standing was reversed and, as a result, so too was the lower court decision to include the previously excluded animals under AWA protection.[29] It is also important to remember that even when the courts grant standing animal advocates often lose cases on their merits, as they did, for instance, in *HSUS v. Hodel*.

While standing remains a major obstruction, it does not affect all suits. Some states have granted enforcement authority to advocacy groups, bypassing the standing problem. Numerous statutes, including more than a dozen federal environmental laws, contain provisions that specifically allow advocacy groups to bring lawsuits (*ASPCA*, Winter 1988/Spring 1989, 10).[30] And suits involving human law are not generally embroiled in standing. Thus, animal advocacy groups can often bring cases without confronting the standing issue.

The above cases demonstrate that challenging the standing obstacle through litigation has been at least moderately effective. First, the legal battle for standing has been reasonably successful in terms of gaining increased access to the courts. With this expanded access, animal advocates can challenge their opposition in new ways. Second, the standing contests have resulted in numerous court victories for plaintiffs on the standing issue. These, in turn, have resulted in the third success: establishing broad and significant legal precedents. These precedents establish a new logic for granting standing, transcending the notion that legal interests stem solely from "personal and proprietary contractual relationships" and suggesting that "longterm moral interests can also be the basis of standing" (*Animals' Agenda*, July/August 1991, 37). As precedents mount, access expands even further, lower courts are increasingly likely to implement decisions, and the movement gains in strength and voice.[31]

The apparent trend toward liberalizing standing regulations has been brought about by means of a continued commitment to employing litigation. Still, this success must be considered in light of the obstacles that limit the utility of litigation. Overall, the standing cases tell a mixed story about the effectiveness of litigation. They illustrate that existing barriers—which appear at times to be rather determinate—make litigation an arduous and often ineffective route. But they also show the malleability of the barriers and demonstrate that litigation can be a useful tool to create openings within those barriers.

Litigation in Animal Law

Lawsuits based on animal law usually involve charging people with violations of anticruelty statutes.[32] Many people have been convicted of cruelty to animals. A Michigan court sentenced two men to 90 days in a work release program for stabbing a puppy. Animal breeders have been charged and convicted of animal neglect and inhumane treatment. A Texas man was fined $2,000 and sentenced to 150 hours of work with the humane society for killing a poodle with a bow and arrow (*Animals' Agenda*, December 1990, March 1991). Along with such convictions, charges of cruelty have been used to halt or delay certain uses of animals. In Washington state, a pigeon shoot was canceled after the attorney of a local animal rights group informed the organizer that the shoot would violate state anticruelty laws. Similarly, a rattlesnake roundup was called off the same day charges were filed (*PAWS News*, September 1990, October 1987). The USDA, in administering the AWA, also blocks cruelty violations through cease-and-desist orders against such things as unlicensed breeding and illegal transportation of animals (*Animals' Agenda*, March 1991).

Animal rights groups commonly stress the cruelty involved in animal experimentation. However, bringing legal charges against researchers is difficult and has generally been unsuccessful. On the other hand, the famous case of *Taub v. State of Maryland* (463 A.2d 819 [1983]) illustrates the potential success of charging researchers with cruelty violations.[33] After animal activist Alex Pacheco reported evidence of abuse at laboratories run by the Institute for Behavioral Research in Silver Spring, Maryland, police investigated and charged Dr. Edward Taub with violating Maryland's anticruelty statute. The district court found Taub guilty of failing to provide necessary veterinary care for six monkeys.

The conviction of Taub was later overturned on the technical grounds that a state animal cruelty statute cannot be applied to research institutions working under a federal program (*Taub v. State of Maryland*, 463 A.2d 819 [1983]). Thus, the initial court victory became a defeat for the advocates involved in the case. Nevertheless, the earlier conviction did create a significant precedent for challenging scientific research procedures. For the first time in this country's history, a court had found an animal researcher receiving federal funds guilty of animal cruelty. In addition, the suit demonstrates how litigation can be used to enforce existing laws. The suit showed that documenting cruelty violations and bringing this documentation to the attention of appropriate enforcement authorities can impel litigation and potentially enforce anticruelty laws.

These cases exhibit the actual and potential effectiveness of litigation in animal law. They demonstrate the ability to access judicial
avenues, to obtain victories in the courtroom, and, at times, to set precedent. In contrast, litigation in animal law does not always, or even frequently, result in success. Lack of evidence on the proportion of cases
that result in judicial penalties makes it difficult to determine the overall level of success. But several factors suggest the limited effectiveness
of suing to enforce animal laws.

First, implementation of anticruelty statutes is quite limited. For
the most part, animal advocacy groups do not have the authority to sue
on cruelty violations and thus lack access to judicial avenues.[34] Moreover, the proper government authorities file few suits that seek implementation of these regulations and display little interest in doing so.
Limited resources available to government agencies and animal advocacy groups further constrain the use of litigation. Restricted judicial
access, combined with a lack of administrative interest in enforcement,
significantly weakens implementation of anticruelty laws.

Second, cases that are brought rarely result in jail terms or significant fines for violators. It has been estimated that of the 10 to 20 animal
cruelty cases prosecuted in the typical major city, less than 10 percent
lead to jail terms of 10 to 30 days (Zak 1990, 6). Moreover, many anticruelty statutes strictly limit the fines that can be imposed on violators.
For instance, a standard maximum penalty provides up to $500–$1000
fine and/or up to six months or one year in jail.

Third, the range of potential suits in animal law is narrow. The
small number of animal laws and their limited extent restricts the range
of suits that can be brought. For instance, animals used in food production are generally excluded from animal protection laws, and, as such,
lawsuits to protect these animals are difficult to bring via animal law.
Similarly, many states exempt scientific research from their anticruelty
statutes. In addition, litigation in this area is of the type that generally
promotes "negative" or "protective" results. That is, litigation in animal law seeks to stop, delay, or limit harmful practices toward animals.
It only rarely advances the more "positive" goals of liberation. In this
way, litigation in animal law is similar to other public interest litigation
in that much of its success is limited to halting and delaying action
(McCann 1986, 250–51).[35]

In light of these limits, it is not surprising that activists have
explored other avenues of law. More surprising is the success experi-

enced within these alternative legal realms. The turn to both environmental law and human law thus provides insight into the creative
potential of litigation in situations in which legal resources are few.

Litigation in Environmental Law

Two segments of environmental law come into play in animal litigation: regulations governing particular species of animals and laws that
require environmental impact studies (EIS). The ESA and the MMPA
provide safeguards for selected animal species. Laws that include EIS
regulations vary greatly, but many relate to the environmental impact
of hunting, recreation, and business ventures. On numerous occasions
advocacy groups employ these segments of environmental law (sometimes in combination) to advance the cause of animals.

Numerous suits have been brought employing the ESA and
MMPA. In 1990, In Defense of Animals (IDA) brought this type of suit
against the U.S. Navy (*Animals' Agenda*, December 1990, 35). IDA won
an injunction and stopped the navy from poisoning squirrels at a California naval weapons station. Employing the ESA, the group successfully argued that the poison threatened certain endangered species of
foxes and mice (Doyle 1990, 9). In a similar case, Defenders of Wildlife,
Friends of Animals and Their Environment, and HSUS sued the
Department of the Interior (*Animals' Agenda*, July/August 1991, 37).
The suit sought to overturn a 1986 directive by the department that
exempted foreign projects from the ESA. The Eighth Circuit Court held
in favor of the animal and environmental groups.

In another case a coalition of animal protection and environmental
groups brought a suit combining the two segments of environmental
law. The suit sought to stop the navy's proposed deployment of dolphins in Washington state's Puget Sound by alleging violations of the
MMPA, the National Environmental Policy Act, and the Administrative Procedures Act (*PAWS News*, December 1990, 11). In May 1990, the
suit was temporarily settled to the satisfaction of animal advocates
(Offley 1990, 1). Under the settlement, the navy suspended deployment
and the further capturing of dolphins pending EIS completion. In addition, the settlement required formal public hearings that would allow
testimony against the planned deployment. The navy continued its
efforts to deploy dolphins, prompting the Progressive Animal Welfare
Society's Laurie Raymond to suggest that despite the settlement the

issue will likely have to be settled in court (*PAWS News*, December 1990, 11). However, in the spring of 1991, a navy spokesperson confirmed that the deployment had been canceled. Although the navy asserted that the cancellation was a result of "changes in the world situation and defense spending reallocations" rather than a response to the legal activities, it is likely that the litigation played a significant role in prompting the cancellation (*PAWS News*, April 1991, 1). And, as Raymond reminds us, "[W]ithout the lawsuit, dolphin soldiers would have been deployed in Hood Canal" (*PAWS News*, December 1990, 11).[36]

In another case, a coalition of animal advocacy groups successfully barred a mountain lion hunt in California by suing the Fish and Game Commission for lack of compliance with the California Environmental Quality Act (CEQA) (*Mountain Lion Coalition v. Fish and Game Commission*, 263 Cal. Rptr. 104 [1989]). Both the Superior Court of San Francisco and the California Appeals Court found that the commission had submitted an inadequate EIS, thereby violating CEQA. By strictly enforcing the regulation requiring that the EIS be "supported by references to specific scientific and empirical evidence," the suit makes the initiation of hunts more difficult (108). According to Associate Justice Haning, "The court's review of the proposed 1987 mountain lion hunt rang the environmental alarm bell loud and clear" (110).

These cases reveal the ways in which environmental law can be deployed on behalf of animals. Success has been achieved on numerous fronts. By gaining access to courts, animal advocacy groups have stopped or deterred various practices deemed harmful to animals. These cases demonstrate how hunts have been impeded through enforcement of environmental regulations, how advocates have inhibited dolphin deployment, and how courtroom victories have been achieved on the part of plaintiffs representing animals. In addition, these legal actions illustrate successful implementation of environmental laws. Through these cases, the judicial system enforced written laws and required compliance with established regulations. Thus litigation attained substantive compliance with formal rules. Finally, by enforcing compliance through litigation, these cases established precedents that animal advocates can employ in future cases.

Despite these victories, litigation in environmental law is again significantly constrained. For one thing, the ESA and MMPA protect only certain animal species. Indeed, the majority of animals lack protection under environmental laws. This means that ESA and MMPA have a limited range of application. For instance, two animal advocacy groups sought to halt a deer hunt in Massachusetts on the grounds that the gunfire from the hunt might disturb endangered bald eagles. Since the U.S. District Court rejected the argument that the eagles would be significantly disturbed, the hunt proceeded (*Animals' Agenda*, March 1992, 50). As this ruling demonstrates, the deer never had any direct protection under the law. Similarly, in the IDA lawsuit, had there not been a population of endangered foxes and mice, ESA and MMPA would have been inapplicable. Alternatively, if the navy could have found another way to kill the squirrels, one that did not threaten the endangered animals, such a solution would have been legally acceptable.

A second and perhaps more significant limitation to litigation of environmental law is that such suits may only result in short-term success for the animal rights movement. Judicial decisions to bar hunts and other activities pending EIS completion leave open the option of completing an EIS. If the opposition chooses to fulfill the EIS requirements and succeeds in demonstrating that the environmental impact of the action would be minimal, then, from the perspective of animal advocates, the initial judicial success would give way to judicial defeat. For example, while the Fund for Animals has forced cancellation of several bear hunting seasons by challenging state fish and game departments, in October 1990, a superior court in California reopened bear hunting by ruling that the department had finally provided a sufficient EIS (*Animals' Agenda*, December 1990, 43). Thus, litigation in such cases does not always result in a long-term or final solution to the problem of hunting. Indeed, litigation rarely achieves finality given both the appeals process and alternative means of circumventing judicial decisions.[37]

A third limitation involves implementation of these judicial decisions. In cases in which judges decide to ban hunts or restrict the killing of endangered species, lack of compliance often ensues. Poaching of animals, illegal import of endangered species, and killing spotted owls in protest of judicial and legislative action exemplify the limited ability to implement judicial decisions and existing laws.

Finally, litigation in environmental law does not go far toward the goal of promoting a positive agenda. While successful in the negative sense of halting and delaying certain actions toward animals, environmental litigation has been less useful for directly initiating more positive movement programs such as promoting habitat renewal.

Thus, we again see the equivocal nature of litigating on behalf of animals. Litigation that employs environmental law provides opportunities for direct success. The existence of such laws affords animal activists alternative and effective ways of using the legal system. Unable to apply anticruelty statutes, activists can at times foster the implementation of environmental laws to protect animals and establish precedent. At the same time, the instrumental effectiveness of these alternative routes remains quite limited and will likely be further constrained if the current Republican Congress succeeds in narrowing environmental regulations.

Litigation in Human Law

The limitations of standing, the lack of sufficient laws protecting animals, and the constraints on environmental law have inspired animal advocacy groups to explore creative litigative strategies in challenging human uses of animals. These strategies focus on laws that do not directly address animals. For instance, the Fund for Animals successfully petitioned a superior court judge in Arizona to suspend an elk hunt on the grounds that the state game and fish department had neglected to provide the mandatory opportunity for public comment (*Animals' Agenda*, January/February 1992, 35). Using a human law to initiate this litigative activity, the animal advocacy group was able to halt a hunt that would have otherwise proceeded.

In more specific terms, animal advocates often turn to the Constitution's First Amendment, freedom of information laws, open meetings laws, libel suits, small claims suits, and tort laws to advance the cause of nonhuman animals. Through litigation of these human laws, activists raise issues of animal rights and protection. Thus, despite the small number of animal laws, activists have found a way to creatively and effectively employ litigation. In doing so, they have increased their access to courts and obtained important judicial victories and precedents.

First Amendment Cases

Animal rights advocates have filed several First Amendment cases that relate to animal issues. One type of case involves dissection. A groundbreaking suit was filed in California when high school student Jenifer

Graham refused to dissect a frog in her biology class. Suing the school district on the grounds that forced dissection would violate her moral beliefs, which are protected by the First Amendment, the case went to U.S. District Court. The judge ruled that Graham must be allowed to fulfill class requirements by using frogs that had died of natural causes (Murphy 1988).[38]

Along the same lines, a student sued the State University of New York (SUNY) at Stony Brook when a biology professor would not offer her an alternative to dissecting a frog. The university, in response, reversed its policy that required the dissection of frogs in basic biology courses (Lyall 1990, 19). Similarly, in response to a lawsuit brought by a veterinary student, the Ohio State University College of Veterinary Medicine agreed to establish alternative classes for students who take a moral stand against dissection (*Animals' Agenda*, September 1991, 41).[39]

Another variation of a First Amendment case was brought by a veterinarian who teaches at the School of Veterinary Medicine, University of California, Davis. Professor Nedim Buyukmihci advised students that they did not have to practice surgical techniques on healthy dogs if they had ethical objections to the practice. He also helped students find terminally ill animals in need of surgery. The university took disciplinary action against Buyukmihci by filing formal misconduct charges and removing him from an ethics course. The professor responded with a civil rights lawsuit alleging a violation of his First Amendment right to free speech and expression. The court extended a partial injunction "prohibiting the school from taking disciplinary action against him" (Vogeler 1990, 7). The court later extended a permanent injunction prohibiting punitive action, awarded Buyukmihci $75,000 in compensatory damages, and required the university to pay his legal fees (*Animals' Agenda*, November 1991, 33). After the lawsuit was filed, the university began evaluating the possible use of terminally ill animals or animals that require surgery and decided to create an alternative program by 1993. Until then it allowed students with moral objections to perform their surgical training at Washington State University, which teaches veterinary surgery without the use of healthy animals (*Animals' Agenda*, September 1991, 41). Despite an official statement that the proposed changes were not prompted by the lawsuit, the connection between the lawsuit and the reevaluation process is clear.

Animal advocacy groups also deploy the First Amendment right to free speech in a more general way: by arguing that the Constitution protects protest activities. Members of the Citizens to End Animal Suffering and Exploitation (CEASE) successfully asserted their First Amendment right when they were arrested at Boston's Faneuil Hall marketplace in June 1989 for urging people to boycott veal. Taking their case to U.S. District Court, members of CEASE won a ruling that security guards had violated their First Amendment protections (*Animals' Agenda*, November 1990, 11).

Along similar lines, animal rights strategists have begun testing a new litigative tactic that challenges hunter harassment laws on free speech grounds. Forty-seven states have passed hunter harassment laws that restrict nonhunters from "harassing" hunters in designated areas. For instance, a Montana law prohibits demonstrators from "disturb[ing] an individual engaged in the lawful taking of a wild animal with the intent to dissuade the individual or otherwise prevent the taking of the animal" (*Washington Post*, January 14, 1995, sec. A, p. 24). Animal advocates have intentionally violated these laws and sought arrest in order to challenge the laws' constitutionality (*Animals' Agenda*, January/February 1991, 32). Although protest actions in New York, Texas, Kentucky, Pennsylvania, and Washington failed to result in charges under the hunter harassment laws, activists have been able to test the laws in some states, including Idaho and Montana.

The direct results of these tests have been mixed. In 1994, the Idaho Supreme Court found the state's hunter harassment law to be "unconstitutionally overbroad." But the previous day the Montana Supreme Court had found the opposite, upholding the conviction of a man under a similar law (Motavalli 1994). The Montana ruling, however, is not definitive. The ruling pertained to a man who had jumped between a hunter and his target, shouting "Don't shoot!" In the ruling, the court distinguished between the protester's form of speech and speech involving such things as picketing parking lots and passing out fliers near hunting grounds. Making this distinction, the court "emphasized that its opinion did not preclude further challenges to the statute when clearly protected speech is involved" (*Washington Post*, January 14, 1995, sec. A, p. 24).

In January 1995, the U.S. Supreme Court refused to hear an appeal of the Montana case. The refusal was no doubt a loss for animal rights proponents who argued that the law was "too broad, vague and improperly infringed on their First Amendment free-speech rights"

(Reuters World Service, January 11, 1995). However, despite the court's refusal to hear the case and hand down a definitive ruling, animal advocates are still free to challenge state laws. Thus, the issue of hunter harassment remains a prime area for legal activism on behalf of animals.

Within the various cases outlined above, activists deploy the First Amendment as a resource to obtain entry into the courts in defense of their cause. Lacking other avenues of judicial access, the First Amendment provides an alternative route for raising animal issues within the legal arena. Additionally, the First Amendment has provided important direct victories and precedents in the Graham frog dissection suit, in the CEASE litigation, and in the veterinarian's suit. The hunter harassment suits have yet to be fully tested, but the potential for judicial victory and the further establishment of precedent remains. Finally, judicial involvement encourages implementation of the First Amendment. It is difficult to say how much of an impact this implementation has had on society at large, but, at least on the dissection issue, it certainly has had an impact on schools and students.

Freedom of Information Laws and Open Public Meetings Acts

Over the past few years, activists have successfully advanced a new litigative strategy in the area of scientific research. A 1985 amendment to the AWA requires that federally funded research institutions using animals in experiments have an institutional animal care and use committee (often called the animal care committee or ACC). This committee reviews all proposed experiments and oversees the use and treatment of animals by researchers. Animal advocates in several states have sought to open committee meetings to the public and to obtain research information. Some institutions have consented to these requests. In other cases, litigation has been brought under state freedom of information laws and open meetings acts to force public access and information.

In an early case, PAWS challenged the University of Washington under the state's Open Public Meetings Act (OPMA) (*PAWS News*, May 1987, 1). In response to demands for public access to the committee meetings, the university argued that the ACC was only an advisory committee and therefore did not fall under OPMA. In a lawsuit, the King County Superior Court ruled that the committee functioned as more than an advisory body. Unless the university chose to make the

ACC a purely advisory committee, it would have to open the meetings. The university complied, fearing that a change in the committee would mean loss of federal funding under the requirements of the AWA. In addition, the university chose not to appeal the case or take it to trial. As a result, animal rights activists now regularly attend ACC meetings and have successfully used their presence to pressure animal researchers.[40]

In a later case, the ASPCA brought suit against SUNY-Stony Brook on the same grounds. In 1989, a state Supreme Court judge in Suffolk County held Stony Brook's animal care committee subject to the state's open meetings law. In 1990, the court further ruled that the state's freedom of information law requires general disclosure of research procedures (Anderson 1990). However, a New York State Supreme Court four-judge panel overturned the open meetings ruling on the grounds that the committee does not perform a "government function" and therefore does not count as a public body under the open meetings law (*Animals' Agenda*, July/August 1991, 37).

The success experienced by PAWS in Washington and the initial success of the ASPCA in New York have inspired other groups to take similar steps. According to Gary Francione, other groups around the country have followed the lead of PAWS and the ASPCA (interview). "Similar cases have been heard in at least six states, with the decisions split between universities and animal-rights groups" (Lyall 1989, 4). As a result, we once again see expanded access to judicial processes. Although these suits have enjoyed mixed direct success in the courtroom, the precedents set in the PAWS case, in the early decision in the ASPCA suit, and in other cases establish important foundations for further judicial action and implementation. Judicial activity in these cases fosters implementation of freedom of information laws and open meetings laws, legislation designed to inspire citizen participation in governing. Moreover, the goal of these lawsuits is to gain admission to scientific research meetings, and, in the PAWS case, activists have implemented rulings and have had significant impact on the research community at the University of Washington.[41]

Libel, Small Claims, and Tort Cases

The libel suit is a tool increasingly employed by animal advocates.[42] Advocates charged by opponents with impropriety, misconduct, and the like have at times responded with the judicial force of libel and achieved success. For instance, a University of Pennsylvania anatomy professor retracted an open letter attacking an animal rights activist after the activist threatened to sue for libel (*Animals' Agenda*, March 1991, 37). In a libel suit that moved beyond the stage of threat, a settlement was reached that led to retractions of alleged impropriety against Friends of Animals and Primarily Primates (*Animals' Agenda*, July/August 1990, 37). Similarly, a successful out-of-court settlement was reached in a libel suit brought by PETA against the *Washingtonian* magazine. The magazine had tried to link PETA to laboratory break-ins carried out by the Animal Liberation Front. The settlement required a public apology by the *Washingtonian* and entailed significant monetary costs for the magazine (*Animals' Agenda*, January/February 1992, 36).

Advocacy groups have expanded their use of small claims and tort law as well. Activists bring these suits to challenge veterinary malpractice, wrongful death, and demands by landlords to remove pets from rental premises. In veterinary malpractice and wrongful death cases, compensation is sought for the loss of the pet. Such claims generally equate the loss of a pet with the loss of property, but lawyers are increasingly trying to distinguish pets from property and have had some success getting judges to recognize the "sentimental value" of animals (Stille 1990, 28). In a similar vein, a judge awarded "a precedent-setting $10,000" for damages and emotional pain in a case in which a man promised to give a dog a good home but then sold her for medical research (*Animals' Agenda*, March 1991, 36).

Here we see once again how judicial access, victories in court, and precedents can be fostered by litigative activities. These direct consequences of litigation often advance movement goals in situations in which animal and environmental laws are lacking. Thus, the turn to human law provides creative litigative opportunities in spite of the limited number of animal and environmental laws and the constraints of standing.

Obstacles to Successful Litigation

Using a combination of animal law, environmental law, and human law, advocacy groups have enjoyed numerous litigative victories in the courtroom. On the other hand, not all litigation has resulted in direct wins for animal advocacy groups. Many lawsuits have ended in losses in court. For example, a PAWS and International Wildlife Coalition suit to obtain the release of two captured beluga whales did not succeed.[43] An effort in 1989 to prevent the release of 35,000 helium-filled balloons that could allegedly threaten endangered species failed when federal Judge Thomas Zilly ruled that an immediate threat had not been demonstrated (*PAWS News*, February 1989, 18). An attempt by IDA to block the transport of a gorilla from a Cleveland zoo to the Bronx Zoo failed when the U.S. District Court denied an injunction (*Animals' Agenda*, January/February 1992, 35). In addition, courts continue to deny standing to animal advocacy groups. And in some cases in which standing has been granted, activists have experienced the failure of losing the case on its merits.

In evaluating the instrumental effectiveness of litigation for the animal rights movement, we must consider these direct losses.[44] We must also consider more general obstacles activists confront when taking the legal route. These obstacles can be divided into two categories: resource costs and legal doctrine.

To achieve success through litigation, advocates require specific resources that may be unavailable or in short supply. All social movements employing litigation require money, time, and energy. The litigative process is lengthy and costly, and those engaged in the process must commit serious energy to the enterprise. Many scholars have noted that the lack of these resources limits the utility of the litigative route (Handler 1978; Bumiller 1987; Kessler 1987). Like other social movements, the animal rights movement must overcome these resource constraints. The high concrete costs of litigation make less costly strategies such as protests, boycotts, and lobbying more appealing and viable. This is particularly true for small animal rights organizations that lack the financial resources necessary to sponsor litigation.[45]

In addition to money, time, and energy, scholars emphasize the importance of legal and technical experts. "Expert legal staff allows a group to keep abreast of ongoing case law and select appropriate cases for group intervention" (Neubauer 1991, 178; see also Vose 1959). Technical experts offer the specialized information frequently needed in litigation. While animal rights groups have access to both legal and technical experts, these resources are limited. Although growing in number, few lawyers in this country specialize in animal issues. According to one report, the ALDF works with 320 volunteer attorneys around the country. However, the same report notes that only "13 lawyers around the country devote most of their practice to animal rights" (Hentoff 1990, 23).[46] As for technical experts, the movement has received support from the medical, veterinary, and scientific communities, and it has access to environmental and animal experts.[47] On the other hand, animal rights opponents have greater access to experts. Vested interests within the scientific, medical, and agricultural communities provide solid support—in terms of both finances and expertise—for opponents of animal rights. The opposition, fearful of interference in such areas as scientific research and food production, can draw readily on the perceived legitimate expertise of people like Louis Sullivan, former secretary of health and human services, and groups like the American Medical Association.[48]

Aside from resource obstacles, animal activists also face numerous legal obstacles, obstacles that arise from accepted legal doctrine. Two have already been discussed: the limited number of animal laws and the doctrine of standing. Other legal obstacles can potentially restrict the effectiveness of litigation. Important in this respect is the limited legal language that can be deployed on behalf of animals. Litigation sponsored by animal activists makes little if any mention of animal rights since animals have not been recognized as having legal rights. In the courtroom, the phrase is off-limits. According to Roger Galvin, "Under current law, animals have no rights and so it would be foolish for a lawyer to argue a case on the basis of animal rights" (quoted in Stille 1990, 28). While litigation can be useful in bringing attention to the issue and can be employed in creative ways to assist the cause of animals, litigation by itself is not likely to confer rights to animals. "The current Supreme Court is not going to go for a constitutional argument on animal rights," notes constitutional law professor Roger Goldman (29). Thus, we see the rather ironic situation of a movement that deploys the discourse of rights outside of judicial institutions but, within the courts, rarely applies the discourse to animals.

This limitation highlights an area in which formal law is not very flexible. In fact, within the context of the courtroom and official legal discourse, the law appears to be quite determinate in barring the notion and language of animal rights. Since animal rights claims cannot be explicitly mobilized in formal law and since animals themselves do not have standing, the determinacy of law with respect to excluding animals seems to prevail. Such prevailing determinacy creates a considerable barrier to rights-oriented litigation for animals and restricts the possibility of direct litigative success for animal rights.

Associated with this language barrier is the legal doctrine that defines animals as property. In tort law, this doctrinal tradition limits judicial victories since the courts treat animals in terms of their monetary value rather than their intrinsic worth or sentimental value. Although this legacy may be changing, the continued practice of equating animals with property minimizes the effectiveness of litigation for groups advancing the view that animals have moral status and intrinsic worth.

Additional legal obstacles stem from the Constitution. The Fourth Amendment and the Commerce Clause have been cited by Larry T. Garvin (1988) as potential doctrinal barriers to successful litigation.[49] Some states give local animal welfare societies the power to inspect research facilities without warrants.[50] These warrantless searches have been challenged successfully under the Fourth Amendment in at least two cases, thereby restricting access to research institutions (*Marshall v. Barlow's, Inc.*, 436 U.S. 307 [1978]; *State v. Osborn*, 63 Ohio Misc. 17, 409 N.E.sd 1077 [1980]). Moreover, Garvin suggests that local and state laws regulating research institutions will likely be held unconstitutional if challenged because they violate federal commerce powers and are preempted by various federal laws.[51]

A final legal obstacle is the judiciary's general unwillingness to become involved in policy issues. According to Marci Messett, courts give great discretion to government agencies responsible for enforcement of laws. In particular, Messett points to the Fourth Circuit Court opinion in *International Primate Protection League v. Institute for Behavioral Research, Inc.* (799 F.2d 934 [1986]) in which the court stated the following:

> To imply a cause of action in these plaintiffs might entail serious consequences. It might open the use of animals in biomedical research to the hazards and vicissitudes of courtroom litigation. It may draw judges into the supervision and regulation of laboratory research. It might unleash a spate of private lawsuits that would impede advances made by medical science in the alleviation of human suffering. To risk consequences of this magnitude in the absence of clear direction from the Congress would be ill-advised. In fact, we are persuaded that Congress intended that the inde-

pendence of medical research be respected and that the administrative enforcement govern the Animal Welfare Act. (Messett 1987, 110–11)

Overall, the obstacles created by legal doctrine and resource costs continue to impede litigative success. Combined with the other barriers animal advocacy groups confront, these obstacles greatly contain the efficacy of litigation. In addition, it should be noted that the Reagan and Bush conservative appointments to the federal courts have not boded well for animal advocates who employ the judicial route. As Gary Francione stated at the March for the Animals:

> At least on the level of the federal judiciary, I do not see a great deal of hope for the future. Remember . . . Ronald Reagan and George Bush have basically stacked the federal judiciary with a lot of judges, many of whom don't care about civil rights, women's rights, or gay and lesbian rights. And they're not about to recognize the more progressive step of animal rights.

Conclusion

What preliminary conclusions can be drawn from the litigative activity of the animal rights movement? From an instrumental perspective, has litigation been an effective route for achieving the goals of the animal rights movement? If so, in what ways and under what conditions has this occurred? Is litigation, more generally, a useful route for other social movements?

The foregoing analysis of case law involving animals tells a mixed, complex, and surprising story with regard to effectiveness. On the one hand, much success has been achieved. Activists have increased their access to courts by challenging the issue of standing and creatively deploying various legal resources. With increased access, activists have obtained victories in court and established significant policy precedents, many of which have had some impact on courts, political institutions, and society. Through litigation, important judgments have been reached in favor of the movement, and creative and tactical uses of the laws that do exist have allowed the movement to bypass many existing barriers. On the other hand, direct losses have been experienced at great cost. Moreover, various barriers continue to diminish the potential of litigative success, including resource costs and legal doctrine.

The primary conclusion to be drawn from this case study is that the direct effects of litigation are often mixed, and hence ambiguous. It is extremely difficult to determine whether litigation has, on the whole, been an effective route. Since we cannot precisely measure the tangible costs of various litigation efforts or quantify the direct benefits of gaining access to courts, setting precedent, or achieving implementation of particular statutes, we cannot say with definitiveness that the benefits of litigation have outweighed the costs. We can say that, taken together, these litigation efforts have been neither overwhelmingly successful nor overwhelmingly disastrous. Litigation's instrumental effectiveness, it appears, is uncertain.

Despite this mixed story, there do seem to be some additional conclusions we can draw from litigation on behalf of animals. From the discussion so far, it appears that litigation has been effective in certain important respects. Lawsuits have been especially effective in gaining access to the judicial realm. The standing cases are notable in this way. In addition, environmental law and human law have opened the courtroom door to animal advocates. Without this access, important judicial victories and precedents would not have been achieved. Moreover, these victories and precedents, although mixed with defeats, have been realized in the face of serious constraints and obstacles.

Along with effectively achieving access, lawsuits have been useful in achieving "negative" movement goals: to delay, limit, or prevent harmful practices toward animals. Litigative actions have prevented the navy from deploying dolphins and from poisoning squirrels. Lawsuits have halted and limited mountain lion hunts, bear hunts, rattlesnake roundups, elk hunts, and more. Injunctions have been successful in delaying animal experiments. Although suits are sometimes initiated to promote directly positive results and on occasion achieve these results,[52] for the most part, litigation is deployed to stop rather than to promote action.

This type of "negative" success is not unique to the animal rights movement. Litigation in many social movements is frequently associated with halting activity, like stopping race and gender discrimination in the workplace and preventing lumber companies from logging in forests. Indeed, in direct terms, litigation may be more effective as a prophylactic measure than as an affirmative step for constructing social relationships (McCann 1994). And the animal rights movement supports this point.

The final and maybe most important conclusion to be drawn from the discussion so far is that, to be directly effective, litigation must be employed creatively and strategically. The animal rights movement is a case in which there are few laws that can be litigated. Even more significant is the fact that this movement cannot even use animal rights language in the courtroom. Litigation would seem ineffective under these circumstances—or at least less effective than it is for movements that can mobilize a wider body of existing law. What has increased the effectiveness of the legal route for the animal rights movement has been the strategic appropriation of environmental and human law. This appropriation has enlarged the potential area of litigation, thereby expanding the strategic choices of movement activists. With this strategic appropriation of law, animal advocates have been able to strengthen the direct effectiveness of litigation.

This creative and strategic approach may be more important for movements like the one studied here than for movements that can rely on broader legal foundations. Nonetheless, the importance of creatively manipulating existing laws through litigation is generalizable to other social movements, even those that have access to a wider body of existing law. Numerous social movements can, for example, benefit by creatively using First Amendment claims, freedom of information acts, libel laws, and so forth.[53] The fact that a movement has a specific law that speaks directly to its concerns does not mean that the law will always be the most effective resource. In certain situations, other laws, strategically deployed, may be more effective and may offer opportunities for resisting prevailing legal meaning.

As we shall see in the next chapter, this strategic and creative deployment of law has done more than enhance the direct effectiveness of litigation. It has further provided the animal rights movement with the opportunity to benefit from the multiple, indirect uses of litigation. With a strategic and creative approach to litigation, animal advocates have generated "cultural space for liberating activism" (Scheingold 1989, 86). Activists have advanced strategic legal battles within this space and, in doing so, have created a larger space for further struggles in both the judicial and nonjudicial realms.

To sum up, this preliminary assessment of instrumental effectiveness suggests that activists have been at least moderately successful in efforts "to pound a square peg in a round legal hole" (Wise, quoted in Stille 1990, 1). However, several questions remain. How far has the peg been pounded? Has the square peg become round, suggesting co-optation into the dominant system? Has the round legal hole become square, implying attainment of some fundamental changes? Or have the peg and hole both changed during the pounding process?

These and other questions about the utility of litigation cannot be adequately answered by looking only at the direct consequences of case law. As suggested earlier, looking at instrumental effectiveness through a constitutive lens will highlight the multiple, indirect conse-quences of litigation and lead us to an alternative method of evaluating instrumental effectiveness. Moreover, examining the constitutive char-acter of litigation will prove immensely important in the assessment of litigation and for understanding the interaction between the judicial and nonjudicial spheres. Therefore, before fully addressing these ques-tions, we must first move to a broader assessment of litigative activity.

Chapter 6

Beyond the Courtroom: The Multiple Uses of Litigation

Astute organizational leaders should be able to take advantage of a lawsuit to generate publicity and legitimacy for their groups. Litigation is often newsworthy, and a press conference held to announce a development in a lawsuit may bring the organization and its goals to the attention of potential new supporters.

—Susan M. Olson

Most law-reform activity serves multiple purposes. Even if the social-reform groups and the law reformers are counting on direct tangible benefits from litigation, the litigation usually will help publicize the organization and the law reformers, legitimize values and goals, stimulate purposive incentives, and hopefully result in obtaining outside resources from elites, foundations, other organizations . . . and public agencies.

—Joel F. Handler

[T]he very presence of a lawsuit and the information it reveals promote attention in the press, which serves to alert citizens that an issue is arising which deserves their attention. In this way, too, litigation helps to realize a truly democratic process.

—Joseph L. Sax

The examination of the instrumental effectiveness of litigation suggested in mainstream scholarship and elaborated in the preceding chapter would be critiqued by those approaching law from a constitutive perspective. To fully appreciate the law, a constitutivist would say, we need to consider its broad effects, its power to make meaning, and the way law influences self-understanding and action. On this view, instrumentalism focuses too narrowly on the direct and immediate effects of litigation, thereby neglecting the more wide-ranging implications of legal languages and practices. Thus, looking to criteria such as judicial access, courtroom victories, precedents, and legal implementation does not tell us enough about the power and significance of law.

The constitutivist's critique of instrumentalism's narrowness is, I believe, correct. A more extensive understanding of the law is revealed when we look beyond the four criteria elaborated earlier. However, the constitutivist approach tends to take its critique of instrumentalism too far by discarding concern for effectiveness and neglecting consideration of the instrumental uses of law.

I suggest in this chapter an instrumental approach that takes seriously the constitutivist concern with the broader effects of law. As applied to litigation, this means that we need to explore not only the direct effects outlined earlier but the multiple indirect effects and uses of the litigative process.

> Indeed, given the copious evidence demonstrating that judicial victories often produce uneven or negligible impacts on targeted social practices, such indirect effects and uses of litigation may be the most important of all for political struggles by most social movements. (McCann 1994, 10)[1]

Within the context of social movement activism, I suggest that these indirect effects and uses of litigation form at least three significant categories: (1) the advancement of education through publicity and consciousness-raising, (2) movement building and mobilization, and (3) the creation of political pressure and leverage against the opposition.[2]

This chapter explores these important secondary effects of litigation as displayed by the animal rights movement. It should be stressed that these effects of litigation must be considered instrumental effects. They are certainly secondary or indirect compared to the direct outcomes of litigation addressed in chapter 5, but they are nonetheless instrumental consequences that contribute to the assessment of litigative effectiveness. Hence, applying constitutivism to instrumentalism does not turn the latter into the former; rather, it broadens the definition of effects in the latter and brings constitutivism and instrumentalism closer together.

At the same time, we should not disregard the constitutive component of these effects. The direct and indirect effects of litigation are implicated in the production of meaning and must therefore be examined in this regard. Most importantly, these effects constitute meaning for animal rights activists and, in turn, influence the attitudes, expectations, and practices of these movement proponents. Exploring the constitutive character of litigation while taking seriously the concerns of instrumentalism will highlight the ways in which the construction of meaning is importantly tied to strategic action. The analysis of the constitutive character of litigation will be taken up in chapter 7. The remainder of this chapter offers a reexamination of animal rights litigation informed by constitutive instrumentalism.

Education, Movement Building, and Leverage

Although most scholarly analyses of litigation emphasize direct effects, increasing attention has been paid to the multiple consequences of litigative activity. Scheingold's *The Politics of Rights* (1974), which conceptualizes rights-oriented litigation as a political resource, offered the foundations for other scholars to move beyond the direct effects of litigation. Using that foundation, I suggest here the importance of looking at litigation's relationship to education, movement building, and political leverage.

Promoting education comprises an essential part of social movement activity. To attract attention and support, movements must educate and raise the consciousness of the public, government officials, and potential supporters on relevant issues. The tactical methods used to advance education and consciousness-raising are numerous, and litigation plays a significant role in this regard. Activists have come to realize that litigation fosters education and consciousness-raising. Moreover, they understand that publicity surrounding litigation is central to education. As a result, activists often use litigation tactically not only to win cases and set precedents, but to encourage education, advance publicity, and heighten awareness.

Several scholars point to the connection between litigation and the secondary effects of education, consciousness-raising, and publicity. Joel Handler argues that publicity and consciousness-raising comprise two of the "multiple purposes" of law reform activity (1978, 210). Susan Olson (1984) contends that assertive litigating groups have found new goals in advancing lawsuits, including educating the public. "Litigation can produce new information through processes such as discovery, create new forums for additional debate . . . [each] of which can be used by organizers" (25). These types of indirect goals are, according to

Olson, an "appropriate part of the 'politics of rights'—educating the potential beneficiaries of the litigation and the wider public about the issues in hopes of mobilizing their support" (26).

In conjunction with education and publicity, litigation can promote movement building and mobilization. Litigation can foster fund-raising and mobilize outside resources and thereby contribute to organizational goals (Handler 1978, 210). In addition, litigation frequently spurs other forms of movement activity, prompting such things as rallies, educational campaigns, letter-writing drives, and lobbying activities. As Scheingold (1974) asserts, litigation and rights language can be useful political resources for the goals of movement mobilization. Used to foster mobilization, they can activate citizens and promote organizational growth and efficacy. In turn, political mobilization can "build support for interests that have been excluded from existing allocations of values and thus promote a *realignment* of political forces" (131). While Scheingold remains skeptical about the effectiveness of rights-oriented litigation in itself, arguing that the "dominant tendency [of the myth of rights] is surely to reinforce the status quo," he concludes that litigation is a political resource that may be used to create change and promote a redistribution of power (91).[3]

Drawing on Scheingold and others, McCann elaborates a model of "legal mobilization" that also recognizes the relationship between legal activism and movement building. This model analyzes the multiple and complex motivations of law, legal discourse, and litigation. It also explores the many direct and indirect effects of legal discourse and legal activism. One of the primary motivations and outcomes of using litigation is *"the movement building process* of raising expectations regarding political change, activating potential constituents, building group alliances, and organizing resources for tactical action" (1994, 11). In studying the pay equity movement, McCann finds that legal mobilization in the early stages of reform activism contributed to movement formation.

[L]egal rights discourse has provided reform activists a compelling normative language for identifying, interpreting, and challenging the unjust logic of wage discrimination. Moreover, litigation has been used by movement leaders as a tactical resource to raise expectations among women workers that wage reform was possible. As a result, legal action greatly enhanced the opportunities for effective political organizing around the pay equity issue. (48)

Litigation also can contribute to mobilization by providing a potent source to advance a movement's credibility and to internally build the confidence of membership and activists. Advancing credibility suggests making the movement appear believable and trustworthy to outsiders and potential supporters. But, more than that, credibility connotes mainstreaming a movement, moving it out of the margins and extremes and placing it in the mainstream. Enhancing confidence works internally to bolster morale and reinforce the conviction that change can be achieved.

By raising expectations, enhancing credibility, and bolstering confidence, legal activism may influence the way a movement defines itself. As Elizabeth Schneider asserts, rights-oriented litigation can be used to "express the politics, vision, and demands of a social movement, and to assist in the political self-definition of that movement" (1986, 605). In so doing, litigation may contribute to the important formative stages of a movement.

A final consequence and tactical use of litigation involves the creation of political pressure and leverage against opposing forces and alleged wrongdoers. Litigation may be used as leverage, allowing groups to mobilize resources and enhance their strength and bargaining power in the use of nonlitigative tactics (Handler 1978, 210). Litigation, or simply the prospect of it, can pressure opponents into action beneficial to movement goals. As Olson claims, "Hand in hand with other political tactics, plaintiffs . . . use litigation to pressure their adversary to the negotiating table when he or she was not willing to negotiate without such pressure" (1984, 9).[4] For Olson, this means that "litigation becomes as important for the pressure it can put on nonjudicial policy makers as it is for the actual decision of the court" (35). Similarly, McCann asserts the importance of leverage and pressure in legal practices.

Such a leveraging role to some degree represents the flip side of law's role as a catalyst to movement building. Just as legal rights advocacy can generate affirmative support for reform from various constituencies, so can it be employed as a "club" to compel concessions from unsupportive state officials and dominant social groups. . . . [T]he mere potentiality of judicial intervention . . . can provide very important, if often unacknowledged, resources for social movements. (1994, 138)

When we consider the relationship between litigative practice, education, movement building, and leverage, the broader context and goals of the legal process are illuminated. Studying litigation in this way highlights not only the courtroom, the state, and official legal activity but also the broad realms beyond the state where legal practices shape and are shaped by social struggle. In addition, such a study of litigation reveals the politics inherent in legal activity. Litigation (and "the law") should not be viewed as separate and distinct from politics. Instead, litigation is a political activity, connected to political aspirations and practices. As such, lawsuits and the sphere of activity and outcomes surrounding legal cases are important not only with respect to their official legal ramifications but also with regard to political and strategic activism, regardless of whether this activism takes place on a grand or small scale.

It is worth stressing that broadening the analysis of litigation does not imply that litigation will always or even generally provide a solid avenue for social change. On the contrary, we must maintain a strong skepticism toward the litigative process and recognize its tendency to reinforce existing power structures. At the same time,

we should be sensitive to how different legal norms and institutional arenas over time offer varying degrees of opportunity or space for creative challenge. . . . [Law's] role in sustaining traditional hierarchies, and hence in structuring potential strategies of resistance, varies significantly among different terrains of social struggle. As such, attention to tactical options concerning the particular sites, terms, and timing of struggle are an important concern. (McCann 1994, 9–10)

It is also worth noting that attention to these tactical options makes the assessment process more difficult. It becomes more difficult not simply because there is more to study but because of problems associated with verifying the indirect ramifications of litigation. How can we measure the indirect effects of education and publicity that may result from litigation? How can we quantify the credibility that use of the legal system provides? How can we evaluate the benefits arising from placing pressure on the opposition and enlightening judges on a new way of thinking about a legal issue?

Indirect effects often cannot be precisely quantified. As Handler notes, "as we move farther away from focusing on direct, tangible results, the use of the theoretical framework and evaluations will become increasingly imprecise" (1978, 210). Nonetheless, indirect effects should not be ignored. I will approach the measurement problems by drawing on a wide variety of evidence that suggests the importance of these indirect uses.[5] This evidence is especially strong with regard to the internal effects litigation has had on the animal advocacy movement itself. By examining movement activism, movement literature, media coverage, and the perspective of animal advocates, I have gathered strong evidence suggesting that litigation has significantly influenced internal movement education, mobilization, and a sense of empowerment. There is also a good deal of evidence suggesting that litigation has had a broader, external effect in advancing movement goals. Although the evidence in this area is less conclusive, I present it in order to demonstrate litigation's indirect potential to contribute to social change.

Secondary Uses of Litigation: The Cases Explored

In the legal cases discussed in chapter 5, animal advocates sought not only to win in court but to produce and capitalize on the multiple uses of litigation. A broadened analysis of these cases illustrates that animal advocates attempt through the litigative process to educate the public, government administrators, judges, and animal supporters. The publicity promoted through lawsuits assists in this education process and can mobilize other movement activities. By educating the public, litigation can foster recruitment of new members, inspire other groups to use litigation and alternative strategies, advance movement credibility and leverage, and prompt government officials to adjust laws and activities. In these various ways, the direct negative victories in court could be transformed indirectly into positive initiatives to promote animal rights and liberation.

The following discussion revisits three specific legal cases and two general areas of litigation addressed in chapter 5. Within this more detailed revisitation, the instrumentalist lens is widened so that we may explore the broad ramifications of legal practice and evaluate the potential of litigation's numerous secondary uses.

The Silver Spring Monkeys

As noted in chapter 5, the Silver Spring monkeys case began when Alex Pacheco, now chair of PETA, provided police with evidence of animal cruelty in Dr. Edward Taub's laboratory. Pacheco's 1981 investigation led to an extensive court battle that lasted ten years. The battle was costly and time-consuming, but it was used to foster education, publicity, and consciousness-raising regarding the animal rights movement in general and the particular issue of animal abuse in scientific research.

In order to find out how animals were treated by researchers, Pacheco sought and found work in Dr. Taub's research laboratory. When he began in 1981, Pacheco learned that he would be working with seventeen monkeys, several of which had been surgically disabled in a process called deafferentation. Deafferentation involves the cutting of nerves that carry sensory communication from a part of the body to the brain. In order to study the nervous system and its regenerative capacities, Taub cut the nerves of one arm in each of eight monkeys. He then restrained the monkeys' good arms to see if they would learn to use their deafferented arms. He found that they did (Carlson 1991).

Although Pacheco was opposed to such experimentation, he had no grounds to directly challenge the experiment. He did, however, begin to document the conditions under which the monkeys were kept, surreptitiously bringing in cameras, veterinarians, and scientists to validate his findings. Pacheco brought his affidavits and photographs to the police, and on this evidence Circuit Court judge John McAuliffe issued a "precedent-setting search and seizure warrant" (Pacheco 1985, 141). On September 11, 1981, the police raided the lab, discovering seventeen monkeys, each in a cage less than eighteen inches wide that had not been cleaned for several days. "Several of the monkeys had bitten off fingers, and some had chewed into their limbs, leaving raw, open wounds the size of silver dollars, wounds that were covered with filthy bandages or not covered at all" (Carlson 1991, 15).

The police seized the monkeys and charged Taub with seventeen violations of the state anticruelty statute. Judge David Cahoon returned custody of the primates to Taub but reversed that decision after one died from mysterious causes. The monkeys were placed in a National Institutes of Health (NIH) facility in Maryland, and Taub was convicted of six cruelty violations for failure to provide appropriate veterinary care for six of the monkeys. On the first appeal, the verdict was changed, and Taub was found guilty of only one cruelty violation. On the second appeal, in 1983, the Maryland Court of Appeals overturned the earlier verdicts on the technical grounds that a state anticruelty statute cannot be applied to a federally funded research program.

Judicial involvement with the Silver Spring monkeys did not end in 1983. The issue of what to do with the monkeys remained. NIH had been given custody of the monkeys, and PETA challenged to obtain possession, demanding that the monkeys be placed in a primate center for rehabilitation. Unable to obtain the monkeys, PETA turned to the courts, but it failed in the custody battle after the court denied legal standing. PETA then sought congressional action, but despite much support only five of the monkeys found new homes in the San Diego Zoo.

In 1988, the Delta Regional Primate Research Center—home of the remaining nine monkeys—threatened to euthanize three (ostensibly because of the primates' declining health) and perform further experiments on the dead animals. PETA and the Physicians Committee for Responsible Medicine (PCRM) again went to the courts, this time to block the euthanization. However, U.S. District Court Judge John Garrett Penn denied requests for a preliminary injunction. In 1990, researchers killed three of the primates and performed the experiments (Pink 1990).

By 1991, four of the Silver Spring monkeys remained in the custody of the Delta Center. NIH decided to kill and experiment on two of these primates. Although Supreme Court Justice Anthony M. Kennedy initially blocked the project and demanded that the Justice Department file arguments explaining why the experiments should proceed, two days later the high court lifted the bar and the monkeys were killed (*New York Times*, April 11, 1991; *New York Times*, April 13, 1991).

Evaluating this case, we first look to the direct benefits of this lengthy judicial activity. The early judicial activity against Taub created an important direct precedent: the conviction of an animal researcher. For the first time in U.S. history, a jury found a scientific researcher guilty of animal cruelty (Stille 1990). Even though the court later overturned this conviction, the fact that the overturning came on technical grounds upheld the impression that Taub was indeed guilty of cruelty. Another direct benefit involved the five primates who were saved from further experimentation and certain death. Although not all the monkeys were so fortunate, at least some of the original seventeen were rehabilitated and socialized into a more normal life.

The later judicial activities involving custody of the primates were far from successful. Animal advocates failed to obtain custody and the remaining Silver Spring monkeys were killed. Judicial access was limited, favorable precedents were not achieved, and direct judicial loss ensued.

If we were to judge the success of the Silver Spring monkeys case simply by looking at direct outcomes, we would have to conclude that it was a failure. The extremely high costs outweighed the direct benefits. Years of legal battles with the associated costs in money and time did not achieve the desired direct outcomes in court. However, when we consider the indirect ways litigation was used during the many years of legal battle, our assessment changes. Despite the overturning of Taub's conviction, despite the eventual failure to obtain custody of the remaining monkeys, the animal rights movement employed litigation in multiple and broad ways to advance many indirect goals.

For one thing, the animal rights movement successfully used this case to obtain publicity. The publicity associated with the case was significant, and the media covered the episode throughout its ten-year history. According to a *New York Times* article, the original case against Taub was "widely publicized" (April 11, 1991, sec. A, p. 19). The Silver Spring monkeys case became famous, certainly the most famous animal case in this country. The British science magazine *Nature* referred to the monkeys as "the most celebrated icons of the U.S. animal rights movement" (Carlson 1991, 15). According to Alex Pacheco, in 1989, a White House reporter asked on which subject the president was receiving the most mail. The White House official responded that the third-largest number of letters related to the Silver Spring monkeys, following letters on abortion and catastrophic health. Pacheco went on to say that, responding to a 1990 news article on the subject, more than 43,000 people wrote to Mrs. Bush requesting her assistance in freeing the monkeys.[6] Thus, at the center of an intense legal and political battle, the primates "became a cause celebre . . . [and] a rallying point for the fledgling animal rights movement" (Pink 1990, 12).

PETA and other animal rights organizations have capitalized on the case to create publicity, to educate, and to mobilize activists in the movement. Activists invoked the Silver Spring monkeys to both educate and gain support in speeches, marches, meetings, and movement literature. The 1990 March for the Animals provides an example of activists drawing on this case to educate and mobilize. In his speech to an estimated 24,000 people, Pacheco reviewed the case, stating that 1990 marked "the ninth anniversary of the police raid on the IBR laboratory, and the confiscation of those animals, and the first conviction of an animal experimenter on the charges of cruelty in this country." Pacheco also noted that the injunction obtained to prevent NIH from harming the monkeys "was the first of its kind." Another example came at an April 1991 talk given at the University of Washington. Ingrid Newkirk, cofounder and national director of PETA, was scheduled to speak. That weekend the Supreme Court had lifted the bar against NIH regarding two of the primates, and as a result Newkirk remained in Washington, D.C., attempting to find alternative ways to free the primates. She sent a videotaped message in which she described the case to an audience of approximately 200, once again raising issues, mobilizing support, and educating at a time when a loss in court had just been experienced.

The case also prompted PETA and others to mobilize members of Congress, some of whom assisted in the efforts to free the monkeys. Through the intercession of Congressman Robert Dornan five of the monkeys were placed in the San Diego Zoo.[7] In 1986, 58 senators and 253 House members signed a letter to NIH director James B. Wyngaarden, which requested that NIH give up custody of the primates (*Animals' Agenda*, July/August 1986, 15). More than 140 members of Congress joined in cosponsoring legislation to remove the primates from NIH custody (*Animals' Agenda*, September 1986, 24), and, according to Pacheco's comments at the March for the Animals, 55 members "wrote personally to President Bush asking [him] to intervene to free these animals."

Beyond mobilizing Congress, the case has served as a catalyst for other movement activities. Rallying around the primates, groups have sponsored protests and letter-writing campaigns. PETA set up a "Conscience Camp" on NIH grounds to protest on behalf of the monkeys. In addition, the case has inspired activists to launch investigations of abuse at other research laboratories. Becoming a model for further investigation, the case has led to numerous challenges of the ways animals are used in research endeavors.

Movement building and mobilization has also been enhanced as a result of the credibility and confidence engendered by the Silver Spring monkeys litigation. From an outsider's perspective, the clear demonstration that abuse does occur in scientific research afforded the movement some measure of credibility. Although it is difficult to ascertain the extent to which this external credibility affected popular perceptions, it is at least likely that congressional support for the Silver Spring monkeys was stimulated by the credibility that attached to the movement after the initial court ruling. The initial conviction of a researcher extended credibility at a time when the movement was considered to be on the extreme fringes. It also challenged the credibility of the research community and, in turn, enhanced the credibility of animal rights claims. As Pacheco notes:

> It is hard to describe our feelings when the [guilty] verdict was announced, but at last now, whatever might happen to the monkeys as we continued to fight for their safety, the public would know that something was definitely wrong with the way in which some segments of the scientific community operated. The criminal conviction had chipped a hole in the wall that protects animal experimenters from public scrutiny. (1985, 144)

Whether or not Pacheco is correct in suggesting that the court decision advanced public knowledge and opened up experimenters to scrutiny, the point is that he and others could use the judicial decision to support movement claims, promote the movement as trustworthy, and initiate further action to challenge experimentation. An external, purportedly unbiased body had validated the assertions of animal activists who were popularly viewed as extremists and fanatics. At the same time, this external judicial body convicted a respected member of the research community of abuse. While the public may have continued to view animal rights activists as a marginal group of fanatics, the conviction of a scientist combined with judicial support for an animal advocacy claim most certainly aided the movement's credibility.

The Silver Spring monkeys litigation also worked internally on the movement's sense of confidence and self-assurance. From an insider's view, the demonstration of abuse and the support it received from the external community and the legal system raised the expectations of animal rights activists. This translated into mobilization, as the Silver Spring monkeys case was continually used as a symbol of the movement's success and as a basis for further mobilizing activity against experimentation.

Since the initial ruling, activists have continually used the case to challenge the credibility of researchers and to bolster the movement's internal morale. In almost every report on the Silver Spring monkeys in *Animals' Agenda*—the foremost animal rights magazine in the country—Taub's conviction is mentioned, thus fostering mistrust of researchers and reinforcing the victory of the movement. When describing the overturning of the conviction, the reports always state that it rested on a technicality, thereby perpetuating the perception of Taub's guilt. Moreover, activists refer to the Silver Spring monkeys litigation to challenge the credibility of animal experimentation. One example came during my interview with Dr. Neal Barnard, director of the Physicians Committee for Responsible Medicine. Barnard discussed his organization's litigative attempts to stop NIH from killing the primates. He spoke of the proposed study as "a garbage experiment," thereby questioning the credibility of NIH. In addition, he bolstered distrust of experimenters, stating that a letter had been written to NIH by opponents of the movement suggesting that the animals should never be released because of the effect it would have on animal rights issues.

Finally, the Silver Spring monkeys case granted the movement new leverage with which to pressure the research community. The publicity surrounding the case, the pressure exerted by Congress in reaction to it, and the fear that similar cruelty charges would be brought has contributed to the movement's potential leverage. The case placed pressure on NIH over the course of the ten-year battle, leading its director to say that the single most enervating case during his tenure had been that of the Silver Spring monkeys.[8]

Despite the losses in court, the combination of these indirect effects made the case of the Silver Spring monkeys a symbolic success. The initial lawsuit, the continuing legal battles, and the additional strategies employed in conjunction with litigation placed the primates and actions on their behalf at the center of the animal rights movement. As such, the primates, through the combination of legal, legislative, media,

and protest activities "became a symbol for the animal rights movement" (New York Times, July 8, 1990, 10). This symbol of success was
particularly important in the first half of the 1980s, as the marginal and
weak animal rights movement sought to gain political strength and
support. The symbolic success provided by the Silver Spring monkeys
enhanced the movement's sense of power. Moreover, the symbol has
and continues to be deployed, both internally and externally, to
advance movement goals.[9]

The events surrounding the Silver Spring monkeys thus display
numerous and significant uses of litigative activity and depict how
activists can capitalize on the potential of litigation. The difficulties
involved in quantifying the intangible benefits mean that it cannot be
precisely determined whether the benefits (both direct and indirect)
outweighed the costs of the actions. However, it can be said that without the numerous legal battles surrounding the primates, without the
initial cruelty suit and the custody suits that followed, and without the
nonlitigative strategies used in conjunction with litigation, the Silver
Spring monkeys quickly would have lost media attention and fallen
out of the public eye. Considering the multiple consequences of litigation that appear to have been significant in this case, it seems easy to
conclude that in spite of the eventual judicial losses the litigation was
an overall success. What is certainly clear is that once we recognize the
indirect uses of litigation we must at minimum reconsider our assessments of litigation's effectiveness.

Jenifer Graham and Frog Dissection

Like the Silver Spring monkeys case, the Jenifer Graham dissection
lawsuit instructs us on the important and broad ramifications of litigative practice. The success of dissection suits like Graham's rests not
simply on the direct outcomes of exempting some students from the
requirement of dissection and saving a few frogs. Instead, success
stems from the secondary purposes of litigation, including the media
attention the cases receive, the education they inspire, and the movement building they encourage.

When California high school sophomore Jenifer Graham first
refused to dissect a frog in her biology class, she was probably not
thinking about how to sponsor litigation and strategically produce its
multiple consequences. More likely, her feelings about animals told her

that it was wrong to perform the dissection. When the school's principal declined to accept her moral stance and threatened to penalize her, Ms. Graham and her mother turned to the legal system. This resulted in a new route of activism for animal rights supporters. Thus, while Graham's deployment of litigation was not consciously tactical for the movement, it inspired future strategic use of both litigative and nonlitigative tactics in the realm of dissection.

Graham's refusal to dissect came in 1987. In 1988, she achieved partial judicial success when U.S. District Court judge Manuel Real held that the school would have to find a frog that had died of natural causes.[10] More important for the animal rights movement, this success was accompanied by several indirect successes that continue to be important.

Like the Silver Spring monkeys case, the Graham lawsuit was successfully deployed to foster significant media attention. As Graham comments in *Objecting to Dissection: A Student Handbook,* "In a matter of weeks I became the subject of dozens of newspaper articles and television stories" (ALDF, 7). The case fostered "impromptu press conferences, school board confrontations and a few demonstrations by animal rights activists," which were also covered by the media (Murphy 1988, 3). Moreover, the CBS television network produced an afternoon school special based on the story. According to John Kullberg of the ASPCA, Graham's objections and the lawsuit "did a tremendous thing at the high school level. . . . Now children all over the country have watched this marvelous story of a high school student who refused to dissect and won" (interview).

Graham's stance, the lawsuit, and the activism that flowed from both fostered education on the issue of dissection. The general public was given a forum for hearing the dissection debate. According to Pat Graham, Jenifer's mother, "Every time a student exercises his or her right not to dissect animals, the consciousness of the entire academic community—including teachers, administrators and classmates—is raised" (ALDF, 2). In addition, Ms. Graham provided an example for students—in California and around the country at both the high school and college levels—to follow. Furthermore, the case contributed to the animal rights community's awareness of the subject. Animal rights organizations reported the case in newsletters and took up the dissection issue. For instance, *NAVS,* the bulletin published by the National Anti-Vivisection Society, reported on the legislative efforts that arose following Graham's lawsuit. *NAVS* suggested that "Like many courageous leaders before her, Jenifer Graham's efforts will without a doubt be recorded in animal rights history" (*NAVS Bulletin*, no. 2 [1988]: 8). Using this student's action as an example, animal advocacy groups could encourage people to take the stand—both morally and legally—that Ms. Graham took.[11]

This case also shows how legal activity can foster mobilization through the instigation of other strategic actions. Graham's lawsuit encouraged further litigation. It attracted the ALDF, which took the case to the federal level in search of a decision that would extend to students the right to refuse dissection on moral or religious grounds (Wells 1989). It has also inspired lawsuits such as the one against SUNY sponsored by the ASPCA. Moreover, other animal advocacy groups now offer legal advice to students who refuse to participate in dissection.[12]

In addition to acting as a catalyst for further litigation, the Graham case has fostered other nonlitigative activity. The incident prompted Graham and her mother to take a more active part in the animal rights movement. In conjunction with the ALDF, they established a dissection hotline for people wanting to learn about ways to avoid dissection. This hotline provides information for people who refuse to dissect and stresses that students have a right to conscientious objection. The hotline also encourages the use of alternative methods for learning animal anatomy. According to ALDF, about 100 callers use the hotline each day (Wells 1989). In addition, the Grahams collaborated with ALDF in putting out a publication on dissection. In this publication, Pat Graham states: "I started the Hotline and designed this handbook so that other students could benefit from what Jenifer and I learned through long hard experience" (ALDF, 1).

Beyond the Grahams' personal nonlitigative activities, their actions seek to encourage students in other schools to form animal rights groups. Included in their 10-step plan for refusing dissection, they suggest that students organize others to advance the ethical issues concerning animals. Additionally, the Graham case has been successful in mobilizing other organizations to become active in this area. According to the *Washington Post*,

> People for the Ethical Treatment of Animals, the sniper in this conflict, is mailing out a booklet called "Dying for Biology" and a

videotape charging that a North Carolina supplier of preserved animals violated the Animal Welfare Act. The district attorney declined to investigate the company, but the undercover tapes, showing acts of brutality against cats and rats, got onto ABC news last fall. (May 3, 1991, sec. A, p. 24)[13]

Most importantly, perhaps, the dissection case further demonstrates how a lawsuit can mobilize legislative activity on an issue. According to *Wall Street Journal* columnist Ken Wells, in the California legislature "Ms. Graham's plight proved a catalyst in the adoption of a law that requires schools to provide alternatives to students who object to dissection on moral or religious grounds" (Wells 1989, 1). Graham took part in this activity, testifying before the California state legislature.

This encounter with the legal system further contributed to the credibility of this individual's moral stance. Graham received little respect from school officials when she initially refused to dissect a frog. Even with her mother's support, which was communicated to the school's administration, Graham's commitment was not deemed credible. It was only with the court's involvement that Graham, and those with similar commitments, received credibility. As noted in the *Wall Street Journal*, "what might have been passed off as just another incident involving a squeamish kid has evolved instead into a case with national implications for education, science and civil rights law" (Wells 1989, 1). This does not imply that no one respected Graham's beliefs before she resorted to the legal system. Nor is it to say that engagement in lawsuits is the only way to gain credibility or that it necessarily achieves this goal. What is being suggested is that lawsuits and legal judgments often confer public credibility that may otherwise be lacking.

This type of legal activity has also advanced credibility by appealing to the First Amendment rights of humans. This appeal bases the movement's claim upon a fundamental constitutional principle. By shifting the discussion from the interests of animals (which the courts and the public are less inclined to accept) to the interests and rights of humans, the movement mainstreams its concerns toward animals in a more popularly acceptable, albeit circuitous, manner. Objections to dissection are now continually made in terms of the student's right to refuse it.[14] The moral force of the First Amendment right is then connected to animal rights. For instance, attorney Joyce Tischler appeals to students in the following manner: "I want to talk to you now about animal rights, and your legal right to stand up for animals and *against* dissection" (ALDF, 3). Connecting the legitimate claim to constitutional rights with demands for animal rights helps to extend the notion of credibility to the latter.

Finally, the Graham case accorded leverage to students refusing dissection, to organizations supporting these students, and to the movement as a whole. It certainly exerted pressure on school officials in Graham's high school. On a more general level, the California case set a precedent for protecting a student's right not to dissect. From this precedent, others can pressure schools and teachers into granting consideration to those who take a moral stand against dissection. As noted by the *Washington Post*,

> The case was perhaps the beginning of a war that has been waged quietly but fervently ever since. Animal rights activists, who argue that dissection has no merit at the pre-collegiate or any other level, are now pressuring schools to quit the practice and are offering legal advice for students who wish to pursue litigation. (May 3, 1991, sec. A, p. 24)

In sum, the Graham case was overwhelmingly successful in terms of promoting multiple indirect benefits for the animal rights movement. The direct outcome of the case was initially successful, although it remains to be seen whether the courts will apply the First Amendment's guarantees to students who have moral objections to dissection. No matter what the eventual legal outcome, the substantial indirect uses and consequences of this case created important victories for the animal rights movement. As a columnist for the *Wall Street Journal* reports, "Whatever the court decides, Ms. Graham has succeeded at least in getting a hearing before the public" (Wells 1989, 4).

Freedom of Information Acts and Open Meetings Laws

Cases that seek to provide animal advocates with access to animal care committees through freedom of information and open meetings laws exhibit multiple indirect uses and benefits of litigation. The PAWS case against the University of Washington—"the first case in the country where animal care committees were opened to the public through litigation"[15]—prompted groups in other states to sponsor both litigative and nonlitigative activity, thereby mobilizing movement endeavors.

> As the national animal-rights movement broadens and its techniques grow more sophisticated, similar suits using state freedom-of-information laws are springing up nationally. . . . "I think we're going to open up 25 to 30 states," said Stephen M. Wise, president of the Animal Legal Defense Fund. (Lyall 1989, 1–4)

As each of these cases proceeds, other groups around the country can draw appropriate lessons from litigation to advance their suits. Moreover, activists involved in this form of litigation explicitly encourage others to challenge university ACCs.[16]

During the progress of such suits, media attention can and has fostered publicity and education. Moreover, with a win in court, a new avenue is created to publicly examine proposed scientific research. This, as a result, establishes further education, publicity, movement building, and pressure. "For advocates of animal rights, success in court would enable them to arouse public opinion against an experiment involving animals before it was approved" (Lyall 1989, 1). With the opening of ACC meetings, animal advocacy groups can act as watchdogs over researchers and use leverage in a realm that has been generally free from oversight. As Gary Francione noted during an interview,

> Just the fact that we're there in those meetings and looking at those documents, and [researchers] know we're there cause them a great deal of anxiety. And that's fine, that's what we ought to be doing. We need to be creating as much anxiety in them as we can.

At the University of Washington, animal activists have capitalized on the lawsuit to advance education, publicity, and pressure. PAWS regularly makes use of the access to the ACC. For instance, PAWS challenged a proposed maternal deprivation experiment that would have isolated rhesus macaque monkeys in order to promote self-injurious behavior. This challenge generated much movement activism, created significant publicity, fostered debates on campus between animal advocates and supporters of research using animals, pressured some on the ACC to vote against the experiment, and by some accounts contributed to the denial of NIH funding for the experiment.[17] Without access to the ACC meetings and information, such challenges would be much less effective.

Even with a loss in court, these suits can ultimately be successful. For example, a decision handed down in New York state held that SUNY's ACC does not fall under the state's open public meetings law because it is an advisory body. Although this claim lost in court, the result threatens the university with a loss of federal funding for research given federal laws requiring that the ACC be more than just an advisory body.

These types of lawsuits, furthermore, encourage movement building through their potential to advance credibility. During these legal challenges, university demands to keep the ACC meetings closed create the appearance of secrecy and give the impression that researchers have something to hide. This questions the credibility of the research community and, in turn, potentially promotes the credibility of animal advocates. Moreover, given that these lawsuits rest on demands for openness, claims for public input and debate, and the general argument for the right of the people to know, the animal rights community can advance its credibility by once again connecting animal rights issues with more commonly accepted notions of human rights and democratic ideals.[18] When attorney Francione states that "We as a society have to make independent assessments rather than deferring to these people all the time and letting them do what they want," his appeal is not directly to animal rights but to the publicly accepted values of democratic forms of decision making (Lyall 1989, 4).

Finally, this increasingly common legal tactic extends the movement's leverage. The pressure placed on universities by these suits, by past precedents that have forced ACCs to open, and by fear of becoming the object of such suits lends leverage to animal rights groups. The animal rights movement can capitalize on the fear associated with lawsuits and employ litigation as a "club" against the opposition.

Libel Suits

Like the cases detailed above, libel suits reveal litigation's indirect purposes and possible benefits. In discussing these, we must first distinguish between those suits brought by animal advocates against opponents and those brought by opponents of the movement. In both of these instances, we can discern important indirect uses of litigation, in particular, the possibility of advancing education, publicity, and credibility.

Like the other suits discussed above, libel cases of both types can promote education and publicity for the movement. Education surrounding the particulars of a case can be significant, as is illustrated in the case *Immuno A.G. v. Moor-Jankowski* (77 N.Y. 2d 235 [1991]). That case involved a libel claim against an animal advocate who wrote a letter criticizing Immuno's plan to capture chimpanzees for research. The substance of the suit fostered education and publicity on the environmental effects of capturing chimpanzees (Lewis 1991). In addition, libel suits against activists educate other activists on how to avoid such suits. In organization newsletters, in *Animals' Agenda*, and at meetings and protests, movement leaders inform other activists on the dangers of libel and educate the membership on ways of avoiding such suits.[19] This education gets promoted through publicity, both in the media at large and in the publicity sponsored by movement organizations.[20]

Probably the most important indirect use of libel suits rests in the credibility they can promote. Successful deployment of the libel suit against the opposition potentially fosters a dual credibility function.[21] First, libel suits have the potential to question the credibility of the opposition. This function is particularly helpful when the public perceives the opposition as authoritative and reputable. Winning suits against scientific researchers, government administrators, and professors might prompt public speculation about their honesty and trustworthiness. The second credibility function of the libel suit is the flip side of the first. While raising doubts about the opposition, the successful libel suit concomitantly lends credibility to the animal advocacy movement, which is crucial for a movement continually searching for public acceptance and trust. As one animal advocate suggested during an interview, in order to maintain and advance credibility, sometimes it is necessary to sue. Although this activist noted that his group does not like to sue for libel, he went on to say: "Sometimes you're just stuck doing it."

Defending movement credibility is also a significant component of defending activists against libel suits. Activists note that settling a libel (or SLAPP)[22] suit out of court may create the impression that the movement and its activists are guilty and therefore lack credibility. For instance, John Kullberg stated: "The unfortunate thing is many of these [SLAPP] suits get settled for like $6,000 to avoid the cost to our attorneys of doing court work. And some people getting those settlements will herald it as a victory" (interview). Attorney Joyce Tischler goes even further: "I can't stress enough that these lawsuits should *never* be settled, but vigorously fought" (quoted in Bring 1991, 42). Thus, rather than settling suits when the opposition brings libel charges, activists have increasingly taken to fighting in court even though the costs are high. During the course of libel suits, activists and movement supporters publicize what they see as the illegitimacy of the suit.[23] Even with a loss of the suit, defending oneself in these instances may help to prevent a loss of credibility.[24]

Standing Suits

The suits that have extended standing to animal rights groups demonstrate the concrete benefits that accrue when activists gain access to the courts, obtain a judicial victory, and set important precedents. In addition, these suits—both those that achieve victory and those that end in direct defeat—are used to foster indirect benefits. While these suits, like others, can foster publicity and education, the three most significant indirect benefits here include expanding mobilization, enhancing credibility, and increasing the movement's leverage.

Mobilization generated by standing suits results from the fact that gaining standing allows more suits to be brought. But more interesting is the fact that, even when they result in a loss of standing, these suits have inspired further attempts to gain it. In *Animal Lovers Volunteer Association, Inc., v. Weinberger* (765 F.2d 937 [1985]), for instance, the court denied standing but explained what standing requires.[25] As such, the decision allowed other groups to come to the court in search of standing.

This mobilization contributes to the leverage of the animal rights movement. Gaining standing means that the movement can file suits and defeat motions to have the case dismissed. With standing, and even with the mere possibility of getting it, the animal rights movement has more leverage with which to act against its opposition. Activists have more leverage with which to challenge hunting, cockfights, pigeon shoots, and the rest since the opposition is aware that there is a possibility that activists will be given standing.

The standing issue can also contribute to the movement's credibility and to its internal sense of efficacy. Justice Douglas's original dissent in *Sierra Club v. Morton* (405 U.S. 727 [1972]) extended moral force to the argument that environmental groups should be granted standing by providing a justification based on legal reasoning and precedent.[26] Likewise, the well-known Stone article, cited by Douglas, granted a measure of credibility to this view. Some members of the judiciary have picked up on this perspective, albeit slowly and only incrementally. The courts have increasingly accepted and applied the view that advocacy groups should act as representatives of nonhuman entities. In doing so, the courts have, to some extent, given a stamp of approval to the notion that animal advocacy groups defend animals in court. This probably helps the movement gain credibility, and it certainly contributes to advocates' own sense of efficacy.[27]

Conclusion: Instrumentalism Reconceived

Within each of the types of suits discussed above, we see litigation's diverse uses and ramifications. Litigation, employed as an instrumental device, has the potential to foster numerous goals. Narrowly and broadly, directly and indirectly, litigative activity contributes to a host of instrumental consequences that may aid in the advancement of a movement's agenda.

What is most important to note about this revisit to the legal cases discussed in the preceding chapter is the significantly altered view of litigation that emerges once we widen the scope of analysis. If we view litigation activity only in the light of its direct outcomes, its instrumental effectiveness appears tenuous. In contrast, seen in the light of both its direct and indirect uses, the strength of the litigative instrument increases. Of course, this does not mean that litigation will always or even generally be effective. Litigation remains a constrained tool despite the possibilities of using it to achieve multiple effects. Nevertheless, the point to be stressed is that, with a broader scope of analysis, the equation for evaluating litigation's effectiveness changes.

Our view of litigation is altered not only in terms of effectiveness but also in terms of its location and role within practical reform activity.

When litigation is examined within the context of its broad effects, we see that it is just one of many instrumental resources, one that is located within and among other political resources. Litigative activity does not stand outside of politics; its uses and effects are not strictly a judicial or legal matter. Instead, litigation is embedded and implicated in the widespread strategic and political activities of social movement organizations. Seen in this light, litigation is neither the sole nor even the most prominent component of social reform activity. Litigation neither begins nor ends the process of social struggle. Rather, litigation is an avenue that potentially opens up many other roads for progressive activity. It forms one part of a multitude of strategies that, when combined consciously and strategically, can foster change by offering "varying degrees of opportunity or space for creative challenge" (McCann 1994, 9).

Viewed in this manner, we also see litigation as an activity that extends well beyond formal state structures and legal institutions. The above examples depict how law extends to the political and grassroots levels. Litigation affects and is affected by multiple factors within the political, social, and economic arenas. Accordingly, our assessment of litigation must recognize its interactive and complex role.

All of these adjustments in our view of litigative activity remain within the terrain of instrumentalism. However, this instrumentalist terrain has been widened, deepened, and made more complex by the move beyond direct instrumentalism. This move, I suggest, is one that is and should continue to be informed by the constitutive view. With the insights of a constitutive approach, we can see the significance of considering legal practice in broad terms. We can see the importance of examining legal practice not as an activity separate and distinct from politics. In short, an instrumentalism that takes constitutivism seriously recognizes the broad, interactive, and multifaceted relationship between the practice of litigation and social reform activism.

Still, this type of exploration does not go far enough. By remaining within the albeit broadened instrumentalist terrain, we have only just begun to delve into the depths of litigative practice. We need not simply to move away from direct instrumentalism toward an instrumentalism informed by constitutivism; we must move closer to a constitutivism informed by instrumentalism. It is to this that we now turn.

Chapter 7

Litigative Practice and the Constitution of Meaning

[L]egal interpretation happens not just in official acts by official actors but also through resistance, compliance, and investment of old forms with new meanings. Legal interpretation happens when nonofficials seek to hold officials to account, either in terms the officials themselves have offered as rationales or in new terms embodying normative commitments that have not before made their way into the official canon of meaning.

—Martha Minow

Litigation, as we have seen so far, produces various effects that may directly and indirectly contribute to the advancement of a social movement's agenda. What has yet to be explicitly investigated is the relationship between these effects and the constitution of legal meaning. In other words, what has been disregarded to this point is a discussion of the constitutive character of litigation: the way litigation, in its prevailing form, shapes human definitions and perceptions of animals; the way litigation frames the perspectives and practices of animal rights activists; and the way movement activists reconstruct the meanings and practices of litigation.

As was noted in chapter 5, the constitutivist perspective moves us beyond the instrumentalist focus on effectiveness into the realm of meaning. When applied to litigative practice, it encourages questions pertaining to how litigation structures understandings, definitions, and practices. However, in its standard form, constitutivism tends to neglect the flip side of constitution, that is, the way individuals and groups engaged in litigative endeavors can reconstitute litigation and its meaning. With this neglect, constitutivism overstates the hegemonic character of law and understates strategic and instrumental challenges to the law that are embroiled in the construction of meaning.

This chapter seeks to remedy this neglect and offer a constitutive interpretation of animal rights litigation informed by instrumentalism and cognizant of both top-down and bottom-up constructions of meaning. To do so, the discussion begins by exploring the construction of meaning that appears to flow out of animal rights litigation. This exploration suggests that the formal legal discourse associated with litigation primarily reinforces predominant meanings and offers little in the way of reconstitution. The discussion then delves into the perspectives of the people who have turned to litigative practices in the effort to advance the cause of animal rights. By investigating the views of activists, we can examine whether they accept or challenge predominant litigative constructions. In doing so, the following pages explore how the direct and indirect effects of litigation discussed in preceding chapters are implicated in the production of meaning for animal rights activists, that is, how litigation has shaped the legal consciousness and practices of movement activists and how the consciousness and practices of activists, in turn, reconstruct the meaning of litigation.

In the end, this analysis will lead us back to the myth of rights and to the questions posed in chapter 4, restated here within the context of litigation. Does the prevailing meaning of litigation constitute movement advocates in a way that detrimentally encourages the use of a problematic process? Or, in contrast, are movement advocates conscious of the problematic nature of the prevailing meaning and effects of litigation, and do advocates reconstitute the meaning of litigation in a manner productive to movement goals? I will argue here, along the lines of what I argued within the context of rights language, that, while the views and practices of movement advocates are surely constituted by standard constructions of litigation, these advocates do not appear to be misled by the myth of rights. Instead, they strategically deploy and thereby reconstitute in their own terms the practice of litigation.

Constituting Legal Meaning and the Legal Subject

The constitutivist approach points us to considering how law, and here the practice of litigation, are implicated in constructing meaning. For the present discussion, this consideration is relevant for understanding how litigation constructs the relationship between humans and their nonhuman counterparts and how these constructions define values and worth. The constitutivist approach also points us to considering

how the practice of litigation is implicated in constructing the legal subject. As Sarat and Kearns describe the view, "Perhaps the most stun-
ning example of law's constitutive powers is the willingness of persons
to conceive of themselves as legal subjects, as the kind of beings the law
implies they are—and needs them to be" (1993, 28). As law infuses subjects with meaning, people come to perceive of themselves within legal
parameters, within the confines and definitions of law; and these parameters appear natural, neutral, and uncontroversial (Gordon 1982,
286). When applied to social movements, the "crucial point is that rules
made by government infuse and inform the movements themselves by
becoming an essential part of their thought, their identity, and their
social boundaries" (Brigham 1987, 304).

The section explores how the several kinds of litigation addressed
in the preceding chapters figure into the creation of legal meaning and
legal subjects. In exploring legal meaning, the discussion points to how
litigation and associated judicial rulings construct the values of
self-interest, individualism, autonomy, rights, and responsibility. The
legal subjects under consideration are animals and humans, in general,
and also the animal rights activists who turn to litigation on behalf of
the animals they seek to protect.[1]

Standing and the Legal Subject

The battle over standing confronted in various lawsuits offers an interesting source for interpreting legal constitution. This source, like others, illustrates how litigation constrains the boundaries and possibilities of meaning and at the same time provides some openings for
alternative constructions.

It is clear that the standing issue significantly limits the terms
under which legal meaning and legal subjects are constituted. With
regard to the constitution of animals, standing cases reinforce the reality that animals cannot speak in defense of themselves and that, in and
of themselves, animals lack standing within the legal system. In addition, while these cases lend credence to the notion that animals deserve
compassion, protection, and humane treatment, they also lend support
to the view that animals are not worthy of rights. Indeed, standing as
applied in these cases suggests that animals have no real interests independent of the humans who speak on their behalf. Standing suits are
not brought "in the name of the nonhuman *alone*," as Christopher Stone

noted (1987, 7). They are brought in the name of human individuals and organizations with interests in protecting animals and the environment. Under this standing construct, animals are not really legal subjects; they are instead objects of law. Hence, the official legal discourse that emerges from standing cases is more consistent with a welfarist point of view than with a rights-oriented approach.

The subjects of standing law are animal rights proponents. In constituting these legal subjects, standing doctrine upholds the values of individualism and self-interest. A legal grant of standing occurs only when a plaintiff has a "personal stake" in a case that can be demonstrated by showing that the plaintiff "personally has suffered some actual or threatened injury" (*Humane Society of the U.S. v. Hodel*, 840 F.2d 45 [1988], 51). Although advocacy groups have had success in gaining standing, the success remains within the confines of self-interest and sustains the individualistic foundations of the standing doctrine. The self-interest at stake is still not defined in terms of animal interests. It is defined in terms of the individual interests of the organization's membership.

While the standing doctrine primarily constitutes meaning by preserving predominant conceptions of animals, human self-interest, and individualism, standing cases may be interpreted as providing some room for alternative constructions. For one thing, the standing cases do give animals a voice they did not previously have. Movement activists become the voices and defenders of animals who cannot speak for themselves. Humans, too, gain a new voice: movement activists and members gain the ability to speak and be heard within the judicial forum. In addition, within these cases there is at least some recognition of animal interests and of the notion that it is not merely human interest that is worthy of consideration. Consider Justice Wright's comment in *Animal Welfare Institute v. Kreps*.

Where an act is expressly motivated by considerations of humaneness toward animals, who are uniquely incapable of defending their own interests in court, it strikes us as eminently logical to allow groups specifically concerned with animal welfare to invoke the aid of the courts in enforcing the statute. (765 F.2d 937 [1977], 1007)

This statement suggests that, despite their inability to defend themselves, animals do have interests and organizations concerned with the interests of animals are the logical representatives of those interests.

By and large, however, standing lawsuits constitute meaning in ways that do not challenge preponderant conceptions of humans and animals. Standing doctrine, even as it has been altered, upholds the notion that animals are objects of compassion not subjects of interests or rights. As such, standing replicates the hierarchical division between animals and humans, thereby sustaining traditional welfare standards.

Animal Law, Environmental Law, and Legal Constitution

Like standing cases, litigation in animal law constitutes legal subjects and legal meaning in ways generally consistent with preponderant conceptions. The confines of animal laws, elaborated in chapter 5, significantly constrain alternative constructions of animals. Laws and litigation pertaining to animals are bounded within anticruelty statutes, which treat animals as beings worthy of compassion but not of rights. Moreover, litigation under animal laws has done little to alter the view that animals are a kind of property. Litigation in this realm takes animals to be objects of human use. Animals are not considered as ends in themselves but as means to human ends. Animals may therefore be used as humans see fit, as long as the use does not inflict unwarranted suffering. And, even when unwarranted suffering is inflicted, the limited extent of legal penalties means that animals still receive only minimal consideration.

The framework of animal laws also limits the litigative practices that can be undertaken by animal advocates. These laws are not easily enforced via litigation sponsored by the movement. For the most part, such laws are litigated and implemented by prosecutors and government agencies. Few animal advocacy groups have been given the authority to sue under these laws. As such, within anticruelty laws activists are not constituted as the primary guardians or representatives of animals.

Although litigation involving anticruelty statutes offers some degree of protection for animals and some opportunity for activists to enforce this protection, it generally reinforces prevailing meanings. Animals are subordinate creatures to be used by humans. Animals are, once again, legal objects not legal subjects. They may have an interest in not being subjected to suffering, but human interests in eating meat,

hunting, wearing fur, and so forth will always carry the day. Furthermore, protection of animals is justified primarily on the basis of human
interest in being compassionate.

Legal constitution entailed in lawsuits concerned with environmental law is also constrained. Under environmental law, the interests
of individual animals are not the primary consideration. Animals are
subsumed under the environment, and it is therefore the well-being of
the environment that takes precedence. Thus, when the California
Appeals Court in the First District barred a mountain lion hunt on the
grounds that the Fish and Game Commission had not complied with
the California Environmental Quality Act, Justice Haning's ruling
expressed not the interests of mountain lions per se but the impact of
such a hunt on the environment (*Mountain Lion Coalition v. Fish and
Game Commission*, 263 Cal. Rptr. 104 [1989]). This means that if individual animals can be destroyed without harming the environment, such
destruction is acceptable. Litigation in this area thus continues the idea
that animals, in themselves, are not worthy of consideration. They are
only worthy to the extent that the environment is valuable or that protecting species from extinction is a laudable goal.

On the other hand, it might be suggested that, insofar as litigation
in this realm advances protection for the environment and for nonhuman species, it reconstructs the meaning of the environment. Such litigation enforces the idea that humans should not be oblivious to our significant impact on the environment and should not act in ways that
lead to environmental destruction. When litigation balances the environment over economic interests, it may suggest the inherent value and
worth of the environment independent of human self-interest.

Still, this is not the predominant construction of meaning that
results from environmental litigation. Lawsuits seeking enforcement of
environmental legislation generally sustain the supreme status of
human interest over other interests. Human self-interest, usually
defined in terms of property and economic interests, is paramount.
Moreover, even when the environmental interest outweighs economic
interest, the former continues to be constructed in terms of human
interests.

The emphasis on human interest in the environment is nicely
depicted in *Mountain Lion Coalition v. Fish and Game Commission*. When
Justice Haning barred the mountain lion hunt in California, he stressed
the failure of the Fish and Game Commission to communicate with the
public. It was the need for public disclosure and public dialogue on the

potential environmental harm that was at the heart of Haning's opinion. According to the ruling:

> Rather than squarely addressing the subjects that were set out in the court's order and submitting their environmental conclusions to public scrutiny, appellants chose to circulate a document that simply swept the serious criticisms of this project under the rug. It was impossible for the public, which had actively asserted a keen and sophisticated interest in the proposed mountain lion hunt, to fully participate in the assessment of the cumulative impacts associated with this project. (108–9)

Haning concluded by again asserting the public's interest.

> Should [appellants] wish to proceed in the future with another attempt to authorize a mountain lion hunt, they must provide a cumulative impact analysis to the public that encourages rather than impedes meaningful public discussion of these important issues. (110)

A final point to be noted about the constitution of meaning stemming from both animal and environmental litigation emerges from the frequently "negative" results of such legal action. Recall that lawsuits in these realms commonly culminate in the halting or delaying of actions. They rarely lead to the promotion of a positive agenda. How are these "negative" results implicated in the construction of legal meaning? The "negative" thrust of these legal actions perpetuates the notions of noninterference and separation. Hunters may have an obligation to stop a hunt and to leave animals alone, but they have no related obligation to promote the well-being of animals or the environment. Responsibility is thus constructed in terms of nonaction rather than "positive" action. As a result, it might be concluded that such litigation replicates the values of liberal individualism rather than offering alternative constructions of meaning and value.

Human Law and the Construction of Meaning

The construction of meaning associated with litigation in the realm of human law resembles that of standing law. Like standing cases, litigation around human law focuses on human interests and rights rather than animal interests. In its human focus, this range of litigation does not go far in altering standard conceptions of rights, individualism, or responsibility, nor does it do much to directly alter the prevailing conceptions of animals.

The direct meaning of First Amendment lawsuits is relevant to humans, and these lawsuits construct meaning in ways that are consistent with standard definitions and attitudes. The various dissection suits, for instance, protect students' individual First Amendment rights to take a moral stand. When veterinary professor Nedim Buyukmihci sued his university, he sought to protect his constitutional right to free speech and expression. Challenging hunter harassment laws via the First Amendment similarly promotes free speech protection.

In all of the First Amendment cases, the focus of formal legal attention rests on the humans involved. Despite the fact that these cases indirectly revolve around animals, the direct legal terms and meaning of these suits concern human rights. Moreover, the meaning of human rights suggested in these lawsuits does not differ from established meaning. Free speech rights are defined as individual rights, that is, as rights held by autonomous beings that must not be interfered with by state institutions. Established constructions are thus perpetuated.

Freedom of information, libel, small claims, and tort cases focus similar attention on humans and support standard legal definitions. In these suits, it is once again the rights of humans that are of central concern. To be sure, under freedom of information laws it is the right of humans to know what is being done about animals that matters in these cases; nonetheless, it is the right to know that carries the day rather than the right to know about animals. In libel cases, human rights are the centerpiece. In small claims and tort cases, dominant definitions of property rights remain in force.

In none of the lawsuits involving human law is the established meaning of animals significantly changed. Animal rights advocates have been attempting to use tort suits to reconceptualize the meaning of animals as something other than property (Hentoff 1990). However, this attempt has only been marginally successful. By and large, animals are still defined and treated as the property of humans.

It should be stressed that, while the many lawsuits discussed above focus directly on humans, they are symbolically about animals. Indirectly, these legal actions raise animal concerns and imply that animals have interests. In this way, as we shall see below, there may be some room to adjust and challenge established meaning. But, in terms of the direct construction of legal meaning, lawsuits around human law maintain common conceptions of rights, individualism, and autonomy.

Reinforcing the Prevailing Meaning of Rights

Each realm of litigation discussed above contains only limited opportunity to legally reconstruct the meaning of rights and offers no direct way to define or demand animal rights. In fact, there is little if any mention of animal rights in these lawsuits. Since no legal foundation exists for extending rights to animals, animal advocates and lawyers cannot speak in terms of animal rights in the judicial arena. This may be one of the most important limits of litigation on behalf of animals.

It may be true that lawsuits on behalf of animals implicitly and indirectly suggest animal rights. Certainly, this is what animal rights activists ultimately seek to promote. Activists use litigation outside of the judicial arena in ways that call for an extension of rights to animals. Notwithstanding this attempt to extend rights, it is important to note that, in direct terms and within the confines of the judicial system, litigation does not extend rights to animals. Nor does it provide the grounds for viewing animals as rights-bearing beings.

In terms of human rights, litigation on behalf of animals has not been very transformative. On the contrary, litigation generally maintains preponderant definitions and conceptions of rights. The rights demanded and sometimes attained in litigation under human law are rights that attach to individuals as individuals. Litigation involving these rights, while useful in advancing certain animal concerns, has not directly altered the liberal-individualistic foundation of human rights.

In sum, this preliminary constitutive analysis—which emphasizes an interpretation of rulings as they flow out from the judiciary—does not offer much reason to believe that litigation for animals offers anything significant beyond the reinforcement of prevailing definitions of rights, responsibilities, individualism, and self-interest. Hence, to this point, litigation does not appear to have afforded much opportunity to reconstruct meaning.

Reconstructing the Legal Subject and the Meaning of Litigation

The implications of the above discussion are not very promising for those who wish to challenge preponderant conceptions of animals.

However, the top-down focus of the discussion has neglected the perceptions and reactions of the activists involved in litigation. The question yet to be explored is whether animal advocates are able to reshape meaning in the midst of litigation that reinforces prevailing meanings. I shall argue in this section that animal rights activists do not simply accept the received constructions of litigation and legal subjects. Instead, activists challenge the notion of litigation, just as they challenge the notion of rights.

Although activists still conceive of themselves in legal terms, they do not buy into the standard meanings and extent of these terms. Activists, as realists in their views of law, are skeptical of the notion that litigation and its outcomes have some objective or definitive meaning. With this skeptical foundation, activists take advantage of legal flexibility to reconstruct litigation in strategic terms.

It is here that it becomes necessary to examine the perspectives of the activists who make choices regarding movement strategies. Previously we have addressed litigation's direct and indirect effects largely as outcomes of a process without discussing conscious attempts to foster these multiple effects. Although in reviewing litigation we have seen how activists refer to cases in efforts to educate and mobilize, we have not addressed whether activists consider these potential uses of the legal route ahead of time or whether, in making decisions to employ litigation, they weigh the potential indirect effects of the process. Nor have we addressed whether such decision making has implications for the construction of meaning. Overall, the question becomes: Do activists recognize the possible indirect benefits of litigation, make strategic choices in light of this recognition, and, in so doing, reconstruct the meaning of litigation?

The interviews conducted with animal activists shed light on this question.[2] In these interviews, I raised questions about movement and organizational strategies, including litigation. Activists explained, in response to these questions, their views of and experiences with litigation. In general, both lawyer and nonlawyer activists displayed a sophisticated understanding of the multiple effects of litigation. These activists defined litigation as a tactic that, under appropriate circumstances, can be helpful in achieving the goals of the movement. They argued that litigation should be employed in conjunction with other strategies, and, like other tactics, it must be used cautiously and prudently, with a recognition of its positive and negative potentials. All of the possible consequences of litigation—direct and indirect, positive and negative—must be carefully weighed against the potential outcomes of other tactics.

An interpretation of these interviews suggests that, with their strategic approach to litigation, activists seek to reconstruct the meaning of litigation both in terms of the process of litigation and the substantive outcomes of that process. Activists approach litigation as a political and strategic instrument deployed as one of several tools to achieve certain ends. The deployers of litigation redefine the meaning of "successful" litigation and reshape the "messages" litigation sends. Activists recast litigation in their definitions of its drawbacks and limitations. Activists further seek to reconstruct prevailing definitions of animals via litigation.

It is important to stress that both lawyer and nonlawyer activists participate in such reconstruction. Neither group, on the whole, accepts prevailing constructions of litigation. Both engage in the process of redefining legal meaning through language and practice. Neither appears to dominate the process of reconstruction, and, although different constructions of meaning certainly emerge, the overall thrust suggests that litigation is perceived by almost everyone as a political instrument.

The remainder of this section examines the perspectives of activists in more detail. The overall thrust of the interviews and the interpretation offered below suggest that bottom-up reconstruction of litigative meaning does occur. While such reconstruction may not be sufficient to alter prevailing meaning, it does offer challenge and resistance. This resistance indicates that legal meaning is not simply a hegemonic force working upon the minds of legal subjects but is instead open and malleable enough to be reshaped from below.

Reshaping the Terms of Litigative Success

Animal rights activists are certainly influenced by the prevailing standards for defining successful litigation. When asked to discuss litigation, almost all activists referred to the direct effects of litigation, defining success in terms of direct victories in court, setting precedents, gaining access, and forcing implementation of existing laws. However, activists quickly moved beyond these criteria and advanced an alternative construction of successful litigation. The terms of this alternative construction stressed the political and strategic nature of litigation and pointed to the many indirect uses of lawsuits.

Reflecting the predominant definition of successful litigation, activists commonly noted the importance of winning cases in the courtroom. A direct win in court, activists suggested, includes such things as stopping a hunt, inhibiting the use of dolphins by the navy, obtaining convictions under anticruelty statutes, opening animal care committees to the public, and allowing students the freedom not to perform dissections. In defining direct victories, activists further pointed to the importance of setting precedents—precedents that can be applied under other circumstances. According to attorney Lucy Kaplan, winning a favorable ruling that becomes precedent is "very successful litigation. . . . [T]here's nothing as valuable as a legal opinion that states a principle that then can be used forever and ever until the opinion is changed." Putting it in the most basic terms, Neal Barnard stated, "Sometimes lawsuits make law." Law made in favor of animals can go beyond application to similar cases and be used in drawing analogies to divergent situations.[3]

Direct victories do not necessarily require following litigation all the way through to trial. In their interviews, a number of activists described favorable settlements as wins. When asked to assess the success his organization has had in using litigation, Tim Greyhavens of PAWS stated that "we've been actually really successful. . . . Maybe there's been half a dozen or so [cases in which] we've won or reached an agreeable settlement." The navy suit involving the dolphins is one such case. Greyhavens and others from different organizations involved in that suit noted the success of the settlement. Gene Underwood, general counsel for the ASPCA, asserted that the suit had been "very successful. We've settled, which I cannot distinguish from a complete victory."

In discussing litigation, some activists pointed to its direct role in forcing implementation. According to attorney Steve Ann Chambers, litigation is "a wonderful enforcement tool." Attorney Kaplan also noted the implementation aspect of litigation, proposing that litigation can be used with "generic pieces of legislation which could create opportunities . . . to ensure that government agencies don't neglect their duties." Dr. Elliot Katz, a nonlawyer activist who has led many litigative efforts, stated: "There's a great deal of lack of enforcement of federal regulations, whether it's by the federal bureaucracy or the university bureaucracy. The courts are an avenue one has . . . to try to use the system to clean itself up."

In order to win a lawsuit, set a precedent, gain a favorable settlement, or encourage implementation, access to the judicial arena is required. Activists on various occasions noted that standing suits, although often a barrier to access, have been successful at times in creating access. Activists also noted that litigation involving human law provides access to the courts. Access, for activists, comprised part of the definition of litigative success even if a lawsuit was lost on its merits.

When asked to discuss litigation, activists often referred to direct victories, precedent, access, and implementation. Indeed, we should expect activists to express litigative success in instrumental terms. What is surprising is the reconstruction of litigative success apparent in the comments of nearly all activists. Activists placed significant emphasis on alternative criteria of success, noting, in particular, the multiple strategic uses of litigation. As we shall see, activists reshaped litigation within political parameters and, in so doing, offered alternative constructions of themselves and animals as legal subjects.

Education and Publicity

Raising public consciousness through education constitutes a prime goal of the animal rights movement. According to many activists interviewed, litigation works toward this end. When asked about the goals of litigation, attorney Francione stated: "The way you educate people is to get the issue before them," and he cited litigation as one way to perform this task. Nonlawyer Greyhavens responded in a like manner noting that "ideally the first benefit [of litigation] would be for the animals involved. The second benefit is for education and information." Another activist explained that we cannot consider litigation solely in terms of the particular animals saved. If someone using litigation "spent six years fighting over the lives of three animals, that doesn't sound terribly effective. But when you think 'well maybe they educated a million people doing it, that it made such a stir in the news that people heard about it,' that's something."

The educational aspect of litigation is associated with publicity. As nonlawyer Newkirk succinctly noted, litigation "makes good press, which is always important." Another activist, working primarily with litigation, emphasized the importance of publicity by telling a story about learning the lesson the hard way. During a lengthy litigation effort surrounding use of the leghold trap in hunting, this attorney-activist accumulated what she called "state-of-the-art veterinary testimony" on the issue. Not only did the case lose in court, but little publicity was generated by the case and the testimony received little attention. According to the attorney: "It was a bitter lesson because we wanted to do more publicity but we didn't. . . . I will never again do something of that magnitude where those affidavits go to waste." She summed up her view regarding publicity and education by suggesting that "you can lose in court and still win if you're doing sufficient public education by exposing the public to what you have assiduously prepared just in court papers."[4]

Many activists similarly noted the importance of connecting litigation with publicity and education. In doing so, they pointed to the numerous goals and consequences of litigation and stressed the need to use it in combination with other strategies. Dr. Katz summed up this vision by stating:

> If you just filed a lawsuit and you didn't on top of that hold demonstrations, and on top of that hold press conferences, and on top of that try to make the public aware through various means of educating them, then the ultimate outcome would not be as successful. And so if the lawsuit doesn't win then what else is happening is that the public is being educated, legislators are being educated, the media [are] being educated, and the lawsuit is one part of the effort to change the system or to right the wrong.

Katz went on to suggest that litigation effectively promotes media coverage because, once suits are filed, the media are more apt to report the issue: "A lot of times the media will not touch anything because of some allegations; they're always afraid to be sued. Once you file a lawsuit and put down what the realities are, then the media will cover it because it's already in the court document."

For the most part, activists who mentioned education and publicity were referring to educating the public generally on the topic of animal rights. In addition to the general education of the public on animal rights issues, litigation advances other, more specific, educational objectives. One concerns educating the public about the tactical uses of legal strategies in advancing the cause. When asked how she would define successful litigation, one attorney-activist suggested that litigation may teach citizens how to use the legal system and thus provide them with a useful tool to foster change.

Indirectly, if we can help to create a climate in a community in which citizens—not just PETA, but local citizens—understand the usefulness of the court, and formulate their own legal strategies, and figure out how to go to counsel and hire counsel, or learn to recruit volunteer lawyers, and so on, that's a kind of success, too.

A second specific educational goal pertains to judges. A few activists expressed the need to reframe legal discourse and accustom judges to arguments regarding animals, arguments they have never heard before. If litigation is to become a more effective instrument, judges must become familiar with animal issues and experience consciousness-raising. As one lawyer-activist put it:

When you take something into court . . . you realize that you're presenting arguments that a court very likely has simply never heard before. . . . And whether or not you're going to win at this point is something else. . . . But you realize you've done something because that panel has never heard that before.

Even bringing individualized, small cases, such as landlord-tenant disputes over pets, can contribute to the education of justices. One attorney-activist involved in such cases argued that "as the courts begin to see people redressing their rights on a seemingly more trivial level, they get used to it, yes, animals are important. . . . [This] adds to the consciousness-raising of people not normally exposed to it." Newkirk expressed this point in a similar fashion. When I asked her to sum up the ways in which litigation can be effective she stated the following:

[F]or me, you don't have to win the case to have won something. There's a certain satisfaction . . . in having prosecutors and judges and their staff[s] learn the issues even if the judge can't bring him or herself in the end to make the decisions that will change things a bit. If we're not there yet, we're getting interesting comments from the bench, we're getting judges to think, and certainly eyes

are being opened. . . . [This] kneads the dough for somebody else
to make bread down the way.

Kneading the dough takes time. But the courts do seem to be
increasingly accepting of animal concerns. The courts, for instance,
"have begun to consider the 'sentimental value' of animal companions
when assessing damages" (Hentoff 1990, 23). This consideration has
been pushed by lawyers in the courtroom for several years. Although
slow in accepting this approach, the movement is now beginning to
reap the rewards of putting forth new legal arguments, like the sentimental value approach, and educating judges on alternative ways of
viewing animals.

A third particular educational end involves government administrators and legislators. Litigation often produces important expert testimony that can educate officials who make and enforce laws. One attorney-activist cited an example that supports this potential effect of
litigation. During a lawsuit brought to enjoin hunting in New York's
Harriman State Park, expert testimony revealed that no ecological justification existed for the hunting. Although hunting was never officially
enjoined by the court, the state agency made the decision to halt it.
According to the attorney involved in the case, the state officials were
educated, and their decision was greatly affected by the testimony
raised during the lawsuit.

Overall, activists conceive of litigation in part as an educational
and public relations tool. Despite the fact that this tool often does not
substantially alter the way animals are legally construed, activists do
suggest that litigation can contribute to popular reconceptualizations
of animals as legal subjects. As Sheila Laracy of the Animal Rights
Direct Action Coalition put it, trials involving animal issues "serve as a
platform for animal rights" (Animals' Agenda, December 1986, 25).
Although animals may not attain rights via litigation and attorneys do
not even speak of animal rights in the courtroom, the perception that
litigation is really about animal rights contributes to the construction of
animals as legal subjects. As attorney Francione noted, this can even be
achieved through human laws that say nothing about animals. For
example, the case concerning dissection is a students' rights case.
Nonetheless, Francione stated, "it gets press as an animal rights issue,"
and attention is thereby focused on the subject of animal rights. The
subject of a dissection case, in legal terms, is the human involved, but in

popular terms a dissection case raises animals to the level of legal subjects.

Sending Messages to Promote Movement Building

Related to both the general and specific educational functions of litigation, many of the activists interviewed suggested that using lawsuits and the courts communicates numerous messages to various groups. Litigation sends messages to the public at large, to government officials, and to the animal rights community. These messages, in turn, promote movement building and mobilization.

One message promotes the credibility of the movement to the public and government. Credibility is important to a movement whose members have been characterized as fanatics, extremists, terrorists, and animal lovers. Animal activists seek to draw on the credibility that may accrue through use of the court system. According to one nonlawyer advocate:

> [S]ome agencies are big enough that they think we're a kind of fly and they can swat us away. We can protest all we want outside of the navy depot, but it's not going to make any difference to them. But if we sue them over the dolphin issue maybe they'll pay a little more attention and give us more credibility.

A second message conveys the resolve of the movement. The commitment to a litigative strategy demonstrates determination and signals to others the willingness to sue. This type of message may lead people who fear lawsuits to change practices before a suit is filed. Thus, as John Kullberg points out, suing one university on the frog dissection issue informs other universities that they, too, are vulnerable to such action.

A third message, directed not at the general public or the government but at animal advocates themselves, communicates the movement's beliefs, successes, and continued dedication to the cause. Litigation efforts are used to express the movement's values regarding respect for and protection of nonhuman life. In a related manner, litigation activities are used to make the opposition appear unjust. Examples of successful litigation and the misdeeds of the opposition are raised in newsletters, magazines, and during protests. At the March for

Animals some activists spoke of the success of litigation, of using it to express the movement's values and successes, and noting the wrong-doing of the opposition.[5]

Newkirk raised the importance of communicating messages to animal advocates through litigation. In particular, she addressed the need to defend animal activists through the court system and to publicize such defense.

> [T]here's a certain positive element in defending people who are in trouble in a social movement. . . . We have innumerable cases we've defended where people have gotten into trouble for their alleged or proven involvement in everything from civil disobedience, to spray painting fur coats, to placing animals removed by the ALF from labs. I think that quickly running in to protect them and show that there's a force behind them ready to help doesn't allow our opposition to intimidate people within the movement. That sends a positive message throughout the activist community which we want to perpetuate.

Newkirk used this point to emphasize the significant impact litigation can have on internal mobilization, consciousness-raising, and self-definition of the movement itself. Publicizing the legal support extended to activists engaged in civil disobedience

> helps radicalize people within the movement. Not that they might go out and perform similar acts, but that when we present why we defend these people, what their moral stand is, what their beliefs are, what their defense is, . . . people start, instead of being able to dismiss radical acts that they would never commit themselves, they perhaps start to feel less hostile and polarized on these issues and understand that there are depths of emotion and action that you just can't dismiss.

In this way, Newkirk reconstructs the meaning of litigation. Litigation, for her, can be an avenue for defining and expressing the ideas behind the movement, which can in turn politicize, radicalize, and bring movement members together through greater understanding.

The message-sending capacity of litigation is significant in terms of constructing animal advocates as legal subjects. Activists' comments regarding the various messages litigation can send are indicative of their attempts to construct the power of litigation. For animal rights activists, litigation is defined as a form of empowerment and credibility. Litigation is meaningful for activists' sense of power, credibility, and identity, and it is seen as a way to communicate this sense to movement supporters and the public. In these ways, litigation helps activists to construct an image of themselves and to use this image to advance their views of animal rights.

Stretching the Meaning of Law

Beyond the alternative constructions discussed above, a few activists referred to the significance of what one called "stretching the law." A direct goal of litigation already addressed involves raising new principles that may become embodied within the law as legal precedent. These principles include not just the general, overriding principles of a case but intermediate ones as well (such as standing and pretrial discovery rulings). Recognizing this direct aspect of litigation, one attorney-activist defined success in a related but distinct manner, stating that "success could be making sure we have the opportunity to see that the law has been stretched to the maximum, even if we lose." Stretching the law means testing its limits as defined by officials who "police" law's meaning. Through such testing, the boundaries of official law can be pushed and reshaped to allow for the acceptance of new concepts. Since this kind of reshaping may require the pursuit of numerous cases, an important side effect of each case may include pushing the law's boundaries.[6]

Another attorney-activist referred to a similar use of litigation. This activist explained that litigation often arises after society changes its values. The courts frequently lag behind such shifts in values, and litigation can be used to "nudge the judicial system ahead." According to this attorney, the judicial system is "a living, breathing thing," with a "stellar capacity to be adjusting." Given this capacity, she suggests to law students that courts can be persuaded to catch up with shifting values and that litigation provides a way to push the system along.

"Stretching the law," "testing the limits," and "nudging the system ahead" all suggest the incremental process of litigation.[7] These notions imply that litigation must be approached with imagination to seek out areas where the boundaries are soft and malleable. As Francione stated, people must

> be creative, and look for . . . areas in which there are holes in the legal system which you can get into and ways in which you can manipulate the legal system to bring the issue you want into focus without necessarily bringing that issue directly into focus.

These perspectives on the legal system symbolize a particular construction of the role litigation plays in the slow and arduous process of expanding the law. Despite the limited pace, one activist summed up the need for litigation by noting that "it's like throwing gravel down before you pave the road. Someone has to go out front and do a lot before someone wins."

Fostering Leverage

Some activists further pointed to the leveraging effect associated with litigation. The attorneys with whom I spoke were cautious in discussing this aspect and stressed that litigation should not be used to threaten the opposition. For instance, Kaplan maintained that lawsuits should never be brought "simply to harass the other side." However, some activists did point to the pressure and leverage that may be fostered through litigation, supporting Scheingold's assertion that "Although litigation leverage may not determine institutional outcomes, it does provide resources for prodding quiescent agencies to act and for bringing pressure against abuses of power" (1989, 86).

Several interviewees implied the connection between litigation and leverage. In a case in which a high-level university administrator was allegedly harassing an animal rights activist who was also a faculty member, an activist-lawyer threatened to sue. The threat of the suit successfully pressured the university to back down. Another case involved activists who wanted to set up a peace camp on NIH grounds. The threat of a lawsuit by activists against the agency pressured NIH to allow the demonstration to proceed. Katz described a further litigative effort that fostered effective leverage. Katz became active in the movement when he challenged the construction of a $44 million animal research facility on the Berkeley campus of University of California. To block construction, Katz brought suit against the USDA, aware that he and the group he organized would in all likelihood be denied standing. Upon hearing through the media of the proposed filing of the suit, the USDA's head attorney contacted Katz. The attorney asked Katz not to file the suit and requested his help in putting together a case against Berkeley. According to Katz, "I put together the lawsuit that they three days later filed against the university with the information I gave him. . . . At that point we dropped our case because we [had] got what we wanted."

Activists also expressed a more general way in which litigation efforts advance movement leverage. As mentioned above, some activists noted that using litigation conveys a message to the opposition that demonstrates a willingness to sue. This message advances movement leverage by suggesting that activists will use the litigative option as a means to achieve their goals.

Catalyzing the Animal Rights Movement

Several activists suggested that, through education, publicity, and leverage, litigation can catalyze other movement activities, including both litigative and nonlitigative endeavors. Advocacy groups use lawsuit filings as springboards for other events. For instance, a 1985 lawsuit was filed by the ALDF against the Provimi Veal Corporation on consumer interest grounds. The suit sought a permanent injunction to prevent the raising and selling of veal in Massachusetts. The "Farm Animal Reform Movement (FARM) used the event as a springboard for kicking off the National Veal Ban Campaign. Both FARM and ALDF hope that activists in other states will take similar steps" (*Animals' Agenda*, July/August 1985, 23).

In addition, activists noted that education stemming from litigation can influence government decision makers. This potentially includes state and federal legislators as well. Attorney Lauren Smedley suggested that judicial decisions can "serve as a springboard for further legislation." Likewise, another attorney-activist described litigation activity as having three parts: litigation, education, and legislation. Although she does not play a direct role in the third, this attorney asserted that, in conjunction with litigation, "ideally, there should be a piece of legislation ready to go so that an angry public that has just read all about it . . . can say 'now Mr. or Ms. Assemblyperson, vote for this.'"

From this we see litigation defined beyond the realm of implementation and regulatory enforcement. Litigation is viewed and used as a catalyst for legislation. In addition, the evidence and information revealed during trials may provide the impetus for other activity. As Kaplan noted, even if a case does not result in a direct judicial victory, the "emergence of evidence . . . may help us to crystallize the grievance that we have and help us to formulate another strategy either in the courts or not in the courts." In Kaplan's view, litigation has meaning-making power for animal rights advocates. It may contribute to the formulation of complaints and strategies and may foster new ways of thinking about and approaching an issue.

More generally, litigation by one group can catalyze litigative activity by others. As was suggested in *Animals' Agenda*, a court decision that overturned a hunter harassment law in New Hampshire "provides potent ammunition for those who wish to challenge the constitutionality of similar legislation in other states" (*Animals' Agenda*, December 1986, 28).

A final but extremely important construction of litigation relates to the effects one movement's litigation efforts have on other movements. This can be considered an aspect of movement catalyzation and mobilization, but it is distinct because here we refer to external mobilization of other movements rather than internal mobilization. In discussing external mobilization, the reference is not to how the opposition may be catalyzed.[8] Rather, what is referred to is how litigative activities can stimulate other similar types of movements.[9]

As of now, it is unclear how, if at all, the litigative activity of the animal rights movement will affect other movements. What is clear is how the litigative experiences of other social movements have shaped the attitudes and practices of the animal rights movement. Almost all of the activists with whom I spoke mentioned the connections between animal rights and other rights-oriented movements. Most frequently mentioned were the environmental movement and movements for civil rights, women's rights, and human rights. In making these connections, several activists pointed to how they have learned from the litigative histories of these movements. The strongest statement of this was made by attorney Joyce Tischler in an interview conducted by Ellen Bring published in *Animals' Agenda*.

[W]e can learn a great deal from other social reform movements. . . . A book that influenced me was the *NAACP's Litigation Strategy from 1925 to 1950.* In the 1920s, the NAACP decided to use litigation as a primary tool to combat racism. They knew they had to overturn *Plessy v. Ferguson.* . . . Finally, in 1954, in *Brown v. Board of Education,* the court ruled that "separate but equal is inherently unequal." This decision followed sixty years of lawsuits that didn't get anywhere because society wasn't ready to listen to them.

We have to develop animal rights litigation with a sense of this history. We're going to lose some of the cases, but we've got to keep bringing them and use them to educate both the judges and the public. (1991, 40–41)

In recognizing and considering other movements' litigative experiences, animal rights activists demonstrate litigation's potential to shape meaning and practice over the long term. Activists realize that litigation by others has indirectly influenced their movement. Likewise, activists understand that their own litigative activity may have consequences for other movements.[10]

Redefining the Value of Animals

With their strategic approach to litigation, animal rights advocates go beyond the legal meaning suggested by the judicial rulings in specific cases. Rather than simply accepting top-down constructions offered in judicial opinions, advocates redefine legal rulings in political ways. In so doing, they strategically shape the legal meaning of case law to suit their political agendas.

Most important in this process of redefinition is the value placed by advocates on animals. In expressing their interpretations of case law, activists speak of animals as if they are the direct legal subjects of lawsuits. Activists thereby imply that animals are worthy of being treated as legal subjects even though the legal system does not generally do so. Thus, activists use legal cases to suggest that animals are valuable in and of themselves, despite the fact that in most legal cases the human, not the nonhuman, is the centerpiece of legal value.

In presenting alternative constructions of judicial opinions, animal advocates frequently attempt to reshape the legal system into one that recognizes animal rights. Despite the fact that the notion of animal rights stays out of the courtroom and is nowhere to be found in the language of judicial opinions, lawsuits become animal rights suits. Animal advocates are aware that such reconstructions of prevailing legal meaning are political and certainly recognize that the judicial system does not accept such reconstructions. Still, advocates believe that these reconstructions of legal meaning are an important component of the political battle to achieve their aims.

Consider once again the legal cases involving standing, environmental law, and human law. In all of these cases, the legal meaning that appears to flow out of the judicial opinions focuses on human interests and human rights. In standing suits, the emphasis rests on humans who have standing to sue. Animals never receive standing. In environmental cases, human interest in protecting the environment remains at the center. Animals, in and of themselves, are not valued; at best, the environment that happens to include animals is valued. In cases concerning human law, animals are clearly not directly at issue. Human rights matter; animal rights do not.

Notwithstanding these human-centered constructions of legal meaning, animal rights advocates transform these constructions to stress the value and sometimes the rights of animals. All of the lawsuits are aimed at animal interests. A standing suit that succeeds in giving animal advocacy groups a hearing in court is transformed into a suit that gives a hearing to animals. The environmental suit that restricts a mountain lion hunt on the grounds of an insufficient environmental impact statement is redefined in terms of a legal system that protects the interests of individual mountain lions. The suit protecting a student's right to avoid performing dissection becomes the suit that protects an animal's right to be free from dissection.

It does not matter, politically, that the strict legal terms of these lawsuits do none of these things. It does not matter that standing suits do not strictly give standing to animals or that environmental suits are not directly concerned with the interests of specific animals. What matters is that animal activists can redefine the strict terms of a legal case into terms that fit their purposes. What matters is that activists can reshape a lawsuit into an animal rights lawsuit.

What also matters politically is that for movement membership and the public at large it is probably the reconstruction of the legal case that will receive attention. Since most people do not read judicial opinions but instead read and hear interpretations of these opinions, it is the interpretations that gain a hearing. That a dissection suit does not, in direct legal terms, protect animal rights is of little consequence for public opinion. Of course, animal advocates will not be the only ones offering interpretations of legal cases. Since competing interpretations will be expressed, the legal meaning offered by animal advocates will not go uncontested. But the point remains: the legal ruling, subject as it is to redefinition, is not fixed, and animal rights activists along with their opponents have the opportunity to reconstruct the meaning of the legal ruling. Moreover, it is such reconstructed meaning that will likely receive the most attention in the public forum.

Constructing the Limits of Success: Activists' Views of the Problems of Litigation

The interviews make it apparent that animal advocates construct litigative success in terms of the direct and indirect uses of litigation and see significant political power available in these multiple uses. At the same time, activists' constructions of litigative success are tempered by acknowledgment of numerous drawbacks associated with litigation. Acknowledgment of these drawbacks suggests that activists' conceptions of litigation are not blinded by the myth of rights. It further highlights the political orientation of activist perspectives: activists conceive of litigation as a resource to be utilized only after a careful assessment of its potential dangers and costs.

Activists pointed to several general drawbacks of the legal process. Monetary expense constitutes the primary drawback raised by activists. When asked about the problems of litigation, activists almost unanimously noted the high costs of the process.[11] Activists explained that, relative to other strategies, the monetary expense of litigation is significant. Thus, the turn to litigation results in the diversion of resources away from less costly projects and strategies.

In addition to monetary expense, litigation imposes high costs in terms of time and energy. The prospect of spending years pursuing litigation and expending energy on a single case inspires much caution. Several activists commented on the delays often experienced in court proceedings. As John Grandy, spokesperson of HSUS, noted in response to litigation challenging hunting: "The good news is that I think we'll get standing; the bad news is that in the meantime another one million animals will die" (*Animals' Agenda*, December 1986, 29). The time, energy, and monetary costs are all the more problematic when considered in light of the unpredictable nature of litigation. Although, like litigation, activities such as protests, boycotts, and promoting education programs may not always result in direct success, the costs involved in them are low compared to the costs of litigation. Accordingly, the decision to commit resources to litigation involves higher risks since failure to succeed in litigation can imply the waste of years of effort and great sums of money. In contrast, the failure to obtain media coverage at a fur protest is a much more limited defeat.

Given that activists defined a favorable precedent as a direct win, it is not surprising that many activists raised the specter of bad precedents as a primary danger of litigation. When litigation creates a precedent against the movement, the outcome may set the movement back by empowering the opposition. In light of this danger, activists suggested that they carefully assess the likelihood of incurring a bad precedent. As Greyhavens stated when asked about the drawbacks to litigation, "there's always a possibility that you will lose and there will be a precedent set [against you]. So we tend to be real cautious, to research everything carefully first." Even with cautious assessment, the prospect of eliciting contrary precedents from the court worries activists considerably.

Some activists identified the adversarial nature of litigation as another general problem. According to Greyhavens, litigation is "especially not our first choice because . . . it is such a confrontational mode. We'd rather try and get people to compromise with us." Kaplan similarly noted the conflictual aspect of litigation: "It's adversarial in a sense that sometimes you don't want to litigate an issue unless you're absolutely sure you can't get very similar results through negotiation." In making these points, both Greyhavens and Kaplan implied that alternative strategies may be more appropriate when seeking compromise rather than conflict with the opposition.

In conjunction with these general problems, activists mentioned specific drawbacks associated with litigation on behalf of animals. Several addressed the barrier of legal standing. Attorney-activist Chambers expressed her frustration with this impediment: "[When] you see an injustice, you can't just go out and sue because you don't have standing to sue." In a similar vein, activists noted that the scant number of animal laws makes litigation a limited tool. "Since there's no body of law, you can't just start lawsuits," Chambers noted. As a result, many activists recommended focusing attention on the federal and state legislatures with the goal of developing new laws that could then be enforced through the courts.

As for suing to enforce the animal laws that do exist, several activists noted problems that arise from the fact that courts do not recognize animal rights. The legal system still regards animals as property, thereby limiting the types of suits that can be brought. Moreover, activists suggested that the number of conservative appointments to the bench that occurred during the Reagan and Bush years limits the prospects of getting the court system to accept the notion of animal rights.

When asked to discuss drawbacks to litigation, several activists mentioned the problems associated with suits brought against their organizations and membership. In particular, activists noted the dilemma of SLAPP suits. Opponents of the animal advocacy movement bring these suits in search of damages and in the attempt to inhibit future activity. The fact that some of these suits have been successful has made animal advocates even more cautious in their activities.

In the interviews, activists generally commented on the direct problems of the litigative process. Activists infrequently mentioned that litigation might have the indirect effect of being counterproductive in terms of mobilizing the opposition or creating negative publicity. The only time activists noted the danger of mobilizing the opposition was in the area of SLAPP suits. These, however, have mostly been brought not as a response to litigation but as a reaction to other forms of movement activity.

To sum up, activists recognized and discussed various dilemmas linked to the litigative strategy. Moreover, they stated that their perceptions of the legal route are informed by this recognition. How, then, did these activists assess the utility of litigation? In weighing the costs against the direct and indirect benefits, what did activists conclude?

The Political Meaning of Litigation

Litigation is "not the bottom line, but as a tool it's generally helpful" (Virginia Knouse, president of PAWS, interview). This statement reflects the assessment of litigation offered by most activists with whom I spoke. Activists view litigation as a generally effective political instrument, a means to advance movement goals. Litigation is not construed as an end in itself, nor is it construed as a purely legal process. In stark contrast, litigation is constructed as a practice, one of many political means to advance the end of animal rights. Thus, the meaning of litigation is constituted in political, as well as legal, terms; meaning is constituted in terms of the broad, long-term goal of promoting animal rights and the shorter-term goals of fostering consciousness, education, mobilization, and leverage.

Activists agreed that employing litigation requires careful evalua-tion. Awareness of the potential outcomes of litigation was stressed by many. According to Newkirk, "People are choosing litigation carefully in these early days. . . . We'll always look to see what the fallout will be if we fail and weigh that before we proceed." Kullberg mentioned the need to think through the consequences of litigation to avoid setting a harmful judicial precedent. He also noted the need to weigh the differ-ent outcomes, stating that producing a contrary precedent through liti-gation is bad, "even though you have a couple of good public relations pieces."

All activists interviewed on this matter agreed that success requires litigation to be used in conjunction with other tactics. When asked to compare the effectiveness of litigation with other strategies, most responded by saying such things as "it's all part of a menu," "it all goes hand in hand," and "it's part of a total campaign." This supports Schein-gold's statement that "Even under the best circumstances and with the most creative leadership, however, it is wisest to think of rights as an ancillary tactic to be used in combination with other approaches to polit-ical mobilization" (1974, 209). These comments also resonate well with Olson's points about a "new style" of public interest litigation.

> The greater participation of nonlawyers in decision making and the greater realization by lawyers of the limitations of judicial pro-nouncements alone to induce change have resulted in a melding of political and legal strategies. Some litigation has become so inte-grated with political activity outside the courts that its goal is as much to increase bargaining leverage externally as to secure vic-tory in court. (1984, 5)[12]

Moreover, Olson asserts that lawyers have "developed a notion of 'flex-ible lawyering' to encompass the variety of activities in which they [are] engaged" (1984, 9). This appears to be the case for attorneys who advocate animal rights.

As discussed above, the activists interviewed recognized the risks and high costs associated with litigation. Kaplan admitted that, unlike education campaigns, litigation is "much more of a gamble." Nonetheless, the overall assessment suggests that litigation has been successful and will likely be more successful in the future. When asked about the possibilities of future success, most activists responded by saying that the movement's growth will make all strategies increasingly effective in the future. Others suggested that the movement will experience success in the realm of legislation, which should translate into expanded effectiveness of litigation.

Francione responded to the issue of litigation's effectiveness by stating that it has "untapped potential." He believes that lawyers and activists must experiment with creative legal strategies to tap the potential within the present system. Although he noted that the conservative composition of the federal courts will probably limit this potential, he maintained optimism over the possibilities inherent in the existing legal system.

In assessing the costs and benefits of litigation, activists demonstrated some differing opinions. In particular, they were divided over whether litigation should be brought when the chances of a direct judicial victory appear slim. According to Roger Galvin: "As a lawyer you have to find cases that are doable, that are winnable, that will set a precedent" (quoted in Stille 1990, 28). Similarly, Francione stated in his interview that activists

> ought to be looking for areas where we can win. . . . I try to talk people out of it when they come to me and say "I don't care if we lose, I want you to bring this suit." . . . Psychologically I think it's important that we win. . . . There are too many areas which we haven't even tapped yet so it's not clear to me why people are bringing lawsuits they're going to lose.

In contrast to this perspective, Katz suggested a different philosophy. Katz, who is not a lawyer, commented that other groups

> try to take on cases that can either set precedents or that they have a good chance of winning. And I feel that if a wrong is being done then you should try to right it, regardless of whether you're going to win or not. . . . That's what the courts are there for.

Despite these differences, all of the lawyer-activists with whom I spoke raised concerns over the ethical issues of bringing a frivolous case. And all activists (lawyer and nonlawyer) agreed that, even if a case results in judicial defeat, other indirect benefits may be achieved. This latter assessment places lawyers in a difficult position: knowing that cases may foster the indirect benefits of education, publicity, mobilization, and leverage, but at the same time being restricted by the legal code of ethics. However, lawyers overcome this difficulty by noting that one only needs some hope of winning and the confidence that one is in the right to bring a case.

The overall view of litigation presented by activists recognizes the combination of direct and indirect effects. This view provides evidence to suggest that activists do not simply buy into the top-down constructions of litigation that arise out of judicial rulings. Although activists are surely influenced by these legal constructions, their own definitions of the litigative meaning go well beyond judicial opinions. Litigative meaning derives not merely from judicial meaning but from the various political components of legal action and the meanings that can be attributed to these political components. What's more, activists are crucial players in this constructive process. Their activities, attitudes, and definitions contribute to the process of defining litigative meaning and the meaning of legal subjects.

Conclusion: Instrumentalism Revisited

Although we cannot, at this point, measure the extent to which alternative constructions of litigative meaning have modified prevailing meaning, it is clear that these constructions have greatly influenced the activities of animal rights proponents. Animal advocates construct litigation in terms of its political utility, that is, in terms of its capacity to educate various communities, publicize movement concerns, communicate messages, and catalyze, mobilize, and empower the movement. Advocates further construct litigation in ways that contribute to their sense of credibility, power, and feelings of efficacy.

In these ways, activists move well beyond litigative meaning that arises directly out of judicial opinions. The parameters of litigative meaning for activists are not confined by legal texts; nor are they determined by authoritative official interpretations. While aware of these confines and interpretations, activists transform the judicial into the political and thereby re-create meaning for their own purposes. Activists manipulate the terms of official legal meaning and reframe these terms to achieve their political ends.[13]

Activists appear to be quite conscious of, and indeed exceedingly strategic about, this process of meaning making. Interviews with animal rights proponents reveal a skeptical savviness about litigative activity and its power. With this skeptical savviness, activists challenge law's neutrality and resist the notion of legal inevitability.

What is crucial to note is that resistance to and re-creation of top-down constructions of meaning occur through an instrumental approach. It is through an instrumental focus on litigation, that is, through strategic attempts to make litigation politically effective, that activists reconstitute legal meaning. Hence, the process of meaning making, highlighted by a constitutive perspective, is tied to instrumentalism.

This brings us full circle, back to the discussion of litigation's direct and indirect effectiveness explored in chapters 5 and 6. It is through the direct and (especially) the indirect effectiveness of litigation that prevailing meaning can be challenged, resisted, and reconstructed. And, maybe most importantly, it is through strategic instrumentalism that legal meaning is reconstituted. Without a strategic, conscious, and political approach to litigation, the possibilities of reshaping meaning appear significantly constrained.

If this is correct, then we must consider revising constitutivism in a way that incorporates instrumentalism. These two approaches, as I have sought to illustrate in this and preceding chapters, are most useful when integrated. Instrumentalism informed by constitutivism highlights the significance of broad effects; when applied to litigation this means recognizing the varied, multiple, indirect effects of the process. Constitutivism informed by instrumentalism highlights how meaning is constructed from the bottom up in strategic and political ways.

Even if this is right, it might still be argued that the animal rights movement's attempt to reconstruct meaning is relatively meaningless if litigation is too costly or produces harmful results. Why bother reconstructing litigation as an effective political tool if it is not effective? To put this point another way, the issue of effectiveness does not disappear simply because one looks to the constitutive aspect of litigation. It also might be said that the reconstruction of meaning is just another example of the myth of rights in action. If litigation creates harmful outcomes but activists believe it is useful, then the myth of rights is evident.

With regard to these points, it must first be noted that the track record of the animal advocacy movement demonstrates litigation's potential to be the proverbial double-edged sword (Scheingold 1989). Deploying litigation has both a menacing and a promising prospect. On the one hand, the movement's deployment of litigation displays various constraints that inhibit success. The obstacle of standing, the lack of laws and enforcement, and constitutional impediments pose significant barriers to success. These combine with the more general problems associated with litigation such as high costs and the divisive nature of the process. At the same time, positive potential exists upon which the movement can capitalize. Activists explore the creative possibilities available within litigation, employing human and environmental laws to advance the cause of animals. Moreover, activists continue to recognize and capitalize on the significant derivative effects of litigation, using the process to succeed in the particular case and to educate, mobilize, attract attention, expand credibility, stimulate confidence, and create pressure.

Given these mixed prospects, it is difficult to definitively determine whether litigation has been or will be effective on the whole. Notwithstanding this ambiguity, it seems that litigation for animal rights, when examined by joining instrumentalism and constitutivism, has been both effective and significant for the production of meaning. Moreover, it is the strategic and wary perspective of activists that makes litigation effective and contributes to meaning making. Litigation appears most effective when employed consciously and carefully, with an awareness of the costs and benefits entailed in the process. Effectiveness grows when activists use litigation creatively to move beyond existing barriers. In addition, effectiveness greatly increases when the tactic is deployed in combination with other strategies. Pursuing litigation in conjunction with education, publicity, leverage, and mobilization expands the possibilities of success since a loss in the courtroom may lead to advances in these other realms. This approach to the tactical deployment of litigation keeps it in its proper perspective: an interconnected piece of the puzzle rather than the single or central means of solving it.

Regardless of why activists view litigation in this way, this perspective may be one of the most important lessons to learn from their

legal endeavors. Viewing litigation as one among many tactics is crucial. It allows activists to weigh litigation against other strategies and
determine which individual or combination of strategies has the greatest likelihood of success under the given conditions. This approach
increases available options and fosters conscious and cautious analysis
in choosing among those options.

What does this imply for the myth of rights? The discussion above
provides evidence that animal activists do not generally act under misguided optimism created by a myth of rights. To the contrary, their
comments display a solid awareness of the dangers and limits posed by
litigation. Moreover, their actions do not demonstrate a generalized
false hope in the system. Indeed, activists express wariness and concerns regarding litigation similar to those raised by scholars critical of
the legal system.

It may be asked whether this conclusion fosters another myth. Do
we now have an extension of the myth of rights, an extension that recognizes litigation's drawbacks but still holds out hope given the multiple possibilities of the process? Does the suggestion that animal rights
activists manipulate and reconstitute the meaning of litigation create a
new myth of rights and litigation? Is it that law reformers are "entering
into another period of symbolic reassurance" as Handler speculates
(1978, 222)? And does this study of law reformers contribute to such
reassurance?[14]

Answering these questions is a difficult task given that activists
and scholars demonstrate both optimism and skepticism surrounding
the deployment of litigation. We can say that, if a new myth is being
established, it is a myth that is more wary, cautious, and critical than
the myth of rights explored by Scheingold. It would seem that, as such,
this new myth is quite distinct in character, promoting what Olson
(1984) calls a "new style" of litigation. We can also say that, if this is in
fact a new myth of rights and litigation, activists and scholars are less
likely to succumb and be harmed by it because the myth itself stresses
acting strategically, consciously, and critically when using law.

We must also ask whether activists themselves are relying on the
public's faith in the myth of rights in advancing litigation. Although it
may be true, as I have argued, that activists are not caught up in the
myth, their deployment of legal strategies may be relying on the public's faith in the legal system. When attorney Tischler encourages students to exercise their right "to stand up for animals and *against* dissec-

tion" and tells potential movement supporters that in the struggle for animal rights "appeals to conscience often fall on deaf ears—*but direct and effective legal action gets results!*" she may be seeking to capitalize on the myth of rights.[15] If so, the deployment of the legal system by animal advocates may perpetuate and reinforce the myth of rights.

It is difficult to tell whether legal activism for animals has reinforced the myth of rights, and to fully address this issue would move us beyond the confines of the present study. However, it is likely that the animal rights movement's deployment of legal resources has reinforced the myth of rights to a certain degree. Nonetheless, the evidence presented here does suggest that activists themselves have not bought into the myth. Furthermore, in advancing animal issues, activists continually argue that the legal and political systems are flawed in their treatment and consideration of nonhumans. As such, activists may be doing two things at the same time: relying on the myth of rights while concomitantly challenging it.

This may seem like a problematic contradiction. Yet, as legal scholar Mari Matsuda (1987) argues, it is possible, and it may even be necessary, for people to believe both that they have rights and that rights are whatever those in power say they are. In other words, it may be possible to have both faith in and critical consciousness of the legal system at the same time. Drawing on the minority experience, Matsuda points to a dual consciousness that accommodates both the idea of legal indeterminacy and the core belief in a liberating law that transcends indeterminacy.

Further study of popular attitudes toward animal rights would have to be pursued to determine whether movement supporters maintain such a dual consciousness. Regardless, we can say that, even if activists are perpetuating a myth of rights, they are doing so within a context in which rights may still be the most effective instruments available to advance their cause.

In conclusion, it cannot be said that litigation is intrinsically either helpful or harmful, effective or ineffective. Despite our desire to obtain such a clear-cut result, the complex conditions under which social movements operate prohibit easy solutions. We can, however, conclude that complex conditions require analysis of both the direct and indirect uses and effects of litigation. We can further conclude that, beyond effectiveness, litigation entails a process of meaning making. This meaning making occurs at various levels and locations. Most importantly, it is a significant component of social movement activism that challenges, resists, and reconstitutes prevailing conceptions of litigation. As Minow suggests:

> Rights pronounced by courts become possessions of the dispossessed. We can listen to rights as a language that contains meaning but does not engender it, as sounds that demonstrate our sociability even while exposing the uniqueness of the speaker. Legal language, like a song, can be hummed by someone who did not write it and changed by those for whom it was not intended. (1990, 310)

Chapter 8

Conclusion: Meaning and Identity

A struggle for rights can be both a vehicle of politics and an affirmation of who we are and what we seek. Rights can be what we make
of them and how we use them.
—Elizabeth M. Schneider

The preceding pages have sought to illustrate the power and concomi-
tant indeterminacy of prevailing legal meaning. This combination of
power and indeterminacy constrains social movement activism but
also creates openings that allow for resistance and reconstruction of
prevailing perspectives. This same combination has important implications for the construction of movement identity. In this chapter, after
reviewing the foregoing analysis of rights language and litigation, I
will argue that legal meaning as it is predominantly constructed and
resisted shapes social movement identity. Given the indeterminate
nature of legal meaning, the shaping of movement identity is itself
indeterminate and pluralistic. Movements therefore have the room to
form their own identities from within, and, using an altered vision of
rights, this is what animal rights advocates have sought to do. However, movement identity is also subject to construction from the outside. Since the public's understanding of rights remains framed by
Lockean liberalism, the shift to animal rights has generated a negative
public perception of the movement's identity. Thus, the relationship
between movement identity and rights is two-sided: movements have
the power to define their own identities, but this power is significantly
constrained by public constructions of meaning.

After discussing the relationship between legal meaning and the
identity of the animal advocacy movement, I will reflect upon what the
preceding analysis might tell us about other social movements. These

speculative reflections will consider, in particular, movement activism aimed at protecting those who cannot protect themselves. The chapter will conclude with some final thoughts about the myth of rights.

Rights, Litigation, and the Politics of Animal Rights

The central argument of this work can be stated as follows. While legal meaning in its predominant form constrains the understandings, definitions, and practices of social movement activists, indeterminacy and strategic action offer the opportunity to reconstitute meaning. This argument, I have suggested, sheds significant light on the way to approach a study of the law. If the argument is persuasive, then it is important to reconsider instrumental and constitutive approaches in a way that brings the two together. Moreover, it is crucial to decenter analyses of law so that we may focus appropriate attention on the way law is manifest in extrajudicial spheres of society.

The Two Faces of Indeterminacy

The experiences of the animal rights movement suggest that there are two sides to the indeterminacy of rights and law. On one side, because rights and other legal principles can yield various and often opposing results, their existence has no determinate impact on the future (Kennedy 1986; Singer 1984). The recognition of a right does not establish, for instance, whose rights will be protected or how those rights will be enforced. As a result, indeterminacy makes rights language a generally unreliable vehicle for those wishing to challenge the powerful (Tushnet 1984).

Often neglected, however, is the second, positive side of indeterminacy, that is, the flexibility and malleability of legal languages.[1] Recognizing the varied and competing ideals within liberalism helps us to understand the flip side of indeterminacy. As was suggested in chapter 4, the liberal values that form the foundation of rights are themselves indeterminate. Locke's liberalism emphasizes individualism, autonomy, and self-interest. In contrast, variations on liberalism stress the public good, community, and responsibility. Critics of rights language generally point to its Lockean, individualistic underpinnings, and rightly so, given that the American cultural heritage echoes Locke's writings.[2] Nonetheless, the existence of values that compete with Lockean liberal assumptions, combined with the fact that these competing values do comprise a part of American culture and thought, point to the indeterminacy of liberalism itself.

Thus, when scholars critique the indeterminacy of rights and imply that more determinate liberal values form the basis of rights, they underestimate the indeterminacy of liberalism.[3] Once we recognize the indeterminacy of liberalism, two important points follow. First, the alternative values that exist within indeterminate liberalism furnish the opportunity to emphasize values that challenge traditional, individualistic liberalism and to infuse rights with new meaning. Second, if such an opportunity exists, the indeterminacy of both liberalism and rights language makes rights adaptable and versatile not just for those in power but for those who seek to challenge the status quo.

It is surely true that the powerful have a greater ability to manipulate rights language than do the powerless. Those with power tend to have considerable control over the meaning of legal languages. It is also correct to note that indeterminacy poses a constraint for those who wish to appropriate rights language in challenging the status quo. Nevertheless, neglecting the flip side of indeterminacy implies that those in power control all uses of the language.

The second face of indeterminacy highlights the potential flexibility of rights language for the powerless. It underscores the opportunity to appropriate the language of the dominant in a way that challenges those in power and the very underpinnings of the language itself. Furthermore, deploying the prevalent and flexible language of the community in order to change the community can be quite effective, particularly for excluded and oppressed groups. It allows the marginalized to enter the conversation and to speak with authoritative words (Williams 1987; Matsuda 1987; Schneider 1986). As Minow suggests:

> The rights tradition in this country sustains the call that makes those in power at least listen. Rights—as words and as forms—structure attention even for the claimant who is much less powerful than the authorities, and even for individuals and groups treated throughout the community as less than equal. (1990, 297)

Although recognizing the two faces of indeterminacy illuminates the ability of the marginalized to capitalize on the versatility of legal languages, it also allows us to maintain awareness of the constraints surrounding legal forms. While both powerful and powerless groups can manipulate indeterminate legal languages, the ability to manipulate is unequal. Those in power have the advantage of controlling the terms of debate. Moreover, despite flexibility, rights are constrained by traditional understandings and usages. Hence, the ability to alter the terms of the language remains limited by tradition.

In sum, scholars pointing to indeterminacy persuasively suggest that rights language and judicial decisions provide no determinate outcome. They also provide insight in their observation that the ability to manipulate legal languages generally benefits the powerful. However, the animal rights movement indicates that we must also recognize the second face of indeterminacy. Rights talk provides the opportunity to reconstruct legal meaning and, in so doing, to challenge the existing relations of power and the traditional foundations and uses of rights.

Rights Language as a Catalyst of Political Action
and Debate

Some critics of rights language argue that rights have been extended too far. They warn that the continual multiplication of rights claims by various groups trivializes the concept and empties the language of its meaning and strength (Glendon 1991). On this view, the extension of rights to nonhumans exemplifies the problematic overflow of the language.

When examining this view, we ought not to neglect a significant benefit that may arise from this overflow: the potential catalytic impact rights language can have on generating other movement activity and dialogue. The animal rights movement underscores this important secondary effect of rights deployment. Analysis of this movement points to its development in the aftermath of other rights-oriented movements. At its inception in the 1800s, the notion of animal welfare grew out of philosophical and political debate surrounding natural and human rights. In the realm of movement activity, early animal advocacy was allied with suffragettes, abolitionists, and workers (ASPCA 1990, 94). In its more recent rebirth, the animal rights movement sprouted from the political seeds sown by civil rights, women's rights, and other movements in the 1960s and 1970s. Of course, these movements did not consciously seek to advance animal rights, and their

members may have had little interest in actively protecting nonhumans. Nevertheless, the catalytic impact upon animal rights is clear
and was echoed by several activists. As one interviewee observed, "the
gay rights movement, the women's rights movement, and the civil
rights movement made it acceptable for people to talk about animals
having rights."

It is important, then, when examining rights mobilization, to consider the entire picture—a picture in this case that includes other social
movements and recognizes the impact rights deployment can have on
ideology and organization. Unfortunately, it is too soon to tell what
other movement activities the present animal rights movement may
generate.[4] However, the fact that animal rights has been catalyzed by
other movements should invite some reassessment of movements that
have advanced various forms of human rights.

The generative aspect of rights language is even more significant
when we consider its catalytic effects on dialogue, alternative languages, and alternative constructions of meaning. The attempt to
extend rights to nonhumans has fostered significant debate on what
kinds of beings can be rights holders. Just as the "use of rights and legal
struggle by the women's movement started the 'conversation' about
women's role in society," animal rights talk has instigated conversation
and debate on new fronts (Schneider 1986, 650).

The debate and dialogue over animal rights has materialized in
many different locations: in the spheres of philosophical analysis, in
legislatures, in the media, in the board rooms of the cosmetics industry,
and in schools. Much of the debate is heated, and, to a large extent, the
notion of animal rights continues to be rejected. But, as John Stuart Mill
observed: "Every great movement must experience three stages:
ridicule, discussion, adoption" (quoted in Regan 1983, epigraph). If
Mill is correct, the animal rights movement has made the move from
the first to the second stage. While the notion of animal rights once may
have contributed to the ridicule, it now contributes to the discussion.

The debate over animal rights and the attempt to extend rights
beyond animals has highlighted the need for alternative languages.
This, in turn, has fostered reconstruction of meaning. For scholars who
fear that rights necessarily reinforce individualism and separation, animal rights language displays the opposite potential. While we must
admit that the dominant tendency of rights in this culture leans toward
individualism, we must also recognize that this tendency is far from

absolute or uniform. When applied to nonhumans, the language of rights has emphasized sentience as the key factor in defining membership in the moral community. In addition, rights in this movement have increasingly stressed the values of responsibility, care, relationship, and a broad notion of community. To be sure, much of this emphasis is, at this stage, implicit. But, as the language expands and fosters further dialogue, the potential exists to advance these alternative ideals and re-create rights.

In short, the deployment of animal rights has sparked conversation and debate and has helped catalyze alternative languages. Furthermore, debate over various human rights issues played a generative role in activating animal rights talk. But, the generative impact of earlier rights-oriented movements has not determined the way rights language has been deployed by animal rights advocates. Unlike some earlier movements, animal rights language has begun to challenge the individualistic assumptions of much traditional rights language itself.[5] Hence, while animal rights has been spurred by other rights-oriented movements, at the same time the movement's experience underscores the opportunity to reframe rights language in a way that incorporates communitarian, relational, and nonhumancentric values (Minow 1990; Lynd 1984; Campbell 1983).

A Strategic Understanding of Litigation

The animal rights movement has sought to advance legal protection for nonhumans. Since there are few laws that provide such protection, and standing regulations limit the ability of movement activists to enforce these laws, we might assume that a judicial strategy would be ineffective. Examination of the direct outcomes of litigation, by itself, lends credence to this assumption. Nonetheless, the experiences of this movement demonstrate that a creative, strategic, and broad approach to litigation can be instrumentally productive despite the limits of official law. Moreover, this movement illustrates that indeterminacy does not apply only to rights language; it also applies to judicial rulings that arise out of litigation and to litigative practices in general. This indeterminacy offers animal advocates the latitude to reconstruct the meaning of litigation just as they reconstruct the meaning of rights.

With regard to instrumentalism, we have seen how the animal rights movement has generated the multiple effects of litigation. Using

litigation in ways that capitalize on its ability to educate, foster publicity, mobilize movement support, and create leverage expands the effectiveness of a legal strategy. Combining litigation with other tactics and
approaching lawsuits with a broad and strategic view greatly increases
the productive capacity of the legal route. With regard to the constitutive character of litigation, the animal rights movement illustrates that
activists reconstruct legal rulings in strategic ways. With the indeterminate nature of legal language, activists often have room to interpret and
reconstitute judicial rulings. Activists use this room to advance their
own political and strategic constructions of legal meaning.

Not only do activists reconstruct judicial rulings, but they also
demonstrate critical sensitivity toward litigation. While it is certainly
true that legal battles and languages may mislead, deceive, and distort,
activists appear to possess an increasing awareness of litigation's pit-
falls. Lawyer and nonlawyer activists alike are cognizant of the various
drawbacks of a legal strategy and suggest that, in making tactical decisions, organizations must take these drawbacks into account. Overall,
activists approach litigation as a political tool to advance their cause,
not the primary or sole tool but one among many to be used under
appropriate circumstances.

The animal rights movement thus demonstrates that concerns
regarding the use of litigation may be overstated. Tushnet (1984), for
instance, warns that social movements conducting politics in the courts
may get used to such a strategy and, in turn, fail to employ extrajudicial
means. While this warning should be heeded, the animal rights movement appears to be taking a strategic, multifaceted approach to litigation that reduces the danger of neglecting extrajudicial strategies. In
doing so, this movement manifests Olson's "new style of litigation,"
which recognizes the multiple goals of lawsuits, the importance of
combining litigation with other political strategies, and the general contribution of litigation to a politics of rights (1984, 25–26).

The Decentered Approach Revisited

It is when we look at the law with a decentered approach that we see
the two faces of indeterminacy. It is when we analyze litigation beyond
the courtroom that we see the multiple uses of the process. It is when
we examine the perceptions of movement activists that we discern their
strategic and critical approaches to using the legal system. In short,

when we begin with a broad, decentered view—exploring the local levels of practical political thought and activity—our attention is drawn to both the opportunities and the limitations provided by the deployment of law.

The top-down approach characteristic of much public law scholarship overemphasizes the official legal system and the designs of judicial officials. For scholars optimistic about the opportunities offered within the judiciary, the court-centered approach overlooks potentially problematic secondary effects that reverberate beyond the judiciary. For scholars critical of that system, the top-down approach suggests a hegemonic view of law. On this critical view, employing the legal system replicates existing power structures, co-opts progressive movement forces, and undermines attempts to advance change. In contrast to the optimistic assessment, but like the critical evaluations, the decentered approach reminds us of existing inequalities and disparities in power and thus recognizes the hegemonic tendencies of the given system. However, the decentered approach also stresses the often overlooked ways in which hegemony can be challenged. By turning our analysis of law inside-out, the decentered, or bottom-up, approach recognizes the potential power of law for those who lack power and resources (Matsuda 1987).

The decentered approach further stresses the importance of considering context. Analyzing the deployment of law from the perspective of those choosing between the various ways to effect change allows us to see the factors that both constrain and expand choices. In the animal rights movement, the historical context of rights-oriented movements provided the opportunity to further develop the language of rights. The historical use of the language of compassion, which reinforced paternalism, protectionism, and the notion of human superiority, inspired the turn to a new language. And the lack of viable alternative languages certainly contributed to the choice of rights language.

One of the most crucial contextual variables influencing the animal rights movement is its unique position, one that is politically and ideologically at the margins but occupied by advocates and supporters who are relatively mainstream and privileged in terms of wealth and education. When we consider this positioning, we see the importance of addressing context. On the one hand, recognizing the composition and characteristics of the movement's constituency and leadership highlights the resonance and appeal that rights language and philosophical debate over rights have for supporters. At the same time, since movement supporters and leaders tend to be more privileged than the rest of the population, the appeal of the philosophical attempts to alter rights may be less successful beyond this white, educated, professional, affluent constituency.

On the other hand, the marginalized position of the movement as a whole signals the importance of addressing the view from the outside. As the minority critique of Critical Legal Studies suggests, scholars should "look to the bottom," that is, to the perspective of the oppressed, in order to develop a more complete understanding of the turn to law (Matsuda 1987; see also Williams 1987). Delgado (1987) makes this point by arguing that rights continue to be useful for minorities who experience racism because they may make the oppressors pause before they oppress and inhibit further oppression. To dismiss rights, Delgado observes, might be easy for scholars theorizing about a more ideal future. But, for outsiders experiencing oppression in their everyday lives, rights offer a weapon that cannot yet be discarded. Along these lines, the marginalized position of the animal rights movement stresses the present-day utility of rights. Rights continue to provide an entry point through which the marginalized can challenge the system. Rights offer a language with which to communicate within the system. Given animal advocates' views of the tremendous abuse and oppression nonhumans experience each day, the need to employ all the tools at their disposal is crucial.

Of course, it must be admitted that employing the language and institutions of the existing system may foster co-optation. Upon entry into the mainstream, the possibility of co-optation increases. This may be the biggest danger of using the legal system and its prevailing languages. At the same time, it may be the biggest danger of using any part of the existing system. Short of revolution, all methods of challenge are vulnerable to co-optation. And revolution is not always the best or even the most viable way to achieve social change. Hence, when the legal system is critiqued for its co-optive tendencies, we should not forget that it is not the only part of the system that has such tendencies. Furthermore, there are various ways to minimize the dangers of co-optation when using law. Examining the animal rights movement from the bottom up points to two important ways of minimizing co-optation: maintaining a critical and strategic understanding of law and deploying law in multiple ways and multiple locations.

Still, the following questions remain. When we look at the animal rights movement's deployment of law from the bottom up, do we find that the movement is progressing from the bottom, up? Has the turn to legal resources been useful in fostering change? These questions are difficult to answer. The movement is still young and, when analyzing its short-term successes, we cannot definitively separate the effectiveness of legal strategies from the effectiveness of other strategies. It can be said that the animal rights movement has, beyond a doubt, made significant breakthroughs in attitudes toward and the treatment of animals. Numerous achievements in battles against cosmetics testings, scientific research, and the fur industry demonstrate the movement's success. Growth in movement size, support, and resources signifies further success. However, there is no doubt that the battle for animal rights has just begun. And, despite some victories, the position of nonhumans in this society has not significantly changed. Opposition is strong and will continue to grow as the movement advances. And activists agree that, while there is reason to be optimistic about the potential for success, there is also reason to believe that success is a long way off.

Rights and Identity

Even if success remains only a distant hope, rights language and litigation have contributed to the movement's development and growth. In addition, the deployment of legal practices and languages has contributed to the shaping of movement identity. In particular, the turn to rights has moved it beyond the conservative and conciliatory stance of animal welfare to the radical notion of animal rights. This transformation has been significant in influencing the internal sense of identity for activists and equally significant in affecting the public's perception of the movement's identity.

Elizabeth Schneider contends that rights discourse can "be a means to articulate new values and political vision" and "can be a way for individuals to develop a sense of self and for a group to develop a collective identity" (1986, 611). For animal advocacy, the appropriation of rights has expressed new values and visions and has, in turn, contributed to the development of movement identity. By adopting an altered version of rights-based language, the movement has reshaped its identity at the same time that it has sought to reshape the meaning of rights. But the shaping of identity has also been structured and significantly limited by the prevailing meaning of rights. Given the flexible character of legal meaning and rights, the shaping of movement identity has itself been indeterminate. The result has been a movement that continues to struggle with its identity and with problematic public perceptions of it.

The Shift to Rights

The notion of animal welfare subscribes to specific identity images of humans and nonhumans. Rationality separates humans from nonhumans and creates a hierarchy of identity in which human identity is superior to nonhuman identity. Although superior, human identity is also compassionate and considerate. Thus, treatment of nonhumans is guided by the dual sides of human identity: compassion and rationality. Aside from the fact that nonhumans lack rationality, nonhuman identity is of little relevance; human identity is what matters for animal welfare.

The notion of animal rights puts forth alternative identity images for both humans and nonhumans by suggesting a relative equality between the two. Sentience becomes the crucial identity characteristic that dissolves the gap between humans and nonhumans. With sentience, activists maintain that animals gain an identity worthy of rights. Not only must humans be caring and considerate to animals, but they must also be restrained by the rights of animals. These alternative identity images contained within animal rights are noteworthy because they resist the dominant conception of rights and the identity images normally associated with rights.

The alternative identity images of humans and nonhumans are noteworthy because not only do they elevate animals to the level of rights-bearing entities, they further speak to human rights. On the one hand, identifying animals as rights-bearing beings places considerable limits on what we now take to be human rights. If animal rights are accepted, the right of humans to eat and wear what we choose is no longer viable. On the other hand, as argued in earlier chapters, animal rights reinforce certain human rights and, in turn, human identity. Because the notion of animal rights goes beyond rationality, it maintains the rights and identities of those humans who lack rationality, including the rights of the mentally disabled and children.

Movement identity is also significantly influenced by these alternative identity images. With the move to rights, animal advocates seek to cast their movement's identity in a new light. From the animal advocate's perspective, the choice of rights creates a positive, progressive, and life-affirming identity for the movement. It is an identity that stresses the values of liberation, equality, community, relationship, and caring. In addition, for animal advocates the movement's identity does not diminish human identity but uplifts animal identity.

The move to rights attempts to align the identity of the animal rights movement with the identities of movements for civil, women's, and gay and lesbian rights. Like these movements, the animal rights movement seeks to extend moral and legal rights to a group that has been excluded from consideration. But the animal rights movement is, in an important sense, distinct from these other movements. Since the concept of animal rights moves beyond the prevailing notion of rationality, the movement's identity lies closer to the identities of movements for the rights of children and the mentally disabled.

However, animal rights go beyond all of these movements by steering away from the strict emphasis on human rights. The identity of the animal rights movement is therefore unique. To be sure, this movement, like others, has appropriated and internalized a dominant mode of speaking. As such, its identity has certainly been shaped by the prevalence of rights language and its commonplace meaning. But this movement's uniqueness suggests that a movement's identity can resist dominant constructions of meaning. The movement, assuming a rights-oriented identity, has not straightforwardly subscribed to accepted notions of rights. The indeterminate meaning of rights thus provides the movement with space in which to shape its own identity.

Problems of a Rights-Oriented Identity

Even with the space to shape its own identity, the shift to rights language has been problematic for movement identity. From within the movement, dispute over a rights-oriented approach and the meaning of rights has led to internal divisions. These divisions have inhibited the development of a unified movement identity. From the outside, the prevailing meaning of rights generates unfavorable public perceptions of movement identity. Thus, it seems that the indeterminate nature of rights and predominant understanding of the language has problematic implications for movement identity.

The shift to rights language has fostered splits among animal advocates. The most prominent split is located between traditional animal welfare groups that seek humane treatment of animals and the newer, more radical groups that strive for animal liberation. There are also important divisions within the contemporary radical branch of the animal advocacy movement. As was discussed in chapter 2, competing frameworks have developed that attempt to justify animal liberation. The rights-oriented framework competes with Peter Singer's utilitarianism and with feminist and holistic approaches. Although the rights-oriented paradigm has come to symbolize the contemporary animal advocacy movement, the movement as a whole has not internally accepted a rights-oriented identity. With these conflicts, the identity of the animal advocacy movement has been under challenge from within.

It is important to note that internal movement splits are not peculiar to rights. Divisions within a movement, and therefore within movement identity, could result without the turn to rights. Had liberation become the dominant label and framework for animal advocacy, that, too, would have split the movement's identity. While the turn to rights certainly affects the way the lines are drawn and defined, rights themselves are not the sole reason for internal disunity.

Still, the meaning of rights is an important component of the continuing divisions in movement identity. Many feminists within the animal advocacy movement believe that rights are inherently individualistic and competitive. These feminists generally do not accept the notion that the standard conception of rights can be altered or that rights can be separated from Lockean liberalism. Utilitarians also have fundamental problems with a rights-oriented approach. Since utilitarians base their views on maximizing happiness, rights are essentially nonsense (Bentham 1962). The meaning of rights, whether based on individualism, rationality, sentience, or anything else, is hollow. For those who buy into a holistic approach, rights based on rationality or sentience do little to recognize the interconnectedness of the planet. Rights, limited as they are, do not extend to plants, trees, or nature as a whole. Rights talk thus does not fit well within a holistic approach. Finally, animal welfarists maintain traditional conceptions of the meaning of rights and do not accept the view that rights apply to nonhumans.

Along with internal conflicts, the shift to rights language has led to some crucial problems with the public's perception of movement identity. Because the public perceives rights as applying only to humans, the notion of animal rights appears absurd. Animal rights are equated with what the public takes to be human rights—the right to free speech, the right to the free exercise of religion, the right to vote, and so forth. Translating these for nonhumans, one arrives at the ridiculous notions of dogs having a right to bark, cats having the right to pray, and cows having the right to elect political representatives. Given the popular perception that animal rights means animals having the same rights as humans, the movement's identity takes on the appearance of absurdity.

As if this were not bad enough, additional problems associated with public perceptions stem from the competing claims rights often foster. Because the notion of animal rights implies a human obligation to cease most if not all current uses of animals, the movement's identity is associated with a challenge to such human rights as choosing the clothes we wear, the food we eat, and the sports in which we engage. Most importantly, the identity of this movement is connected to the assertion that it is immoral to experiment on animals. This, in turn, identifies the movement with a challenge to the human right to life.

The move from welfare to rights thus transforms the publicly perceived identity of animal activists from the traditional, somewhat derogatory image of animal lovers to the new, extremely disparaging image of human haters. Animal rights activists have come to be viewed as people who prefer animals to humans, who fight for animals when humans are still in need of protection, and who would sacrifice human lives for the lives of animals. This image is captured nicely by animal rights opponents who ask the question: Your child or your dog?

To a large extent, such public perceptions of movement identity would have occurred had animal liberation rather than animal rights come to symbolize this movement. Animal liberation, like animal rights, seeks to end the way we presently use and conceive of animals. However, the language of animal rights is especially problematic for public perceptions. It pushes the public toward the belief that the movement's identity is about giving cows the right to vote. In so doing, the rights-oriented identity amplifies the absurdity of animal rights and reinforces common perceptions of rights.

There are more problems with the external perception of this movement's identity. When the animal rights movement aligns itself with other human rights-oriented movements, those movements often see the alignment as degrading. To compare animal rights to the rights of African Americans, women, gays and lesbians, the physically and mentally disabled, and children is, from an external perspective, to reduce those groups to the level of animals. Such alignment is therefore often met with resistance from members of those rights-oriented movements.

An additional alignment dilemma stems from the fact that the identity of the animal rights movement is often perceived to be similar to the identity of the pro-life movement. Both of these movements seek to grant rights to beings who cannot protect themselves, and these rights come at the expense of human rights. This similarity is problematic since the animal rights movement does not wish to directly align itself with the pro-life movement. The perceived similarity is also a drawback because it may dissuade pro-choice proponents from supporting animal rights.

From the outside, the prevailing meaning of rights has structured the perceived identity of the animal rights movement. This structuring has not been very favorable to the movement. From the inside, dispute over the meaning and importance of rights has inhibited the development of a unified identity. While a transformed version of rights that emphasizes sentience, responsibility, and community has been an important factor in redefining the identity of animal advocacy, the internal and external struggles over movement identity remain challenging. And these struggles are importantly connected to and constituted by the contested meaning of rights.

Rights for Others

While it would be inappropriate to develop definitive generalizations from a single case study, the analysis developed in the preceding chapters offers some foundation for the consideration of other movements. In particular, a study of animal rights activism may shed some speculative light on movements that seek to gain rights on behalf of those who cannot speak for themselves.

As has been noted throughout this work, animal rights activists frequently connect themselves to other reform efforts. Activists refer to an expanding circle, identifying animal rights as the next step in the extension of rights. Within this reference, activists explicitly seek to associate animal rights with movements for women and people of color.

The link between animal rights and the rights of women and people of color is significant for comprehending the development of this movement and its philosophy. However, as argued earlier, the notion of animal rights has become distinct from the notions of rights developed for women and people of color. With the move toward sentience and away from rationality, arguments for animal rights attempt to do more than simply include nonhumans in the community of rights-bearing beings.

Activism for animal rights is also distinct from activism on behalf of civil rights and women's rights, despite some important similarities. The latter movements, like animal rights, have struggled to secure respect for their constituents. They have, in addition, employed similar legal and political strategies to gain power and protection. But a significant difference rests in the fact that the activists for and members of the civil rights and women's rights movements are often (although not always) the direct beneficiaries of the movements. These are not movements comprised of people who work solely for the benefit of others.

This difference is significant because of the common view that rights ought to apply only to beings who can assert and comprehend rights and fulfill obligations for the rights of others (i.e., moral agents). For the concept of animal rights to gain acceptance, it must successfully counter the philosophical argument that rights can extend only to moral agents. In addition, to gain acceptance activists must counter the popular argument that it makes no sense to protect deer from being hunted by humans if those same deer are going to be hunted by mountain lions. Why should humans respect the rights of animals if animals themselves do not respect those rights?

The fact that activists for animal rights are not the direct beneficiaries of their advocacy is also significant because of the legal issue of standing. Unlike civil rights and women's rights, for which standing can be attained directly by individual movement members, animal rights must confront the substantial obstacle of standing. This obstacle presents a problem for activists not only with regard to gaining a judicial hearing but because it sustains the idea that animals have no rights.

The difficulties noted above are unique to movements that attempt to achieve rights on behalf of beings who cannot assert their own rights.[6] Thus, while advocacy for animals follows in the path of civil rights and women's rights activism, it may have more in common with activism for children, fetuses, the environment, future generations, and people with severe mental disabilities. How, then, might the experiences of animal rights activism inform these other movements?

The attempt to revise the concept of rights along the lines of sentience may be most important for activism that seeks to protect the rights of people with severe mental disabilities. Humans with profound mental handicaps often lack rational capacities and some may never develop them. For these humans, rights based on rationality guarantee little. Rights based on sentience may offer greater protection, as they would for nonhumans.

For children and fetuses, a notion of rights based on sentience may not be necessary. Children and fetuses can be classified as potential rational creatures. Their potentiality, some would argue, offers sufficient grounding for bringing them into the moral community and under the protection of rights. Because they only have the potential to be rational creatures, children and fetuses would not gain the same rights as adult humans enjoy, but they could gain significant rights guarantees even without a revised conception of rights.

Nonetheless, the construction of rights offered by animal advocates might be appropriated and revised for children and fetuses. If potentiality is not a convincing framework for extending rights, sentience might offer an intriguing alternative. Certain rights for children, such as the right to be protected from physical and psychological abuse, might be persuasively grounded on sentience. If it is found that fetuses experience physical pain during abortion, the sentience argument might be applicable.

For fetuses, though, rights founded upon sentience probably do not offer much help. Basing rights on sentience does not necessarily lead to a right to life. While it does lead to a right to a life free from suffering, this does not straightforwardly imply an actual right to life. This remains a problem for animal rights advocates who want to guarantee nonhumans a right to life. It would also be a problem for those who wish to grant fetuses a right to life.

For the environment and future generations, rights based on sentience offer little. This, as was noted in earlier chapters, is recognized by animal advocates who take a holistic approach to ethics. Rights, even as reconstructed for animals, remain bound to certain individual and current capacities that the environment does not possess and that future generations only have the potential to possess.

Along with considering how a sentience-grounded notion of rights works for other movements, we should reflect upon what animal advocacy tells us about how a rights approach generally affects reform efforts. In particular, the conflicts of rights generated by a rights-oriented approach is noteworthy. The animal rights movement highlights the difficulties associated with counterrights claims. Certainly the abortion battle between the pro-choice and pro-life movements is similarly illustrative. Movements for the rights of children and for the mentally impaired also confront conflicts of rights.

We should not forget, however, that our examination of the animal rights movement has demonstrated that counterclaims will arise even without the turn to rights. For example, even if reform efforts for children were couched in terms of welfare rather than rights, conflicts between the interests of children and the interests of parents would, in many instances, arise. Furthermore, we should not ignore what the animal rights movement illustrates about the absoluteness of certain rights, that is, that stressing the absoluteness of certain rights may be desirable. We may want to be absolute in claiming a right that prohibits experimenting on humans without their consent. This emphasis on absoluteness may be of special interest for humans with profound mental disabilities.

What is probably the most significant insight to be drawn from animal rights activism is that the attempts to revise rights offer reinforcement of certain values. The emphasis on a broadened notion of community and on the responsibility we have in our relations with members of the community may be important in advancing causes beyond animals. What is noteworthy for these other causes is the fact that the effort to extend rights to animals has not simply maintained an individualistic version of liberalism but has challenged that version. In other words, it is the general challenge and resistance to dominant constructions of meaning from which other movements may learn and draw support.

Still, several problems remain with the practical goal of connecting animal rights to other movements. One problem stems from the perception that associating the rights of nonhumans and humans is demeaning to the latter. In particular, suggesting that humans with serious mental impairments are similar to nonhumans in the sense of lack of rationality may be viewed as a devaluation of human beings. Another problem arises from the political conflicts between animal rights and the environmental movements. Although similar in many respects, environmental activism is often at odds with protecting the interests of specific animals because from an environmental perspective those specific interests may be sacrificed for the sake of the environment.

These and other problems perpetuate the gap between animal advocacy and activism for others. But the practical realities should not overshadow the relevant similarities and differences among these various social movements. Most importantly, activists in movements concerning humans ought not to be blinded by the differences between humans and nonhumans. It is through recognition of the relevant differences *and* similarities between humans and nonhumans that insight might be gained.

The above comments should be taken as preliminary and nonexhaustive reflections on the connections between animal rights and the rights of others. A more comprehensive examination must, unfortunately, be reserved for the future. But I am hopeful that such a future exploration will be informed by the foregoing analysis of animal rights.

Conclusion: The New Myth of Rights?

Legal languages and practices, I have argued, are importantly related to the construction of meaning at various levels. Rights language and litigation are at once constrained by prevailing legal meaning and subject to alternative reconstructions of meaning. Rights language embedded within legal liberalism is confined by notions of individualism, autonomy, and rationality, but the indeterminacy of rights keeps the language open to varying constructions of meaning. The rules, structures, and practices of litigation, constrained as they are by such things as standing and precedent, construct and confine the terms within which litigative activity can take place. Yet a creative, strategically oriented approach to litigation can challenge these confines and reconstruct the terrain of litigation and legal meaning.

In making these points, this study has sought to qualify the various critiques of rights and litigation. By contextualizing the experiences of the animal rights movement, I have attempted to provide an alternative interpretation of the relationship between law, meaning, and social change. On this interpretation, rights language and litigation, subject to reconstitution, are resources that may contribute—directly and indirectly—to various social movement goals. This study has not, however, sought to suggest that the deployment of legal resources necessarily advances social change. The experiences of the animal rights movement do not suggest that legal language and activity guarantee success. Legal resources cannot be used without incurring potentially significant costs, and the context within which these resources are deployed impinges upon the chances of success. It is therefore crucial to realize the dangers and costs of legal language and litigation.

Along these lines, legal scholarship, which has exposed these dangers, must be commended. However, critiques of rights and litigation are often too categorical. The preceding pages have therefore been an attempt to "salvage" legal languages and practices in the face of attacks from both the right and the left.[7]

This salvaging attempt and the generally optimistic thrust of these pages must be placed in context. For one thing, much of the apparent optimism presented here is misleading. I have argued continually that rights language is useful, given the lack of alternatives. If there were reason to be hopeful about alternative avenues of social change, the assessment of rights provided here would be quite different. Furthermore, the optimism suggested in these pages rests within a context that continues to recognize immense power disparities and continuing inequality. It is an optimism that expresses the possibility of the powerless challenging the powerful, but there is no suggestion that legal languages and activities comprise the slingshot with which David slew Goliath.[8] In short, this is an attempt to salvage the legal route as one among many means of promoting change in the face of continued inequality and oppression and in light of limited alternatives.

This work is not alone in its attempt to salvage rights and legal avenues of change. Several scholars have responded to recent critical assessments by attempting to salvage and rescue rights. These scholars maintain hope in the legal system and legal language. For instance, Schneider (1986) argues that the battle for rights is a form of praxis that allows for both the expression and affirmation of human values. Minow (1987) contends that rights language helps foster community. McCann (1994) and Scheingold (1989) provide evidence that rights and litigation contribute to movement mobilization and the advancement of a politics of rights. And several scholars suggest that rights talk continues to be powerful and persuasive (Appleby 1987; Haskell 1987). In light of such benefits, and in the face of continued inequality, Matsuda (1987), Crenshaw (1988), and others assert that oppressed groups cannot yet afford to discard rights and other legal resources (see Williams 1987; and Delgado 1987).

While attempting to salvage legal practices, these scholars at the same time recognize the contingencies and limitations of the law. They take seriously the critique of rights and maintain skepticism toward the judicial process. From this perspective, legal avenues offer the potential for change, but in general they tend to reinforce existing relations of power. As such, the attempt to salvage and rescue the law is checked by a critical awareness of law's hegemonic tendencies.

Despite the continued concerns and skepticism, legal scholarship demonstrates a renewed hope in the law. Given this renewed hope, one might conclude that a new myth of rights is being created. Scholars, in working to deconstruct and reconstruct rights and in trying to find some worth in the rights-oriented social activity of the past half-century, have developed a new faith in rights. If this is true, then I, too, have contributed to the advancement of a new myth.

However, if this new myth is coming into being, we must recognize it as distinct from the myth of rights elaborated by Scheingold (1974) and distinct from the false consciousness implied in critical scholarship (Tushnet 1984; Freeman 1982; Gabel 1982; Gabel and Kennedy 1984). This new myth of rights is at once hopeful and wary, optimistic and skeptical, encouraging and doubtful. What's more, the new faith in rights fosters a critical and strategic approach. Rather than advancing a guileless, unreflective belief in the promises of the law, this new myth recognizes contingencies and dangers. It realizes that rights talk or litigation alone cannot remake the world and warns that law may only re-create existing power inequities.

Fear of a new myth of rights should not lead us to discard legal practices. While it is tempting for activists seeking social transformation to throw out the old and bring in the new, such a strategy involves significant costs. And the fear of a new myth of rights should not provide the sole justification for scholarly dismissal of rights. Scholars who may find it easy, in the abstract, to dismiss the old should not forget the tangible and significant benefits offered by rights and litigation. On the contrary, scholars should reevaluate the potential gains to be made as a result of legal activism and an extension of rights language. Indeed, scholars should, with critical reflection, consider the advice of Patricia J. Williams.

> In discarding rights altogether, one discards a symbol too deeply enmeshed in the psyche of the oppressed to lose without trauma and much resistance. Instead, society must *give* them away. Unlock them from reification by giving them to slaves. Give them to trees. Give them to cows. Give them to history. Give them to rivers and rocks. Give to all of society's objects and untouchables the rights of privacy, integrity and self-assertion; give them distance and respect. Flood them with the animating spirit which rights mythology fires in this country's most oppressed psyches, and wash away the shrouds of inanimate object status, so that we may say not that we own gold, but that a luminous gold spirit owns us. (1987, 433)

Although this advice raises questions regarding the extension of rights, it is advice worthy of discussion and consideration. Considering it within the context of animals has been the goal of this book, and we have seen that the unleashing of rights can strengthen both the language itself and the communities for whom the language provides meaning.

Notes on Data Gathering

As discussed in chapter 1, the data employed in this research project were gathered by means of a multidimensional methodology. In particular, I employed five types of methods to examine the deployment of legal resources by the animal rights movement: content analysis, analysis of philosophical writings, analysis of litigative experiences and legal writings, participant observation, and in-depth interviews. This appendix reviews my approach in employing these multiple methods.

Content Analysis

To examine the deployment of legal resources by the animal rights movement and the media's participation in this deployment, I performed content analysis on three sources: newspapers, popular periodicals, and movement literature. In examining newspapers, I reviewed stories relating to animal rights and welfare issues covered in eight newspapers: the *New York Times*, the *Washington Post*, the *Los Angeles Times*, the *Wall Street Journal*, the *Christian Science Monitor*, the *Seattle Times*, the *Seattle Post-Intelligencer*, and the *University of Washington Daily*. I selected the first five because of their national stature. I selected the *Seattle Times* and the *Seattle Post-Intelligencer* for their local coverage, and I chose the final paper to explore collegiate coverage of the issues. In all, I reviewed more than 125 news reports, editorials, and letters to the editor appearing in these papers between 1987 and 1992. These articles covered a wide range of topics, including animal use and movement activism against animal use in the fur industry, factory farming, cosmetics testing, scientific research, and entertainment.

In examining popular periodicals, I reviewed articles in the *Nation*, the *New Republic*, *New York*, the *Village Voice*, and *Newsweek*. Unlike newspaper coverage, the coverage in these periodicals was much more limited. I reviewed fewer than ten articles in these periodicals. However, the stories were lengthy and provided in-depth coverage of animal rights activism.

My content analysis of movement literature drew on three types of sources: the foremost animal protection magazine in the country (available through subscription), organization newsletters, and organization pamphlets. The first source, *Animals' Agenda*, offers information and articles on a whole range of animal issues and animal activism. I examined more than twenty issues of this magazine. In the second source, I reviewed newsletters from various organizations, including PETA, PAWS, the Fund for Animals, the ASPCA, NAVS, AAVS, FARM, HSUS, HFA, FAR, and PCRM. My focus in these rested largely on the newsletters of the first two organizations, PETA and PAWS. I chose to focus on PETA because it is the largest and best known animal rights organization in the country. I chose PAWS for its local focus and because it is a "progressive" welfare organization that has made the move from welfare issues and discourse to rights. I reviewed fifteen editions of *PETA News*, ten of *PAWS News*, and ten of *PAWS Action*. Of the other organizations, I examined a total of twenty newsletters. In all, I explored fifty newsletters, mostly those of animal rights organizations but including at least five from animal welfare organizations.

In reviewing pamphlets distributed by animal protection organizations, I categorized the abundant pamphlets and circulars published by the organizations listed above and others under the following issues: animal experimentation and dissection, cosmetics testing, fur farming, factory farming and vegetarianism, animals and the environment (including wildlife and endangered species issues), hunting, animal use in entertainment (zoos, rodeos, movies), and domestic animal issues. In addition, I categorized pamphlets under strategic approaches, including legislative, litigative, and protest activities and educational and media campaigns. Finally, I organized pamphlets under two special headings: animal organizations' statements of purpose and animal rights justifications. Of course, in categorizing pamphlets in these ways, there was a good deal of overlap; for example, some pamphlets on animal experimentation included animal rights justifications.

Analysis of Philosophical Writings

My review of philosophical writings was straightforward and needs little discussion. Since the philosophical work regarding animal issues is relatively limited, I was able to examine a significant portion of this material. I reviewed both classical and contemporary writings. My stress in the contemporary sphere was on the works of Singer and Regan, who are the two most important philosophers within the animal protection movement. I also investigated the writings of many other contemporary scholars, including Carol Adams, Josephine Donovan, Joel Feinberg, Michael W. Fox, Marti Kheel, Mary Midgley, John Robbins, Bernard Rollin, Stephen Sapontzis, and Marjorie Spiegel. The primary exclusion in this review were writings from the Eastern philosophical and religious traditions. I neglected these works because they do not impinge significantly, at this point, on the American context in which animal rights activism is carried out.

Analysis of Litigative Activities and Legal Writings

Like the philosophical writings, legal writings and activities regarding animals are rather limited. I examined numerous cases relating to animal issues, including the most significant ones of the last two decades. My examination of these cases came from various written sources: judicial opinions, law journals, media coverage, and movement coverage. In addition to examining cases, I explored the potential avenues for future litigation and the barriers to litigation discussed in several law journals.

Along with written sources, my examination of litigative activities relied on interviews with animal rights activists, both lawyer and non-lawyer. Since many litigative activities of the animal rights movement never make it near the courts, reliance on written material alone was insufficient to understand use of the litigative route. Thus, as I will discuss below, my interviews with advocates probed their experiences and views regarding litigation.

Participant Observation

I gathered a good deal of information on the animal rights movement from participant observation of organizational activities. Participant observation is a common form of data gathering used within ethnographic studies (Geertz 1983; Scott 1985; Gaventa 1980). It allows scholars to examine their subjects from within, and often provides data not accessible by other means.

In performing participant observation, I was able to maintain sufficient distance from my object of study. This was possible because all of the activities in which I participated allowed for anonymity on my part. The meetings, talks, protests, and other events I attended were all large enough to allow for this type of distant and anonymous observation.

I attended several meetings of animal rights groups in the Seattle area. These meetings dealt with organizational issues and strategies and sometimes included talks by activists from other organizations. In addition, I attended talks given by various leaders within the movement, including Tom Robbins, president of EarthSave; Dr. Neal Barnard, head of PCRM; and Kim Stallwood of PETA. I participated in several protests and marches, including small demonstrations in front of fur stores and larger protest marches that targeted animal use in the fur industry and scientific experimentation.

The 1990 national March for Animals and the PETA 101 Seminar were the two most significant activities that I observed. The former was a day-long event held in Washington, D.C., which close to 25,000 people attended. At this event I was able to listen to and record the speeches of a multitude of animal protection leaders from around the country, including Priscilla Farrell, Dr. George Cabe, Lawrence Carter, Alex Pacheco, Wayne Pacelle, Dr. Nedim Buyukmihci, Bernard Unti, Holly Hazard, Gary Francione, Peter Linck, Congressman Tom Lantos, Cleveland Amory, Congressman Charles Bennett, Peggy McCabe, Coleman McCarthy, Michael W. Fox, Gretchen Wyler, Berke Breathed, Peter Singer, John Kullberg, Andrew Lindsey, Ingrid Newkirk, Carol Adams, Bill Sterling, Gil Michael, Tom Regan, and others.[1] These speakers represented a host of animal protection organizations, including NAVS, Friends of Animals, PETA, Fund for Animals, AAVS, Doris Day Animal League, HSUS, ASPCA, FAR, and more. In addition to the speeches, the March for Animals provided me with the opportunity to mingle and speak informally with movement supporters, to observe reactions to the speakers, and to note what kinds of signs were carried and what chants were yelled.

The second most significant activity I observed was the PETA 101 Seminar designed to educate would-be activists. This day-long seminar reviewed the various strategies that advocates can use to advance the cause of animals. Several speakers covered different topics, including establishing new organizations; using the media; organizing protests, letter-writing campaigns, and legislative activities, and so forth. This seminar, like the other activities I observed, provided me with the opportunity to speak informally with movement supporters, to examine their perspectives and ways of speaking about animals, and to investigate organizational strategies.

Interviews

The richest component of my data came from intensive interviews conducted with animal advocates. Like participant observation, interviews are a common form of data gathering used within the social sciences (Lane 1962; Hochschild 1981; Rubin 1976; Luker 1984; Gilligan 1982). Interviews provide scholars with the opportunity to delve into the perspectives of actors central to the subject of study and to obtain information not available by other means.

Twenty-five people participated in these interviews. All but one of the participants can be classified as activists within the animal protection movement.[2] They all devote significant time to an animal protection organization, through full-time, part-time, or volunteer work. The decision to limit the interviews to activists was based on the research questions that guide this project. These questions focus on the actors who make choices regarding discourse and movement strategies. Thus, my interest in probing the actions and perspectives of those who lead the movement stemmed directly from the research questions, which emphasize the players who define, shape, and mobilize the movement.

The selection of interviewees was based on five factors: location, association with an organization, type of activist, references, and availability. In terms of location, I chose interviewees in three parts of the country: the Northeast, the San Francisco Bay area, and the Seattle area. I selected these locations in order to obtain a broad geographic base. Within these locations, I sought out activists associated with two basic types of organizations: large, national, well-known organizations and smaller, local organizations.[3] In all, I interviewed activists from PETA, ASPCA, the Fund for Animals, PCRM, FAR, PAWS, Legal Action for Animals, IDEA, IDA, Action for Animals, and a local Virginia-based humane society.[4] With regard to type of activist, I sought to speak with a broad range of actors, from the leaders of organizations to staff and active supporters. Half of the participants can be classified as leaders and the other half as staff and active supporters. In addition, I sought out several attorneys and interviewed five of them.[5]

In addition to location, association with an organization, and type of activist, two factors influenced the selection of participants: referrals and availability. At the end of each interview, I asked activists to refer me to other potential interviewees. As a rule, I only followed up on two such references to avoid potential bias connected with referrals. Finally, my selection of interviewees was limited by availability. Several advocates I sought to interview were unavailable for a variety of reasons.

In most of the interviews, I initially approached activists with a letter, noting my association with the Political Science Department of the University of Washington and explaining, in broad and vague terms, my research interests. I followed up the letter with a phone call asking the activist to participate in an interview. In some instances, my initial approach was via a phone call. This type of approach was used with referrals and when a shortage of time did not allow for the initial letter.[6] In most instances, the activists I called agreed to meet me for an interview. However, five activists did not participate. Of these, three were willing to speak with me at a time when I would not be available.[7] Two were unwilling to speak with me at all.[8]

The interviews were conducted at a variety of locations, depending upon the desires of the interviewees. Most were conducted at the participants' workplaces or at restaurants and cafes. A few were conducted at other locations, including activists' homes and hotels. Each interview lasted between one and two hours. Four were conducted with two people;[9] the remainder were individual interviews. All but three were tape recorded, with the approval of the interviewees. All taped interviews were later transcribed. The three untaped interviews were off the record at the request of the advocates. In the taped interviews, there were occasions during which advocates wished to speak off the record. On those occasions I temporarily turned off the tape recorder.

At the outset of each interview, I briefly introduced myself and gave a very general statement about the purpose of the interviews. This statement noted that I was conducting academic research at the University of Washington for a study on the politics surrounding the movement concerned with animals. I also noted that, since I wished to avoid biasing the interviewee, I did not want to provide too much detail regarding the specifics of my research but would be happy, after the interview, to give the interviewee more information. I further stated that my work was not sponsored by any group working against the movement.[10] Finally, I asked if the activists would agree to be quoted in my written work. Only three did not wish to have their names cited.[11] One, over the course of the interview, became uncomfortable with speaking on the record, at which point I turned off the recorder and said that the rest of the interview would be confidential.

The interviews were conducted with a standard questionnaire that sought to discover how advocates view and deploy legal resources. However, on the whole, the interview format was open-ended rather than survey-oriented. The format was designed to allow activists the opportunity to expound on their own views and thoughts about move-ment activism. Hence, the standard questions guided and structured the discussion but left sufficient opportunity for interviewees to use their own words and express their thoughts at length.[12] As a result, the interviews varied, depending upon how each advocate responded to the questions. For instance, certain questions were not asked if partici-pants had already raised a particular topic on their own. In addition, I frequently probed participant responses, asking for elaboration and clarification.[13]

The interviews always began with the open-ended "How did you get started in activities concerning animals?" This question frequently prompted interviewees to describe consciousness-raising experiences that had led them to become active in the cause of animals. Quite often, this question led interviewees to independently raise the notion of ani-mal rights. In those instances, I then asked advocates what they meant by animal rights and followed up with a question probing whether they thought the language was useful. If advocates did not mention rights on their own, later in the interview the question was asked: "How do you justify the belief that animals should be protected?" Activists responded to this question either by raising the topic of rights or not. In the few instances in which activists did not mention rights on their own, I, toward the end, asked what they thought about the notion of animal rights.

To examine the strategies deployed by the movement and solicit advocates' thoughts on these strategies, I asked interviewees about their organization's activities and asked them to rate the effectiveness of their various strategies. I queried them on their organization's litigative activities, asked how they felt litigation compared with other strategies, and asked them to describe the ways in which litigation is and is not effective.

In addition to the general open-ended format, the interviews ended with a set of survey-style questions, including: "How would you classify your political orientation on a continuum?" "Are you a vegetarian?" "What is your level of education?" "Do you consider yourself a feminist?" "Are you familiar with any philosophical literature regarding animal issues?" In the earlier stages of certain interviews, participants answered some of these questions on their own.

Overall, the intensive interview process was aimed at exploring the perspectives of activists who play a central role in mobilizing the animal rights movement. The data gathered through these interviews, combined with the information obtained through the other methods, provided a textured and expansive body of evidence. Although there is no doubt that further data gathering would prove useful, for the purposes of this study the multifaceted body of evidence provided a solid foundation for examining the deployment of legal resources by the animal rights movement.

Animal Advocacy Groups

Information supplied by the following animal advocacy groups was employed in this study.

Action for Animals
Activists in the Lafayette Animal Rights Movement (ALARM)
American Anti-Vivisection Society (AAVS)
American Society for the Prevention of Cruelty to Animals
    (ASPCA)
Animal Legal Defense Fund (ALDF)
Animal Liberation Front (ALF)
Animal Protection Institute (API)
Animal Rights Mobilization (ARM; previously Trans-Species
    Unlimited)
Animal Rights Network (ARN)
Association of Veterinarians for Animal Rights (AVAR)
Berkeley Students for Animal Liberation (BSAL)
Citizens to End Animal Suffering and Exploitation (CEASE)
Culture and Animals Foundation
EarthSave
Farm Animal Reform Movement (FARM)
Feminists for Animal Rights (FAR)
Friends of Animals (FoA)
The Fund for Animals (FUND)
Humane Farming Association (HFA)
Humane Society of the United States (HSUS)
In Defense of Animals (IDA)
Institute for the Defense of the Earth and Animals (IDEA)
International Society for Animal Rights (ISAR)
Legal Action for Animals (LAA)
National Alliance for Animal Legislation (ALLIANCE)

National Anti-Vivisection Society (NAVS)
Northwest Animal Rights Network (NARN)
People for the Ethical Treatment of Animals (PETA)
Physicians Committee for Responsible Medicine (PCRM)
Progressive Animal Welfare Society (PAWS)
Students United Protesting Research on Sentient Subjects
    (SUPRESS)
United Action for Animals (UAA)

Notes

Preface

1. Several of these questions were developed in a paper I coauthored with Robert Van Dyk, entitled "Social Movements in the Courts: Power and the Problems of a Legal Strategy" (1989).

2. I was especially heartened when my mother confirmed my expectations about this point. After reading an early version of the first chapter, she explained to my father that I was not arguing for or against the animal rights movement.

Chapter 1

1. According to Hart (1961), a legal system is characterized by the presence of authoritative rules. These rules are formal and are made authoritative through institutions. For a critique of this approach, see White 1985b. According to White, "the conception of law as a set of rules merges with the conception of law as a set of institutions and processes" (686).

2. For instance, studies of judicial decision making explore various factors that may influence judges' perspectives and attitudes. The law, as established within judicial opinions, is dependent upon the factors that shape judges' views. See, for example, Frank 1930.

3. Emphasis in the original.

4. Sarat and Kearns further describe the constitutive perspective as follows: "So conceived, law is inseparable from the interests, goals, and understandings that comprise social life. Law is part of the everyday world, contributing powerfully to the apparently stable, taken-for-granted quality of that world and to the generally shared sense that as things *are*, so *must* they be" (1993, 30, emphasis in the or:ginal).

5. Alternative dispute resolution literature varies in its assessment of the effectiveness of these informal techniques. For critiques of alternative dispute resolution, see Abel 1981 and Harrington 1985. For a more positive assessment, see Henry 1985.

6. It should be stressed, as it will be in later chapters, that the constitutive investigation suggested here ought not to neglect instrumentalism. Indeed, instrumental uses of the law are a crucial component of the construction of

meaning. Understanding the constitutive character of law requires awareness and consideration of its instrumental character. Thus, the constitutivism described here and in what follows is a constitutivism informed and revised by instrumentalism.

7. I am grateful to Wayne Fishman for helping me think through these three points.

8. Indeed, if this were not the case, there would be little need for courts. See Galanter 1983.

9. Emphasis in the original. White made this statement while talking to a group of first-year law students. Thus, the *you* in the final sentence may have referred narrowly to law students who would later become legal practitioners, although I cannot be sure of this. Regardless of what White may have intended, I suggest a broader understanding of law as an activity in which the *you* includes all members of a culture who must learn to function within that culture.

10. For Scheingold, these dangers include limiting grassroots activism, generating inertia that constrains the restructuring of movements, and the encouragement of divisiveness and conflict (1989, 85). For McCann, "legal discourses tend to privilege some meanings but to silence, undermine, or transmute others" (1994, 284).

11. This type of interaction is nicely exemplified in recent pro-life blockades of abortion clinics. These blockades generated court battles and prompted the passage of national legislation that made such blockades a felony violation. In turn, these official actions continue to have ramifications on pro-life protest activity.

12. Given that this investigation seeks to shed light on when and how rights language is effective for social movements, and given its focus on the animal rights movement, this study will provide information for groups fighting for animal rights. It should be noted, however, that this is a side effect of the project rather than a conscious goal. This work is not being undertaken to advance the ends of the animal rights movement. My concern is neither to assist nor to thwart the animal rights movement. Instead my intention is to provide information to those who study rights and social movements, and to inform social movements generally (see preface).

13. For philosophical examinations of animal rights, see Singer 1990; Regan 1983; Midgley 1984; Sapontzis 1987; and Feinberg 1978.

14. It is important to use the term *nonhuman* to distinguish humans from nonhuman animals. However, throughout this book I will frequently refer to animals without the applying the adjective *nonhuman*. When I do use the term, I mean specifically to distinguish human from nonhuman animals.

15. With regard to the deployment of rights, the debate ranges from those who view rights as an undeniable good for groups seeking reform, to those who see rights language as ultimately detrimental to real change, and finally to those with a more mixed view who see rights as helpful for certain movement goals but caution against the idea that rights can truly transform prevailing social conditions. For the optimistic view of rights, see Friedman 1985; Dworkin 1978; and Michelman 1973. For those who view rights as detrimental, see Med-

calf 1978; Quinney 1974; and Lefcourt 1971. For the mixed view, see Scheingold 1974; McCann 1986; and Schneider 1986.

16. For a more detailed discussion of the methodology employed in this work, see appendix A.

Chapter 2

The notion of the "expanded" or "extended" circle has been elaborated upon by several scholars. See, for instance, Wynne-Tyson 1985; and Singer 1981. Albert Schweitzer also invoked the extended circle in *The Philosophy of Civilization:* "Until he extends the circle of his compassion to all living things, man will not himself find peace" (cited in Wynne-Tyson 1985, 316).

1. This controversy was captured by Bentham, a utilitarian theorist, who referred to rights as "nonsense on stilts" (1962, 501).

2. This is not surprising. Since rights language is the prominent mode of debate, it makes sense for scholars who wish to advance a different foundation for protecting or liberating animals to formulate their work in contrast to rights.

3. To say that there has been a move away from the language of compassion does not mean that there has been a complete dismissal of that language. Compassion remains a central language within the animal rights movement. However, it is used in combination with and as a supplement to the concept of animal rights.

4. Several scholars suggest that the allure of rights in American culture fosters a naive faith in the language. These scholars suggest that the false promise of rights frequently leads social movement activists to appropriate a language that reinforces existing power structures (see Scheingold 1974; Tushnet 1984; and Gabel and Kennedy 1984.

5. These include *Free Thoughts on the Brute Creation* (1742), *Four Stages of Cruelty* (1742), *An Essay on Humanity to Animals* (1798), and *An Apology for the Brute Creation or Abuse of Animals Censured, Dedicated to T. B. Drayman* (1772). In addition, Niven cites Dr. Humphrey Primatt's *A Dissertation on the Duty of Mercy and Sin of Cruelty to Brute Animals* (1776). According to Niven, "This was the first book devoted entirely to teaching the duty of kindness to animals and is regarded by the R.S.P.C.A. as the foundation stone of their organization because of the influence it had on those who founded the society" (1967, 53).

6. Carson 1972, 50. According to Carson, more than a quarter century later France followed suit, passing a similar animal protection law.

7. This division was the precursor of the present-day split between the moderate animal welfare movement and the abolitionist animal rights movement.

8. The bill required that anesthesia be used in experiments but allowed researchers to waive this requirement under certain conditions (Niven 1967, 84).

9. Despite this minimal concern, some regulations concerning animals existed prior to the 1800s. For instance, a 1641 law passed in Massachusetts by the Puritans directed that "No man shall exercise any Tirrany or Crueltie towards any bruite Creature which are usuallie kept for man's use" (Carson 1972, 71).

10. According to one account, "The publication of Peter Singer's *Animal Liberation* in 1975 signaled the birth of today's animal rights advocacy" (ASPCA 1990, 94).

11. It should be stressed that the issue here is desire, not need. If there is a need to use animals, there may be some justification for causing pain. The question then becomes: How do we define human need?

12. For instance, the ASPCA, the first animal welfare group in this country, has referred to itself as an animal rights group and in 1990 published *The Animal Rights Handbook.*

13. Information on the size and growth of the movement was obtained from Merritt Clifton, news editor of *Animals' Agenda,* in a phone interview which took place in the fall of 1991. He cited the 1991 *Annual Directory of Animal Organizations,* noting that these 900 groups are stable, incorporated organizations. The number does not include ad hoc groups that emerge for short periods of time.

14. According to Clifton (interview), this number excludes animal shelter services provided by cities.

15. For example, in the fall of 1995 a group of Lafayette College students organized ALARM (Activists in the Lafayette Animal Rights Movement) in order to lobby the dining services for more vegetarian and vegan food choices and to challenge the use of animals in experiments conducted on campus.

16. The reason for the lack of evidence in itself suggests the dramatic growth of the movement. Few exact numbers for the early 1980s are available because at the time there wasn't much of a movement. By the latter half of the 1980s, the expansion of the movement provided a reason to begin calculating the level of strength and support.

17. The number comes from the mailing lists of the 900 animal protection organizations. The number accounts for the fact that some people may be members of several organizations.

18. This number is a rough estimate given to me by Merritt Clifton (interview), who admitted that the number probably does not account for various new groups that had been formed.

19. Although furriers deny the impact of animal advocacy, it is quite likely that animal rights activism has affected the profitability of the fur industry.

20. Revlon, Avon, and Mary Kay are some of the cosmetics firms that have either halted testing or placed a moratorium on it following attacks and boycotts by animal advocacy groups.

21. Several television shows have taken up animal issues, including *L.A. Law,* the *ABC Afternoon Special, 60 Minutes,* and *48 Hours.* Doonesbury, Bloom County, Outlands, and the Far Side are comic strips that raise animal issues. And, although few television commercials have anything to do with animal concerns, the Archer Daniels Midland Company, which always advertises during *This Week with David Brinkley,* is promoting meatless hamburgers. The commercial does not depict an older person who is vegetarian for health reasons but a young woman in a restaurant who wishes to order something without meat.

22. The survey from which this and the following data were obtained was

conducted by sociologists at Utah State University (Bartlett 1991, 2). According to this report, "Questionnaires sent to a computer-selected random sampling of ANIMALS' AGENDA subscribers were filled out and returned by 853 of 1,020 addressees—an almost unheard of 84 percent participation rate, indicating a high level of commitment. ANIMALS' AGENDA subscribers were chosen for the survey because 'they provided a valuable cross-organizational profile of animal rights activists as a collectivity.'"

23. According to the Utah State University survey, 4.9 percent are under twenty; 18.3 percent in their twenties; 21.7 percent in their forties; 10 percent in their fifties; and 10 percent sixty and over (Bartlett 1991, 2).

24. About a quarter of the members live in rural areas (Bartlett 1991, 2).

25. The focus here is on Western thought and thus excludes Eastern views of animals. I do not undertake analysis of Eastern thought because it has yet to permeate the contemporary debate and activism to any significant degree. Two exceptions to this should be noted. First, the recent application of holistic views to animal issues draws on Eastern thought. Second, there is at least one animal protection organization influenced by Eastern thought: Buddhists Concerned for Animals.

26. For excerpts on philosophical and religious thought relating to animals see Clarke and Linzey 1990; and Regan and Singer 1976.

27. According to Aristotle, "*There is a principle of rule and subordination in nature at large: it appears especially in the realm of animate creation. By virtue of that principle, the soul rules the body; and by virtue of it the master, who possesses the rational faculty of the soul, rules the slave, who possesses only bodily powers and the faculty of understanding the directions given by another's reason*" (1958, 11, emphasis in the original).

28. According to Descartes, the notion "I think, therefore I am" clearly does not apply to animals. For animals, the phrase would probably take the form "I do not think, therefore I am not," although, of course, as nonthinking machines, animals could not hold this or any other thought.

29. Others from that time period include Porphyry and Seneca (see Salt 1980, 3).

30. Ryder notes that Montaigne, "with some justification, is regarded as the father of the modern movement towards a more compassionate view of the other species" (1979, 3).

31. Ryder lists several theologians of the eighteenth century who advanced this view: John Milton, Robert Fludd, Richard Overton, Joseph Butler, John Hildrop, Richard Dean, and, most prominently, Dr. Humphry Primatt (1979, 6–7).

32. Ironically, while Darwinian thought advanced the connections between humans and animals and contributed to the growth of the humane movement, it also advanced the science of biology, with its use of animals in experimentation.

33. According to Ryder, one of the first mentions of the rights of animals was made by Thomas Tryon. In *The Countryman's Companion*, published around 1683, the birds and fowl of heaven state: "But tell us, O Man! we pray you tell us what injuries have we commited to forfeit? What Law have we broken, or

what Cause given you, whereby you can pretend a Right to invade and violate our part, and natural Rights, and to assault and destroy us, as if we were the Agressors, and no better than Thieves, Robbers and Murtherers, fit to be extirpated out of the Creation?" (quoted in Ryder 1979, 5).

34. In *The Philosophical Treatise on Horses, and on the Moral Duties of Man towards the Brute Creation,* John Lawrence wrote of "the jus animalium, or the rights of beasts to the protection of the law, on the ground of natural justice in the first instance, and in sequel, on that of expedience, regarding both humanity and profit" (quoted in Ryder 1979, 224). Thomas Young actually used the phrase "the rights of animals" (Ryder 1979, 224).

35. See, for instance, the works of Locke, Rousseau, and Kant.

36. Here Singer draws the analogy between severely retarded human beings who lack reasoning abilities to animals. His argument is that if we are not entitled, by superior intelligence, to exploit the mentally ill, then we are by analogy not entitled to exploit animals.

37. In a later article, Singer states: "Why is it surprising that I have little to say about the nature of rights? It would only be surprising to one who assumes that my case for animal liberation is based upon rights and, in particular, upon the idea of extending rights to animals. But this is not my position at all. I have little to say about rights because rights are not important to my argument. My argument is based on the principle of equality, which I do have quite a lot to say about. My basic moral position (as my emphasis on pleasure and pain and my quoting Bentham might have led [readers] to suspect) is utilitarian. I make very little use of the word 'rights' in Animal Liberation, and I could easily have dispensed with it altogether. I think that the only right I ever attribute to animals is the 'right' to equal consideration of interests, and anything that is expressed by talking of such a right could equally well be expressed by the assertion that animals' interests ought to be given equal consideration with the like interests of humans. (With the benefit of hindsight, I regret that I did allow the concept of a right to intrude into my work so unnecessarily at this point; it would have avoided misunderstanding if I had not made this concession to popular moral rhetoric.)" (1978, 122).

38. Although Regan's work is the best-known defense of animal rights, he is not alone in making the case for extending rights to animals. For instance, Sapontzis (1987) argues that rights rhetoric ought to be used in the case of animals despite the problems associated with the concept. He recommends that animal activists use the concept of rights "because it accurately communicates the general and fundamental change they seek in our attitude toward the moral and legal status of animals" (82). See also Fox 1980.

39. According to Regan, perfectionism holds that individuals deserve things based on the virtues they possess. Utilitarianism holds that individuals deserve equal consideration of their interests.

40. Donovan includes utilitarianism within the broad label "animal rights theory."

41. See Diamond and Orenstein 1990; Keller 1985; and Kheel 1988. Kheel states, "Currently, the self is identified with human will and reason, both of which are conceived in opposition to the natural world. Nature, in this world

view, is seen as an object to be used (either conquered and subdued or enslaved and controlled) for the benefit of a self that is detached from the natural world" (16).

42. As Collard describes it, "In patriarchy, nature, animals and women are objectified, hunted, invaded, colonised, owned, consumed and forced to yield and to produce (or not). This violation of the integrity of wild, spontaneous Being is rape. It is motivated by a fear and rejection of Life and it allows the oppressor the illusion of control, of power, of being alive. As with women as a class, nature and animals have been kept in a state of inferiority and power-lessness in order to enable men as a class to believe and act upon their 'natural' superiority/dominance" (1988, 1).

43. Inspiration for this argument comes in part from the work of Carol Gilligan (1982). Gilligan argues that women are driven more by the notions of responsibility and care than rights and obligations.

44. Like Kheel, Collard expresses the notion of holism. In challenging the oppression experienced by women, animals, and nature, she states, "Feminists must articulate this oppression as part of our holistic, biophilic [life-loving] vision" (1988, 1).

45. This chapter focuses on the philosophical turn to rights, whereas the following chapter turns to political activism involving rights.

46. Clearly, certain rights can be denied to irrational human beings. The assumption here is that it would be unacceptable, for instance, to experiment on mentally incapacitated human beings. Or, using the terminology of rights, mentally incapacitated humans have a right to life and a right to be free from unwarranted cruelty and suffering, although they may not have the right to vote.

47. As Professor Christine Di Stefano noted in discussing this point with me, the claims of absurdity targeted against the notion of animal rights are not unlike the claims of absurdity that were made in response to the Equal Rights Amendment (for example, comments that men and women would be forced to share public restrooms).

48. Perusal of philosophical and movement literature on animal rights clearly indicates this type of reaffirmation. See Singer 1975; Regan 1983; and Spiegel 1988. In addition, my interviews with animal advocates revealed their connections with other progressive social causes, including human rights, civil rights, women's rights, and gay and lesbian rights. Of course, this is not to say that all animal advocates "love" all humans. It is simply to say that to be an animal lover is not the equivalent of being a human hater.

49. An expansion of rights to fetuses would not necessarily require a denial of a woman's right to an abortion. It would require some kind of balancing between the fetus's right to be free from unwarranted suffering and the woman's right to control her body, but it is not clear what the resulting balance would be.

Chapter 3

1. In discussing the employment of rights language in movement literature we must keep in mind the distinction between the animal rights and animal

welfare movements. The animal welfare movement makes little use of rights terminology given its focus on welfare and compassion. Recently, deployment of rights language has increased in welfare organizations such as the ASPCA. However, the split between animal welfare and animal rights remains, and it is within the latter camp that rights language prevails. It is this camp that makes the public call for "animal rights." At marches, protests, news conferences, seminars, and information booths, slogans demand an extension of rights to animals. In newsletters, magazines, pamphlets, and editorials the rights of animals are asserted, demanded, and justified.

2. *PAWS News* and *PAWS Action* are newsletters distributed by the Progressive Animal Welfare Society. The former is the general newsletter of the Seattle-based organization. The latter is a more specific newsletter focused on activism. *PETA News* is published by People for the Ethical Treatment of Animals. I chose these examples for extensive content analysis for the following reasons. PAWS is a rights-oriented welfare society. The group runs an animal shelter and was founded as a humane organization with a focus on domestic animals. However, the group has crossed the divide between welfare and rights, as demonstrated in its reference to itself as a "progressive" welfare society. The organization espouses vegetarianism, abolition of animal exploitation, and animal rights. I have chosen PETA because it is the fastest growing and best-known animal rights organization in the country. Finally, I selected *Animals' Agenda*, one of the few magazines that focuses exclusively on animal protection issues. Although the magazine is associated with an animal rights group—Animal Rights Network—the magazine is not a newsletter and can be purchased by subscription. For further discussion of my approach to content analysis, see appendix A.

3. These pamphlets and circulars cover a host of topics, including animal experimentation, dissection, fur production, animals in entertainment, and animals in food production.

4. Numbers were taken from the following randomly selected issues of *PETA News:* May/June 1990, September/October 1989, July/August 1989, Winter 1987, and Winter 1986. Two issues (May/June 1990 and September/October 1989) included a pull-out section called PETA Kids. The total number of pages in these 5 issues (including the PETA Kids sections) is 101 (for an average of approximately 20 pages each).

5. Numbers were taken from the following 5 randomly selected issues of *PAWS News:* April 1991, February 1989, December 1988, October 1987, and May 1987. The total number of pages for these 5 issues is 160 (for an average of approximately 32 pages each). Numbers were also drawn from the following 5 randomly selected issues of *PAWS Action:* May 1991, February 1991, December 1990, November 1990, and October 1990. Each issue of *Paws Action* is 8 pages in length.

6. Numbers were taken from the following 5 randomly selected issues of *Animals' Agenda:* March 1992, July/August 1991, March 1991, January/February 1991, and September 1990. The total number of pages for these 5 issues is 302 (for an average of approximately 60 pages each).

7. The first three articles come respectively from the following issues of

Animals' Agenda: January/February 1992, October 1991, and December 1989. The latter three come from the following issues of *PAWS News:* October 1987, September 1989, and December 1990.

8. Examples include *Animal Rights: What's It All About?* (Trans-Species Unlimited), *The Argument for Abolition* (International Society for Animal Rights), and *A Change of Heart: Former Defender of Animal Research Reconsiders His Positions* (NAVS).

9. As one PAWS pamphlet suggests, "Most people believe that humans have certain innate rights, regardless of their intelligence, skin color, attractiveness, or sex. We agree that it's wrong to hurt people, to kill them, or to use them against their wishes. The concept of animal rights is much the same; in the areas relevant to them (such as pain, fear, life and death, and freedom of movement), animals' rights should be respected. Animal rights is based on ethics not emotion; but it's hard to examine animal rights issues without becoming emotional" (*Animal Rights: Speak for Them*). The pamphlet then goes on to describe animal abuse in ways that appeal to both reason and emotion.

10. Pamphlet advertising the PETA 101 Seminar.

11. The seminar workbook mentions rights on page 5, in an outline entitled "How to Answer Common Questions." Within the outline, the workbook advises students to "learn the arguments," including the "ethical basis of animal rights." Aside from that note, the workbook mentions animal rights only in recommending Regan's work.

12. This increase becomes clear when one looks at newspaper and magazine reporting on the issue over the past decade.

13. This is not to say that overall the media have been respectful to animal concerns. Indeed, from the perspective of an animal rights activist, the media are generally insensitive to animal issues. Although the media demonstrate increasing respect when directly covering animal rights concerns, news reports on such topics as the fur industry, meat production, and fishing often lack any mention of opposition by animal rights activists.

14. According to Caras, "animals have the right not to have pain, fear or physical deprivation inflicted upon them by us. Even if they are on the way to the slaughterhouse, animals have the right to food and water and shelter if it is needed. They have the right not to be brutalized in any way as food resources, for entertainment or any other purpose" (1988, 57).

15. My interviews demonstrate that most activists are familiar with the works of the major philosophical thinkers who have written about animals. In addition, movement literature frequently cites philosophical works.

16. Activists and movement supporters often point to philosophical works as contributors to their own views and activities within the movement.

Chapter 4

1. Although Scheingold elaborated the notion of the myth of rights, which is related to the false consciousness view elaborated within CLS, Scheingold himself is not within CLS.

2. The explicit suggestion of false consciousness is most apparent within CLS (see, for instance, Gabel and Kennedy 1984; and Tushnet 1984).

3. The discussion of the debate is by no means a comprehensive analysis of the critique of rights. In addition to the points addressed above, there are other broad critiques of right-based theories. For an excellent exploration and response to these critiques, see Waldron 1987.

4. See appendix A.

5. Of course, deploying animal rights also provides further evidence for the ubiquity of rights language in this culture.

6. Another activist stated: "If we assign rights to this type of life, then there's a carryover on some philosophical reasons on why we assigned those to humans or to upper-level mammals, or whatever. The reason we assign that right, say, a right to be [free] from pain, . . . [is] because we don't believe that violence is a proper outlet; if we don't believe that causing pain is right, then it's very difficult to say that that applies only to one form of life. Philosophically, and in many ways scientifically, those same concepts we apply to humans apply to other life forms."

7. Along the same lines, another advocate stated: "If someone's going to say that women have rights or humans have rights, then I don't think it's problematic at all to say that animals have rights. As long as we're already using that word and we accept it for one group or two groups or ten groups, then I don't see why we can't use it for twelve or thirteen groups."

8. This activist stated: "If a great proportion of the public accepts a phrase, you start feeling more comfortable using it."

9. This point is supported by analysis of media coverage (see chapter 3).

10. See Milner (1989, 643) for a review of scholarship that stresses the persistence of rights talk.

11. Although, for analytical purposes, I have separated the popularity and acceptance of rights language from rights as persuasive and rousing language, these categories are clearly connected.

12. In making this point, the activist went on to say that the same thing happened when rights were extended to women.

13. Likewise, another advocate stated that "you will hear things like 'you're saying animals have a right to vote. How silly.'"

14. In the spring of 1990, FAR was considering changing its name in order to move away from the notion of rights. However, the group decided to keep its original name despite its concerns over the dualistic and patriarchal aspects of rights (see *Feminists for Animal Rights*, Winter-Spring 1990).

15. This point will be elaborated in detail in the following chapters.

16. Others who believe that rights talk is incompatible with communitarian goals recommend a bold move away from it (see Gabel 1984; and Tushnet 1984). Although Glendon speaks of refining rights talk, the impression she leaves is that we should make a serious move away from what she refers to as an impoverished discourse.

17. In addition to this critique of rights language, there is a common critique of the practical deployment of rights in the legal system. According to this critique, both the legal process and the use of rights in the process are individualizing. Most often, legal claims are advanced on an individual basis, and

rewards are distributed individually. As a result, the legal process transforms social battles into individual battles over rights and thereby reinforces individualism (see McCann 1986; and Scheingold 1989). I will take up this issue in the following two chapters on rights in litigation.

18. Indeed, animal experimentation may be the thorniest issue the animal rights movement confronts.

19. This is related to the indeterminacy of rights.

20. This is true despite the experimentation on Jews conducted by the Nazis during World War II and experimentation conducted on blacks with syphilis in this country. In these experiments, blacks and Jews were viewed as less than human.

21. We might be able to advance a hypothetical case in which this absoluteness is problematic. For instance, if an epidemic were in the process of wiping out an entire population, people might reconsider the absoluteness of the experimentation issue. But this, again, harkens back to the first point: absoluteness, even when desirable, is not completely and under all circumstances absolute.

22. Indeed, it is the importance of such close-to-absolute rights that demonstrates the flaws of utilitarianism.

23. Letters to the Editor, *New York*, January 29, 1990. Indeed 25 percent of the published letters (seven out of twenty-seven) that could be considered profur made explicit counterrights claims, generally in the form of the right to choose. This seems a significant percentage considering that many of the letters that did not refer to rights were from furriers claiming fur is raised and trapped humanely.

24. Another potential problem with liberation is that it may be associated with the pejorative connotations of "women's lib." However, I have not come across this connection in my investigations.

25. See chapter 2.

26. As Delgado asserts, the existence of specific rights may "give pause to those who would otherwise oppress us" (1987, 305).

27. The works of John Stuart Mill are significant in their emphasis of the common good. In addition, the writings of Thomas Jefferson, James Madison, and Thomas Paine stress concern for the community. Even the work of Adam Smith recognizes the need to provide for the public good.

28. In a sense, this argument draws upon Glendon's 1987 work, *Abortion and Divorce in Western Law*, which looks to the European continent's tradition of Rousseau to counter the hyperindividualism of America's Lockean tradition. However, Glendon is much more pessimistic than I am about the possibility of infusing rights with alternative values.

Chapter 5

1. For an overview of the history of law protecting animals, see Ryder 1979. According to Ryder, a 1635 law passed in Ireland that prohibited pulling wool off sheep and attaching ploughs to horses' tails contained probably the

earliest legal reference to the concept of cruelty to animals in the English language.

2. There are many exclusions within the AWA. For example, mice and rats, which constitute the overwhelming majority of research animals, are excluded from the AWA. Moreover, even for those protected animals, the act only provides minimal regulations and leaves researchers free to perform painful experiments.

3. Zak explains that, although reliable statistics are not available, "Dr. Randall Lockwood of the Humane Society of the United States, in Washington, D.C., estimates that a typical major city records 5,000 animal abuse complaints a year out of which 10 to 20 result in prosecutions. Of those, less than 10 percent result in jail terms of 10 to 30 days" (1990, 6).

4. These include, for instance, the civil rights and women's rights movements.

5. Sarat and Kearns describe the constitutive perspective: "Because law is constitutive of the very forms that social relations and practices take, it is embedded in them, so much so that it is virtually invisible to those involved. This invisibility, this taken-for-grantedness, makes legality and legal forms extremely powerful" (1993, 51). It should be noted that Sarat and Kearns are critical of the constitutive perspective.

6. This dimension is particularly apparent in analyses of the Supreme Court that stress the various paths of access and the numerous barriers to entry (see Baum 1989; and Spaeth 1979).

7. Zemans does add the qualification that this access is not equally distributed (693).

8. Burstein's analysis of successful mobilization and winning in court is strongly tied to another component for analyzing litigation: implementation. Burstein's work focuses on using litigation to implement existing law. His work thus exemplifies two of the components for assessing litigation.

9. Unlike what Chayes (1976) calls traditional litigation, policy litigation by public law litigants is future-oriented and concerned with establishing broad policies. Baum (1989) makes a similar distinction between ordinary litigation, which is brought by people who have a direct personal goal they wish to achieve through the courts and political litigation, the goal of which is to advance policy (75). See also Tushnet 1987.

10. Tushnet's work (1987) is a prime example of such an analysis.

11. Johnson and Canon (1984) provide a model of implementation and impact that divides the constituents into five categories: the decision maker, the interpreting population, the implementing population, the consumer population, and the secondary population.

12. Although their works cannot be classified as impact studies, their assessments of implementation and impact are relevant and important.

13. Increasingly, the terms of the debate are being challenged (see, for instance, McCann 1994).

14. The most difficult part of this assessment involves analysis of judicial implementation. A few qualifications are appropriate in this regard. The analy-

sis that follows should not be taken to be an impact study. That would likely require a book in itself. Moreover, it is still too early to assess the overall impact of animal rights litigation. Thus, my comments on implementation are, for now, largely speculative. Nevertheless, the importance of implementation leads me to include the forthcoming interesting, albeit speculative, comments on impact.

15. I do not include in this discussion the history of litigation involving animals that took place during the medieval era. This history is strange and unusual given that litigation frequently involved bringing animals to trial as both defendants and witnesses! "According to the archives of the French criminal courts, pigs in particular seem to have suffered severely at the hands of the law," but stories tell of trials involving "ants, asses, bloodsuckers, bulls, cockchafers, cocks, cows, eels, dolphins, goats, moles, serpents, sheep, wolves, [and] worms . . ." (Carson 1972, 29–30). Frequently counsel was appointed to defend accused animals, and convicted animals often met their fate by public execution. And we consider ours a litigious society!

16. Handler (1978) refers to these secondary legal struggles as "clearing the underbrush," using litigation to "change legal rules that impede mobilization" (210).

17. For an overview of standing regulations, see Orren 1976 and Stewart 1975.

18. Most states have anticruelty statutes that prohibit the infliction of unnecessary or unjustified pain on animals. For instance, the Michigan anticruelty statute reads: "Whoever overdrives, overloads, drives when overloaded, overworks, tortures, torments, deprives of necessary sustenance, cruelly beats, mutilates, or cruelly kills, or causes or procures to be so overdriven, overloaded, driven when overloaded, overworked, tormented, deprived of necessary sustenance, cruelly beaten, mutilated, or cruelly killed, any animal, and whoever having the charge or custody of any animal, either as owner or otherwise, inflicts unnecessary cruelty upon the same, or willfully fails to provide the same with proper food, drink, shelter, or protection from the weather, is guilty of a misdemeanor . . ." (*Mich. Comp. Law Ann.* [1974] sec. 752.21). In several states such things as scientific research and hunting are exempted from anticruelty provisions. For an overview of state anticruelty statutes, see Moretti (1984).

19. In some states, local humane societies have been granted such enforcement power (see Thomas 1986).

20. In *Salorio v. Glaser* (82 N.J. 482 [1980]), the court held that each state court "remains free to fashion its own law of standing consistent with notions of substantial justice" (491).

21. For instance, in an interview with an animal rights attorney published in *Animals' Agenda*, the issue of standing is raised and discussed at some length (Bring 1991). Likewise, the March 1992 issue of *Animals' Agenda* devoted a page-length article to the topic, written by attorney Steven Wise, president of the Animal Legal Defense Fund. In all of my interviews with attorneys, the standing issue arose.

22. In particular, the federal courts appear to show a greater willingness than the state courts do. This is somewhat surprising given the number of Reagan appointees on the federal bench.

23. This depicts one important indirect effect of litigation: the effect of mobilizing other movements (see chapter 6).

24. Although this case did not involve animals, the logic of granting standing to nonhuman entities is easily extended to animals.

25. The article was rushed into print so that the justices could read it before rendering their decision in the case. This haste turned out to be effective, as evidenced by Douglas's citing of the article in his opinion.

26. Stone also points out the irony connected to the fact that "a decade before Soweto erupted the U.S. courts had shown themselves ready to interpose in South Africa's mistreatment of its *seals*" (1987, 8).

27. This case resulted in a mixed win in court. HSUS won on the issue of standing but lost the case on its merits.

28. Prior to the ruling, the USDA had excluded mice, rats, and birds from its definition of animals. The court, in response to the suit, stated, "The defendants' failure to pursue the humane care and treatment of birds, rats and mice . . . allows the mistreatment of birds, rats and mice to continue unchecked by the agency charged with the protection of laboratory animals. The Court cannot believe that this is what Congress had in mind" (*Animals' Agenda*, March 1992, 33–34).

29. This decision was reported by U.S. Newswire Service, December 28, 1994, in an article ironically entitled "Humane Society Declares 1994 an Excellent Year for Animals."

30. It is not clear whether the liberalized judicial opinions on standing have influenced legislators in their decisions to pass these types of laws.

31. In addition to these three successes, we shall see in chapter 6 how standing cases foster additional indirect effects that advance movement goals. We shall also see in chapter 7 how standing cases, in strict legal terms, seem to reinforce the values of individualism and animal welfare rather than animal rights. But these same cases can be reconstructed in ways that challenge individualism and promote the values of animal rights.

32. These suits are brought by both animal advocacy groups and state law enforcement agencies.

33. This case also involved important indirect successes, which will be explored at length in chapter 6.

34. Most advocacy groups with the legislative authority to sue are welfare organizations that are closely associated with city and state governments. It has been suggested by some—including one of the activists I interviewed—that this close connection led to the co-optation of the animal advocacy movement during most of the twentieth century.

35. See also Fuller (1964), who distinguishes between the morality of duty and the morality of aspiration. He contends that law is most useful in the realm of duty, commanding what people should not do. Law is less useful for promoting positive ideals of what people should do.

36. In a related suit, Citizens to End Animal Suffering and Exploitation won a settlement out of court with the New England Aquarium providing that the "surplus" dolphin Rainbow would not be handed over to the navy (*Animals' Agenda*, January/February 1991, 33).

37. On the other hand, the indirect effects of litigation, even when directly effective for only a short time, are important to consider, as we will see shortly.

38. In response to the case, numerous indirect effects were created. For instance, the state passed a law allowing students to be excused from dissections on the basis of religious or moral beliefs. In addition, this case prompted other high school cases that have been successful. For further discussion, see chapter 6.

39. Represented by attorney Gary Francione, the suit was brought by Jennifer Kissinger in November 1990. The university's new policy was established in May 1991.

40. See chapter 6.

41. Similar impacts are likely to be felt around the country as more and more cases open up ACC meetings.

42. Opponents also employ this tool against the animal rights movement.

43. However, the aquarium did agree not to catch a third whale. Moreover, the lawsuit was initiated largely as a last resort, only after protests, letter writing, and a media campaign failed to stop the capture.

44. Unfortunately data are unavailable regarding the percentage of cases that have led to favorable judicial decisions, precedents, and implementation.

45. On the other hand, some scholars note that "Lawsuits are especially attractive instruments for groups whose small size, lack of prestige, and limited cash limit their influence in other political forums" (Murphy and Pritchett 1986, 186).

46. This number has, in all likelihood, increased since 1990.

47. For instance, the Physicians Committee for Responsible Medicine, headed by Neal D. Barnard, M.D., is supported by 2,000 doctors.

48. As secretary of health and human services, Louis Sullivan forcefully came out against the animal rights community. Just prior to the 1990 March for the Animals, Sullivan publicly denounced animal rights activists as "terrorists" (Gladwell 1990, 4).

49. The Fourth Amendment states that "The right of the people to be secure in their persons, houses, papers, and effects, against unreasonable searches and seizures, shall not be violated, and no Warrants shall issue, but upon probable cause." The Commerce Clause—Article I, section 8—gives Congress the power to regulate commerce among the states. Legal precedent regarding commerce holds that states may regulate commerce as long as such regulations do not conflict with federal commerce laws.

50. For example, see *Mass. Gen. Laws Ann.*, chap. 140, sec. 174D (*West Supp.*, 1988).

51. Garvin does argue, however, that despite these limitations activists can be more successful if they focus on the federal level where fewer impediments exist. He also suggests that "though the local and state laws may prove either

unconstitutional or relatively harmless to researchers, they may help bring the public behind more damaging federal measures. In the long run, researchers cannot rely upon constitutional arguments to protect their present rights to perform humane animal research" (1988, 388).

52. For example, Legislation in Support of Animals brought suit against the city of New Orleans in response to its failure to fund animal pickup services. The intent of the suit was to promote the positive goal of funding a program beneficial to animals (*Animals' Agenda,* November 1991, 32).

53. Certainly the civil rights movement exemplifies the importance of First Amendment claims. More recently, the pro-life movement has turned to First Amendment claims in its attempts to continue protesting at abortion clinics.

Chapter 6

1. See also Scheingold (1974) and Handler, who states with regard to indirect effects that "indeed, they may be the most important part of all" (1978, 210).

2. While many scholars recognize the significance of secondary effects, McCann (1994), Olson (1984), and Handler (1978) are among the few who explore such outcomes systematically.

3. Although Scheingold does hold out the hope that rights litigation may foster mobilization, he notes that "Legal tactics do not by any means assure political mobilization" (1974, 209).

4. Given that negotiation involves compromise, Olson points to the suggestion that disputes involving tangible goods are more likely to be negotiated than those involving intangible, symbolic goods.

5. The evidence I use (1) draws on content analysis of newspapers and magazines; (2) investigates particular legal cases and their outcomes as displayed in judicial opinions, law review articles, and news coverage; (3) explores the literature and political activities of animal advocacy groups; and (4) examines the perspectives of activists on the topic of litigation. Any of these alone would not provide sufficient documentation for evaluating litigation. But taken together they provide a solid body of evidence from which we can speculate, with a good degree of confidence, about the indirect effects of the litigative process.

6. Alex Pacheco, speech delivered at the March for the Animals, June 1990, Washington, D.C. Pacheco's statement about the letters to Mrs. Bush is corroborated by Carlson (1991).

7. This information was reported in a PETA pamphlet entitled *Silver Spring Monkeys: A PETA Casework Report.*

8. This was reported by Pacheco at the March for the Animals.

9. For instance, in his speech at the March for the Animals, Pacheco referred to the primates as "symbolic survivors."

10. Graham also refused to dissect the dead frogs provided by the school district, arguing that there was no conclusive evidence that the frogs had died of natural causes (Wells 1989).

11. For instance, PETA published a pamphlet entitled *Dissection: Your Right to Refuse*, in which the notion is expressed that students have the right to speak out against dissection in general and to refuse to participate in classroom dissection.

12. The PETA pamphlet *Dissection: Your Right to Refuse* notes: "If you need legal assistance, we'll help."

13. PETA shows this videotape at other types of events, including "Animal Rights 101," a seminar for activists.

14. For instance, in *Objecting to Dissection*, there is continual reference to "student rights" and to judicial protection of these rights. In the pamphlet *Dissection: Your Right to Refuse*, reference is made to the student's "constitutional right to speak."

15. This statement was made by Tim Greyhavens, executive director of PAWS during an interview.

16. For instance, Gary Francione's article in *Animals' Agenda* recommends legal action that challenges ACCs (September 1990, 44).

17. It is not clear what led to NIH denial of funding, nor will it ever be, given the fact that if animal rights activitism had led to such denial NIH would never admit it. Regardless, because of the publicity surrounding this case and its association with activism, the impression remains that PAWS was at least partially responsible for the denial of funding.

18. In *Animals' Agenda*, one article suggests that opening up ACCs represents a victory for "both animals and civil liberties." The article also notes the secrecy associated with university-sponsored research: "As well as hiding their paperwork, some labs are hiding" (May 1989, 23).

19. For instance, attorney Joyce Tischler states: "We've begun to organize attorneys and develop materials to advise animal activists about the [libel] lawsuits. We want them to know what slander and libel are so that they can protect themselves while working effectively" (quoted in Bring 1991, 42).

20. Several articles in *Animals' Agenda* have publicized the libel issue. (See, for example, *Animals' Agenda*, December 1989, 33; Clifton 1988, 20; and *Animals' Agenda*, May 1989, 23).

21. It is important in this type of libel suit that the suit be "successful," meaning a win in court or a favorable settlement. The loss of a libel suit brought by activists generally does not create legitimacy nor does it delegitimize the opposition.

22. SLAPP stands for strategic litigation against public participation.

23. For instance, columnist Anthony Lewis wrote that the Immuno lawsuit against animal advocates is his "candidate for the prize in outrageousness" in a country that "offers numerous examples of vexatious litigation" (1991, 31).

24. Of course, this is a very costly way of defending the movement's credibility, and it may, in many instances, be too costly.

25. See chapter 5.

26. See chapter 5.

27. As one advocate suggested during an interview, the inability to get into court with the goal of defending animals is frustrating; with greater ability to obtain standing, the frustration dissipates.

Chapter 7

1. It is important to take note of a curious twist associated with examining animal rights activists as they are constituted by animal rights litigation. The twist results from the fact that the legal subjects being constituted are not only the activists but also the animals. Of course, animals do not conceive of themselves in legal terms and strictly speaking are not legal subjects. In contrast, activists do perceive of themselves as legal subjects. Moreover, their turn to litigation on behalf of animals seeks to include animals as legal entities. In effect, then, animals are being treated as legal subjects given voice and subjectivity by animal rights activists. Given this twist, the following discussion will explore litigation as it constructs both human and nonhuman subjects.

2. The activists interviewed during the course of this study represent a wide range of organizations, each employing a different mix of strategies. Some focus almost exclusively on litigation (Legal Action for Animals), others rarely become actively involved in the process (Institute for the Defense of the Earth and Animals, FAR), and still others employ litigation on a somewhat regular basis (PETA, PAWS, Fund for Animals). Despite this varying frequency, almost all the activists I spoke with had a solid understanding of litigation and held surprisingly similar views on the subject.

3. In the interviews several activists specifically addressed this point.

4. At this point it is important to stress that, although the attorneys working on behalf of animals recognize the importance of indirect benefits of litigation, their decisions on whether to bring a case must be based on the belief that there is some potential to win. Each of the lawyers with whom I spoke stressed this issue, which concerns Rule 11 of the code of legal ethics. According to Rule 11, lawyers may face sanctions for bringing frivolous lawsuits. Thus, while attorney-activist Steve Ann Chambers appreciates the importance of publicity, she notes: "I have a real responsibility not to just go out to get publicity. I have to believe that I have a good case that should win."

5. Although mention of lawsuits was not frequent at this march, a few activists spoke of litigation. For example, Alex Pacheco stated that a lawsuit filed against the National Institutes of Health "is showing that NIH has deliberately fabricated an experiment in an effort to justify killing . . . primates."

6. Stretching the law is related to, but broader than, educating judges. Stretching the law suggests not only that judges become educated and accustomed to new ideas and discourses but that they act upon these new ideas.

7. Attorney Gene Underwood, in an interview, noted the incremental nature of the process. Likewise, attorney Joyce Tischler stated: "Elevating the status of animals from property to person will be a step-by-step process involving litigation, legislation, and public education" (quoted in Bring 1991, 43).

8. This is dealt with in the discussion of counterrights claims in chapter 4.

9. For instance, we might explore how the animal rights experiences are influencing the environmental movement.

10. The overall point of recognizing effects on other movements cannot be fully elaborated here since we lack evidence at present that demonstrates

whether the animal rights movement's litigation will affect other social movements. This is, however, an area for future study. This type of study would
involve comparative analysis of social movement activity to discover the extent
to which the movement's litigative activities have affected other movements.

11. One notable exception to this was offered by John Kullberg, who suggested that litigation costs are not a serious problem if one can find pro bono
help, willing lawyers, and groups to join as plaintiffs. Kullberg noted that this
kind of assistance is increasingly becoming the norm.

12. A case involving a Fund for Animals suit seeking to stop the planned
shooting of bison in Yellowstone National Park demonstrates this type of inte-
gration. After the U.S. District Court granted the fund a hearing and a tempo-
rary restraining order, thereby delaying the shoot, the National Park Service
agreed to cancel it. According to one report: "Park spokeswoman Joan
Anzelmo said because of the court action and Monday's public opening of the
park, officials decided they had missed their best opportunity to kill pregnant
bison." According to the fund, this agreement prompted the organization to
dismiss its lawsuit (*Seattle Post-Intelligencer*, April 12, 1991, 6).

13. To the extent that the public is more aware of politics than judicial rulings, this approach is likely to be successful.

14. To put it another way, am I falling prey to the myth of rights?

15. The first statement was made in the ALDF pamphlet *Objecting to Dissection* (3). The second was made in an ALDF mailing. Emphasis in the original.

Chapter 8

1. A handful of scholars responding to Critical Legal Studies address the
flexibility of legal language (see McCann 1994; and Minow 1990).

2. For a discussion of Locke's influence on American culture, see Hartz
1955.

3. Glendon is not guilty of this. She spends much time distinguishing Lockean and Rousseauian values. However, she does distinguish the American
understanding of rights from the use of rights on the European continent. In
doing so, she implies that individualism within the American understanding of
rights is pervasive and extremely problematic.

4. In its early phase, the animal welfare movement did contribute to the
advancement of child protection. Indeed, one of the first child cruelty cases in
this country was prosecuted on the premise that animals deserve protection. In
this case the judge invoked an animal protection law, given the lack of child
protection laws. In the decision, the judge drew upon the testimony of Henry
Bergh, founder of the ASPCA. Bergh argued: "The child is an animal. If there is
not justice for it as a human being, it shall at least have the rights of the dog in
the street." The judge found that the child was certainly an animal and therefore deserved at least the same protection as animals (Clifton 1991, 42).

5. The earliest versions of the civil rights and women's rights movements
did not really challenge these individualistic assumptions. Rather, they sought
simply to apply existing rights to blacks and women. However, over time,

these movements, like the animal rights movement, began to challenge the individualistic underpinnings of rights (see Schneider 1986; and Minow 1990).

6. They are also especially significant for animal rights. The problem of moral agency is particularly critical for animals because—unlike children, for instance—they will never become moral agents. In addition, children can gain standing even though they might be represented by a legal guardian. Thus, while the problems are unique to movements that work on behalf of those who cannot defend themselves, the problems are especially critical for animal rights.

7. Milner (1989) reviews various recent attempts by legal scholars to "salvage" rights.

8. A more apt metaphor might be the chisel that chips away at the foundations of a building in the hopes of eventually eroding it. Of course, the chisel does not work alone; rocks are being thrown at the building, some are submitting plans for renovating the building, and others are trying to have the building condemned.

Appendix A

1. I later transcribed these speeches.

2. The one exception was a lawyer who was brought in during an interview at the initiative of the activist I was interviewing. The occasion then became a double interview. The participant, self-described as a nonactivist, was a staff attorney working for the animal advocacy group.

3. One noticeable exclusion from the organization list is the Animal Liberation Front (ALF), an underground animal rights group that employs illegal tactics to advance its goals. I chose not to seek out anyone from ALF due to the difficulty in obtaining interviews with these activists.

4. The first five of these organizations are national in scope. The latter are local. Of the first five, FAR might be better classified as a smaller, more local organization. Although growing in size and scope, it is the smallest and least known of the first five groups listed here. However, I place it with the other "national" organizations because it has branches in several parts of the country and is seeking to expand its base.

5. One of the five attorneys did not classify himself as an animal advocate (see note 2).

6. Shortage of time became an issue when I was conducting interviews in the Northeast and the Bay area for brief periods.

7. These situations occurred when I was visiting the Northeast and the Bay area for brief periods of time.

8. Both activists stated that they were too busy to do an interview. One had just given birth and the other referred me to another activist within his organization.

9. Three of the four double interviews were conducted at the interviewee's own initiative. That is, when I arrived at the interview location, the person I had contacted thought I would be interested in speaking with another person as

well. The other double interview was conducted at the convenience of the participants.

10. This point, I felt, was important because when I first made phone contact with one activist he asked if I was being sponsored by the opposition and told me that there had been previous attempts to send someone posing as a reporter to obtain information regarding movement activity. As it turned out, most activists were not concerned about my association. Several said that, even if I was with the opposition, they would speak with me because they had nothing to hide. Only one activist was openly distrustful and reluctant to speak with me. However, even he provided me with an interview. In general, the activists were forthcoming, open, and extremely cooperative.

11. These were the same activists who did not want the interview recorded.

12. Lane calls this a "discursive" form of interviewing, which allows participants to follow their own trains of thought. One advantage of this approach, according to Lane, is that it offers "insight into the connotative meanings of words and phrases" (1962, 9).

13. Clarification questions took the form: "Can you elaborate a bit?" or "What do you mean by . . . ?"

References

Abel, Richard L. 1981. "Conservative Conflict and the Reproduction of Capitalism: The Role of Informal Justice." *International Journal of the Sociology of Law* 9:245.

———, ed. 1982. *The Politics of Informal Justice.* 2 vols. New York: Academic.

Abraham, Henry J. 1974. *Justices and Presidents: A Political History of Appointments to the Supreme Court.* New York: Oxford University Press.

Adams, Carol J. 1990. *The Sexual Politics of Meat: A Feminist-Vegetarian Critical Theory.* New York: Continuum.

Anderson, Cerisse. 1990. "Animal Research Data Ordered Released." *New York Law Journal,* May 18, 1.

Appleby, Joyce. 1987. "The American Heritage: The Heirs and the Disinherited." *Journal of American History* 74:798.

Aquinas, Saint Thomas. 1928. *The Summa Contra Gentiles of Saint Thomas Aquinas.* The Third Book. London: Burns, Oates and Washbourne LTD.

———. 1964. *Summa Theologica.* Part II. Cambridge: Blackfriars in conjunction with McGraw-Hill.

Aristotle. 1958. *The Politics of Aristotle.* ed. Ernest Barker. Oxford: Oxford University Press.

ASPCA. 1988–89. *ASPCA Quarterly Report,* Winter 1988–Spring 1989.

———. 1990. *The Animal Rights Handbook: Everyday Ways to Save Animal Lives.* Los Angeles: Living Planet.

Augustine, Saint. [1467] 1981. *The City of God,* ed. David Knowles. Middlesex: Penguin.

Baker, Ron. 1986. "News Shorts." *Animals' Agenda* (December): 28.

Bartholomew, Amy, and Alan Hunt. 1990. "What's Wrong with Rights?" *Law and Inequality* 9:501.

Bartlett, Kim. 1991. "Survey Shows Movement Promise." *Animals' Agenda* (March): 2.

Baum, Lawrence. 1989. *The Supreme Court.* 3d ed. Washington, D.C.: Congressional Quarterly Press.

Bell, Derrick. 1985. "Forward: The Civil Rights Chronicles." *Harvard Law Review* 99:4.

Benney, Norma. 1983. "All of One Flesh: The Rights of Animals." In *Reclaim the Earth: Women Speak Out for Life on Earth,* ed. Leonie Caldecott and Stephanie Leland. London: Women's Press.

Bentham, Jeremy. 1879. *An Introduction to the Principles of Morals and Legislation.* Oxford: Clarendon.

———. 1962. "Anarchical Fallacies: Being an Examination of the Declaration of Rights Issued During the French Revolution." In *The Works of Jeremy Bentham,* ed. John Bowring. New York: Russell and Russell.

Berger, Raoul. 1977. *Government by Judiciary: The Transformation of the Fourteenth Amendment.* Cambridge: Harvard University Press.

Bishop, Katherine. 1989. "From Shop to Lab to Farm, Animal Rights Battle Is Felt." *New York Times,* January 14, sec. A, p. 1.

Black, Donald. 1973. "The Mobilization of Law." *Journal of Legal Studies* 2:125.

Bork, Robert H. 1986. "The Constitution, Original Intent, and Economic Rights." *San Diego Law Review* 23:823.

Brest, Paul. 1982. "Interpretation and Interest." *Stanford Law Review* 34:765.

Brigham, John. 1987. "Right, Rage, and Remedy: Forms of Law in Political Discourse." *Studies in American Political Development* 2:303.

———. 1990. "Bad Attitudes: The Consequences of Survey Research for Constitutional Practice." *Review of Politics* 52:582.

Bring, Ellen. 1991. "Joyce Tischler: Legal Activist." *Animals' Agenda* (July/August): 40.

Brophy, Brigid. 1972. "In Pursuit of a Fantasy." In *Animals, Men and Morals: An Enquiry into the Maltreatment of Non-humans,* ed. Stanley Godlovitch, Roslind Godlovitch, and John Harris. New York: Taplinger.

———. 1979. "The Darwinist's Dilemma." In *Animals' Rights—A Symposium,* ed. David Paterson and Richard D. Ryder. London: Centaur.

Brown, Don W., and Robert V. Stover. 1989. "Compliance with Court Directives: A Utility Approach." In *American Court Systems: Readings in Judicial Process and Behavior,* ed. Sheldon Goldman and Austin Sarat. 2d ed. New York: Longman.

Brumbaugh, Robert S. 1978. "Of Man, Animals, and Morals: A Brief History." In *On the Fifth Day: Animal Rights and Human Ethics,* ed. Richard Knowles Morris and Michael W. Fox. Washington, D.C.: Acropolis.

Bruun, Rita. 1982. "The Boldt Decision: Legal Victory, Political Defeat." *Law and Policy* 4:271.

Bullock, Charles S., and Charles M. Lamb. 1982. "Toward a Theory of Civil Rights Implementation." *Policy Perspectives* 2:376.

Bumiller, Kristin. 1987. "Victims in the Shadow of the Law: A Critique of the Model of Legal Protection." *Signs* 12:421.

———. 1988. *The Civil Rights Society: The Social Construction of Victims.* Baltimore: Johns Hopkins University Press.

Burstein, Paul. 1991. "Legal Mobilization as a Social Movement Tactic: The Struggle for Equal Employment Opportunity." *American Journal of Sociology* 96:1201.

Burstein, Paul, and Kathleen Monaghan. 1986. "Equal Employment Opportunity and the Mobilization of the Law." *Law and Society Review* 20:355.

Campbell, Tom. 1983. *The Left and Rights: A Conceptual Analysis of the Idea of Socialist Rights.* London: Routledge and Kegan Paul.

Caras, Roger. 1988. "We Must Find Alternatives to Animals in Research." *Newsweek*, December 26, 57.

Carlsen, Spence. 1987. "Animals Are Victims of Vast Human-Regulated System of Slavery." *Los Angeles Times*, April 22, sec. 2, p. 5.

Carlson, Peter. 1991. "The Great Silver Spring Monkey Debate." *Washington Post*, February 24, sec. W, p. 15.

Carp, Robert A., and Ronald Stidham. 1990. *Judicial Process in America*. Washington, D.C.: Congressional Quarterly.

Carson, Gerald. 1972. *Men, Beasts, and Gods: A History of Cruelty and Kindness to Animals*. New York: Charles Scribner's Sons.

Casper, Jonathan D. 1976. "The Supreme Court and National Policy Making." *American Political Science Review* 70:50.

Chayes, Abram. 1976. "The Role of the Judge in Public Law Litigation." *Harvard Law Review* 89:1281.

Clarke, Paul, and Andrew Linzey, eds. 1990. *Political Theory and Animal Rights*. London: Pluto.

Clifton, Merritt. 1988. "A Fight for Freedom." *Animals' Agenda* (December): 20.

———. 1991. "Who Helps the Helpless Child?" *Animals' Agenda* (December): 42.

———. 1992. "Urban Wildlife: Reclaiming Their Birthright." *Animals' Agenda* (January/February): 12.

Collard, Andrée, with Joyce Contrucci. 1988. *Rape of the Wild: Man's Violence against Animals and the Earth*. London: Women's Press.

Copelon, Rhonda. 1989. "Beyond the Liberal Idea of Privacy: Toward a Positive Right of Autonomy." In *Judging the Constitution: Critical Essays on Judicial Lawmaking*, ed. Michael W. McCann and Gerald L. Houseman. Glenview, Ill.: Scott, Foresman.

Cover, Robert M. 1986. "Violence and the Word." *Yale Law Journal* 95:1601.

Crenshaw, Kimberle Williams. 1988. "Race, Reform, and Retrenchment: Transformation and Legitimation in Antidiscrimination Law." *Harvard Law Review* 101:1331.

Dalton, Clare. 1985. "An Essay in the Deconstruction of Contract Doctrine." *Yale Law Journal* 94:997.

Darwin, Charles. 1906. *The Descent of Man*. 2d ed. New York: Appleton.

Delgado, Richard. 1987. "The Ethereal Scholar: Does Critical Legal Studies Have What Minorities Want?" *Harvard Civil Rights–Civil Liberties Law Review* 22:301.

Delgado, Richard, Chris Dunn, Pamela Brown, Helena Lee, and David Hubbert. 1985. "Fairness and Formality: Minimizing the Risk of Prejudice in Alternative Dispute Resolution." *Wisconsin Law Review* (1985):1359.

Descartes, René. 1971. *Discourse on the Method*. In *Descartes: Philosophical Writings*, ed. Elizabeth Anscombe and Peter Thomas Geach. Indianapolis: Bobbs-Merrill.

Diamond, Irene, and Gloria Feman Orenstein, eds. 1990. *Reweaving the World: The Emergence of Ecofeminism*. San Francisco: Sierra Club.

Donovan, Josephine. 1990. "Animal Rights and Feminist Theory." *Signs* 15:350.

Doyle, Jim. 1990. "Judge Orders Navy to Stop Killing Squirrels." *San Francisco Chronicle,* October 6, sec. A, p. 9.

Dworkin, Ronald M. 1977. *Taking Rights Seriously.* Cambridge: Harvard University Press.

Engel, David M. 1984. "The Oven Bird's Song: Insiders, Outsiders, and Personal Injuries in an American Community." *Law and Society Review* 18:551.

Everson, David H., ed. 1968. *The Supreme Court as Policy-Maker: Three Studies on the Impact of Judicial Decisions.* Carbondale, Ill.: Public Affairs Research Bureau.

Feinberg, Joel. 1978. "Human Duties and Animal Rights." In *On the Fifth Day: Animal Rights and Human Ethics,* ed. Richard Knowles Morris and Michael W. Fox. Washington, D.C.: Acropolis.

Flathman, Richard E. 1976. *The Practice of Rights.* Cambridge: Cambridge University Press.

Fox, Michael W. 1979. "Animal Rights and Nature Liberation." In *Animals' Rights—A Symposium,* ed. David Paterson and Richard D. Ryder. London: Centaur.

———. 1980. *Returning to Eden: Animal Rights and Human Responsibility.* New York: Viking.

Francione, Gary. 1990. "The Importance of Access to Animal Care Committees: A Primer for Activists." *Animals' Agenda* (September): 44.

Frank, Jerome. 1930. *Law and the Modern Mind.* New York: Brentano's.

Freeman, Alan. 1982. "Antidiscrimination Law: A Critical Review." In *The Politics of Law: A Progressive Critique,* ed. David Kairys. New York: Pantheon.

Friedman, Lawrence M. 1985. *Total Justice.* Boston: Beacon.

Fuller, Lon L. 1964. *The Morality of Law.* New Haven: Yale University Press.

Gabel, Peter. 1982. "Reification and Legal Reasoning." In *Marxism and Law,* ed. Piers Beirne and Richard Quinney. New York: Wiley.

———. 1984. "A Critique of Rights: The Phenomenology of Rights-Consciousness and the Pact of the Withdrawn Selves." *Texas Law Review* 62:1563.

Gabel, Peter, and Paul Harris. 1983. "Building Power and Breaking Images: Critical Legal Theory and the Practice of Law." *New York University Review of Law and Social Change* 11:369.

Gabel, Peter, and Duncan Kennedy. 1984. "Roll over Beethoven." *Stanford Law Review* 36:1.

Galanter, Marc. 1974. "Why the 'Haves' Come Out Ahead: Speculations on the Limits of Legal Change." *Law and Society Review* 9:95.

———. 1983. "The Radiating Effects of Courts." In *Empirical Theories about Courts,* ed. Keith O. Boyum and Lynn Mather. New York: Longman.

Garvin, Larry T. 1988. "Constitutional Limits on the Regulation of Laboratory Animal Research." *Yale Law Journal* 98:369.

Gaventa, John. 1980. *Power and Powerlessness: Quiescence and Rebellion in an Appalachian Valley.* Urbana: University of Illinois Press.

Geertz, Clifford. 1983. *Local Knowledge: Further Essays in Interpretive Anthropology.* New York: Basic Books.

Gilligan, Carol. 1982. *In A Different Voice: Psychological Theory and Women's Development.* Cambridge: Harvard University Press.

Gladwell, Malcolm. 1990. "Scientists Not Backing Animal Rights Rally." *Washington Post,* June 9, sec. A, p. 4.

Glazer, Nathan. 1975. "Towards an Imperial Judiciary?" *Public Interest* 41:104.

Glendon, Mary Ann. 1987. *Abortion and Divorce in Western Law: American Failures, European Challenges.* Cambridge: Harvard University Press.

———. 1991. *Rights Talk: The Impoverishment of Political Discourse.* New York: Free Press.

Godlovitch, Stanley, Roslind Godlovitch, and John Harris, eds. 1972. *Animals, Men and Morals: An Enquiry into the Maltreatment of Non-humans.* New York: Taplinger.

Goldman, Sheldon, and Austin Sarat, eds. 1989. *American Court Systems: Readings in Judicial Process and Behavior.* White Plains, N.Y.: Longman.

Gordon, Robert W. 1982. "New Developments in Legal Theory." In *The Politics of Law: A Progressive Critique,* ed. David Kairys. New York: Pantheon.

———. 1984. "Critical Legal Histories." *Stanford Law Review* 36:57.

Gramsci, Antonio. 1971. *Selections from the Prison Notebooks,* ed. Quinton Hoare and Geoffrey Nowell Smith. New York: International.

Greenhouse, Carol J. 1988. "Courting Difference: Issues of Interpretation and Comparison in the Study of Legal Ideologies." *Law and Society Review* 22:687.

Hackett, Larry. 1989. "Animal Instincts: Squabbling Could Weaken Anti-Fur Groups' Offensive." *New York Daily News,* October 25, 39.

Handler, Joel F. 1978. *Social Movements and the Legal System: A Theory of Law Reform and Social Change.* New York: Academic.

Harrington, Christine B. 1985. *Shadow Justice: The Ideology and Institutionalization of Alternatives to Court.* Westport, Conn.: Greenwood.

Harrington, Christine B., and Sally Engle Merry. 1988. "Ideological Production: The Making of Community Mediation." *Law and Society Review* 22:708.

Harrington, Christine B., and Barbara Yngvesson. 1990. "Interpretive Sociolegal Research." *Law and Social Inquiry* 15:135.

Harriston, Keith, and Avis Thomas-Lester. 1990. "Animal Rights Activists' Day in the Sun." *Washington Post,* June 11, sec. E, p. 1.

Hart, H. L. A. 1961. *The Concept of Law.* Oxford: Clarendon.

Hartz, Louis. 1955. *The Liberal Tradition in America: An Interpretation of American Political Thought Since the Revolution.* New York: Harcourt, Brace.

Haskell, Thomas L. 1987. "The Curious Persistence of Rights Talk in the 'Age of Interpretation.'" *Journal of American History* 74:984.

Henry, Stuart. 1985. "Community Justice, Capitalist Society, and Human Agency: The Dialectics of Collective Law in the Cooperative." *Law and Society Review* 19:303.

Hentoff, Nat. 1990. "Lawyers for Animals." *Washington Post,* April 28, sec. A, p. 23.

Hirsch, James. 1988. "Animal-Rights Groups Step Up Attack on Furriers." *New York Times,* November 27, sec. A, p. 11.

Hobbes, Thomas. [1651] 1986. *Leviathan.* ed. C. B. Macpherson. Harmondsworth: Penguin.

Hochschild, Jennifer L. 1981. *What's Fair? American Beliefs about Distributive Justice.* Cambridge: Harvard University Press.

Hochswender, Woody. 1989. "As Image of Fur Suffers, So Does Profit." *New York Times,* March 14, sec. A, p. 1.

Hogshire, Jim. 1991. "Animals and Islam." *Animals' Agenda* (October): 10.

Hohfeld, Wesley Newcomb. 1919. *Fundamental Legal Conceptions as Applied in Judicial Reasoning.* ed. Walter Wheeler Cook. New Haven: Yale University Press.

Horowitz, Donald L. 1977. *The Courts and Social Policy.* Washington, D.C.: Brookings Institution.

Hume, David. 1898. *A Treatise of Human Nature.* London: Longmans, Green.

Hunt, Alan. 1985. "The Ideology of Law: Advances and Problems in Recent Applications of the Concept of Ideology to the Analysis of Law." *Law and Society Review* 19:11.

Hunt, Ken. 1990. "Animal-Rights Activists Target Gillette." *University of Washington Daily,* October 30, 1.

Hutchinson, Allan C. ed. 1989. *Critical Legal Studies.* Totowa, N.J.: Rowman and Littlefield.

Johnson, Charles A. 1979. "Lower Court Reactions to Supreme Court Decisions: A Quantitative Examination." *American Journal of Political Science* 23:792.

Johnson, Charles A., and Bradley C. Canon. 1984. *Judicial Policies: Implementation and Impact.* Washington. D.C.: Congressional Quarterly.

Johnson, Kirk. 1988. "Arrest Points Up Split in Animal-Rights Movement." *New York Times,* November 13, sec. A, p. 40.

Kader, Rob. 1990. "No Reason Why PAWS' Rescue Should Ruffle P-I's Feathers." *Seattle Post-Intelligencer,* February 6, sec. A, p. 20.

Kairys, David, ed. 1982. *The Politics of Law: A Progressive Critique.* New York: Pantheon.

Kant, Immanuel. 1930. "Duties towards Animals and Spirits." In *Lectures on Ethics,* trans. Louis Infield. New York: The Century Co.

Kasindorf, Jeanie. 1990. "The Fur Flies: The Cold War over Animal Rights." *New York,* January 15, 27.

Keller, Evelyn Fox. 1985. *Reflections on Gender and Science.* New Haven: Yale University Press.

Kelman, Mark. 1987. *A Guide to Critical Legal Studies.* Cambridge: Harvard University Press.

Kennedy, David. 1986. "Critical Theory, Structuralism, and Contemporary Legal Scholarship." *New England Law Review* 21:209.

Kessler, Mark. 1987. *Legal Services for the Poor: A Comparative and Contemporary Analysis of Interorganizational Politics.* New York: Greenwood.

Kheel, Marti. 1988. "Animal Liberation and Environmental Ethics: Can Ecofeminism Bridge the Gap?" Paper presented at the annual meeting of the Western Political Science Association, San Francisco.

Kirkby, Marilyn. 1989. "Fur's A-flying: Furriers Defend Their Industry's Practices as Animal-rights Activists Continue Protests." *Seattle Times,* November 29, sec. G, p. 1.

Klare, Karl E. 1982. "Critical Theory and Labor Relations Law." In *The Politics of Law: A Progressive Critique,* ed. David Kairys. New York: Pantheon.

Knobelsdorff, Kerry Elizabeth. 1987. "Stricter Regulation Sought over Labs Using Animals in Research." *Christian Science Monitor,* January 8, 7.

Lane, Robert E. 1962. *Political Ideology: Why the American Common Man Believes What He Does.* New York: Free Press of Glencoe.

Lefcourt, Robert, ed. 1971. *Law Against the People: Essays to Demystify Law, Order, and the Courts.* New York: Random House.

Lempert, Richard. 1976. "Mobilizing Private Law: An Introductory Essay." *Law and Society Review* 11:173.

Lewis, Anthony. 1991. "Abusing the Law." *New York Times,* May 10, sec. A, p. 31.

Luker, Kristin. 1984. *Abortion and the Politics of Motherhood.* Berkeley: University of California Press.

Lyall, Sarah. 1989. "Animal-Rights Suits Challenging University Panels." *New York Times,* August 22, sec. B, p. 1.

———. 1990. "Student Refuses to Dissect a Frog and Sues University." *New York Times,* May 3, sec. A, p. 19.

Lynd, Staughton. 1984. "Communal Rights." *Texas Law Review* 62:1417.

McCann, Michael W. 1986. *Taking Reform Seriously: Perspectives on Public Interest Liberalism.* Ithaca: Cornell University Press.

———. 1989. "Legal Mobilization, Rights Consciousness, and the Politics of Pay Equity Reform." Paper presented at the annual meeting of the Law and Society Association, Madison, Wisconsin.

———. 1990. "Legal Mobilization and Social Reform Movements: Notes on Theory and Its Applications." Manuscript.

———. 1994. *Rights at Work: Pay Equity Reform and the Politics of Legal Mobilization.* Chicago: University of Chicago Press.

McCann, Michael W., and Helena Silverstein. 1993. "Social Movements and the American State: Legal Mobilization as a Strategy for Democratization." In *A Different Kind of State? Popular Power and Democratic Administration,* ed. Gregory Albo, David Langille, and Leo Panitch. Toronto: Oxford University Press.

McCarthy, Colman. 1984. "A National Force with Moral Basis." *Seattle Times,* April 17, sec. A, p. 8.

———. 1990. "Philosopher of Animal Rights." *Washington Post,* June 9, sec. A, p. 23.

McDonald, Karen L. 1986. "Creating a Private Cause of Action Against Abusive Animal Research." *University of Pennsylvania Law Review* 134:399.

Maggitti, Phil. 1991. "Annette Lantos: Bringing Concern for Animals into Congress." *Animals' Agenda* (January/February): 40.

Matsuda, Mari. 1987. "Looking to the Bottom: Critical Legal Studies and Reparations." *Harvard Civil Rights–Civil Liberties Law Review* 22:323.

Medcalf, Linda. 1978. *Law and Identity: Lawyers, Native Americans, and Legal Practice.* Beverly Hills: Sage.

Merry, Sally Engle. 1985. "Concepts of Law and Justice among Working-Class Americans: Ideology as Culture." *Legal Studies Forum* 9:59.

———. 1986. "Everyday Understandings of the Law in Working-Class America." *American Ethnologist* 13:253.

———. 1988. "Legal Pluralism." *Law and Society Review* 22:867.

———. 1990. *Getting Justice and Getting Even: Legal Consciousness Among Working-Class Americans.* Chicago: University of Chicago Press.

Messett, Marci. 1987. "They Asked for Protection and They Got Policy: *International Primate's* Mutilated Monkeys." *Akron Law Review* 21:97.

Michelman, Frank. 1973. "The Supreme Court and Litigation Access Fees: The Right to Protect One's Rights—Part I." *Duke Law Journal* (1973):1153.

Midgley, Mary. 1984. *Animals and Why They Matter.* Athens: University of Georgia Press.

Milner, Neal. 1986. "The Dilemmas of Legal Mobilization: Ideologies and Strategies of Mental Patient Liberation Groups." *Law and Policy* 8:105.

———. 1989. "The Denigration of Rights and the Persistence of Rights Talk: A Cultural Portrait." *Law and Social Inquiry* 14:631.

Minow, Martha. 1987. "Interpreting Rights: An Essay for Robert Cover." *Yale Law Journal* 96:1860.

———. 1990. *Making All the Difference: Inclusion, Exclusion, and American Law.* Ithaca: Cornell University Press.

Montaigne, Michel de. [1580] 1923. *The Essays of Montaigne,* trans. John Florio. London: J. M. Dent and Sons.

More, Thomas. [1516] 1949. *Utopia,* ed. H. V. S. Ogden. New York: Appleton-Century-Crofts.

Moretti, Daniel S. 1984. *Animal Rights and the Law.* London: Oceana Publications.

Morris, Richard Knowles, and Michael W. Fox, eds. 1978. *On the Fifth Day: Animal Rights and Human Ethics.* Washington, D.C.: Acropolis.

Motavalli, Jim. 1994. "Hunters' Free Speech; Hunter Harassment Laws; In Brief." *Earth Action Network* 5 (October):16.

Murphy, Kim. 1988. "Judge Jumps to Conclusion: Find Naturally Dead Frogs." *Los Angeles Times,* August 2, sec. 1, p. 3.

Murphy, Walter F., and C. Herman Pritchett, eds. 1986. *Courts, Judges, and Politics: An Introduction to the Judicial Process.* 4th ed. New York: Random House.

Neubauer, David W. 1991. *Judicial Process: Law, Courts, and Politics in the United States.* Pacific Grove, Calif.: Brooks/Cole.

Niven, Charles D. 1967. *History of the Humane Movement.* London: Johnson.

Oestereich, James. 1992. Letter to the editor. *Animals' Agenda* (March): 7.

Offley, Ed. 1990. "Legal Hitch for Navy's Dolphins." *Seattle Post-Intelligencer,* May 3, sec. B, p. 1.

Olson, Susan M. 1984. *Clients and Lawyers: Securing the Rights of Disabled Persons.* Westport, Conn.: Greenwood.

Orren, Karen. 1976. "Standing to Sue: Interest Group Conflict in the Federal Courts." *American Political Science Review* 70:723.

Pacheco, Alex, with Anna Francione. 1985. "The Silver Spring Monkeys." In *In Defense of Animals*, ed. Peter Singer. New York: Harper and Row.

Paterson, David, and Richard D. Ryder, eds. 1979. *Animals' Rights—A Symposium*. London: Centaur.

Peterson, Sandra. 1989. "Animal Rights and Human Rights Go Hand in Hand." *Christian Science Monitor*, February 16, 20.

Pink, Daniel H. 1990. "'Silver Spring Monkeys' Die in La. Experiment." *Washington Post*, July 7, sec. A, p. 12.

Piven, Frances Fox, and Richard A. Cloward. 1977. *Poor People's Movements: Why They Succeed, How They Fail*. New York: Pantheon.

Putnam, Ruth Anna. 1976. "Rights of Persons and the Liberal Tradition. In *Social Ends and Political Means*, ed. Ted Honderich. London: Routledge and Kegan Paul.

Quinney, Richard. 1974. *Criminal Justice in America: A Critical Understanding*. Boston: Little, Brown.

———. 1980. *Class, State, and Crime: On the Theory and Practice of Criminal Justice*. 2d ed. New York: Longman.

Rabkin, Jeremy A. 1989. *Judicial Compulsions: How Public Law Distorts Public Policy*. New York: Basic Books.

Rapattoni, Linda. 1988. "Lawyers in Frog Dissection Suit Say They May Appeal." *United Press International*, August 2.

Raz, Joseph. 1986. *The Morality of Freedom*. Oxford: Oxford University Press.

Regan, Tom. 1983. *The Case for Animal Rights*. Berkeley: University of California Press.

———. 1990. "The Struggle for Animal Rights" In *Political Theory and Animal Rights*, ed. Paul Clarke and Andrew Linzey. London: Pluto Press.

Regan, Tom, and Peter Singer, eds. 1976. *Animal Rights and Human Obligations*. Englewood Cliffs. N.J.: Prentice-Hall.

Richardson, Richard J., and Kenneth N. Vines. 1970. *The Politics of Federal Courts: Lower Courts in the United States*. Boston: Little, Brown.

Rollin, Bernard E. 1981. *Animal Rights and Human Morality*. Buffalo: Prometheus.

Rose, Nikolas. 1985. "Unreasonable Rights: Mental Illness and the Limits of the Law." *Journal of Law and Society* 12:199.

Rosenberg, Gerald N. 1991. *The Hollow Hope: Can Courts Bring about Social Change?* Chicago: University of Chicago Press.

Rosenthal, Douglas. 1974. *Lawyer and Client: Who's in Charge?* New York: Russel Sage Foundation.

Ross, Elizabeth. 1988. "Referendum Would Toughen Massachusetts Farm Rules." *Christian Science Monitor*, November 1, 3.

Rubin, Lillian Breslow. 1976. *Worlds of Pain: Life in the Working-Class Family*. New York: Basic Books.

Ryder, Richard D. 1979. "The Struggle against Speciesism." In *Animals'*

Rights—A Symposium, ed. David Paterson and Richard D. Ryder. London: Centaur.

Salt, Henry S. [1892] 1980. *Animals' Rights: Considered in Relation to Social Progress.* Clarks Summit, Pa.: Society for Animal Rights.

Sapontzis, S. F. 1987. *Morals, Reason, and Animals.* Philadelphia: Temple University Press.

Sarat, Austin. 1985. "Legal Effectiveness and Social Studies of Law: On the Unfortunate Persistence of a Research Tradition." *Legal Studies Forum* 9:23.

Sarat, Austin, and Thomas R. Kearns. 1993. "Beyond the Great Divide: Forms of Legal Scholarship and Everyday Life." In *Law in Everyday Life,* ed. Austin Sarat and Thomas R. Kearns. Ann Arbor: University of Michigan Press.

Sax, Joseph L. 1970. *Defending the Environment: A Handbook for Citizen Action.* New York: Random House.

Scheingold, Stuart A. 1974. *The Politics of Rights: Lawyers, Public Policy, and Political Change.* New Haven: Yale University Press.

———. 1989. "Constitutional Rights and Social Change: Civil Rights in Perspective." In *Judging the Constitution: Critical Essays on Judicial Lawmaking,* ed. Michael W. McCann and Gerald L. Houseman. Glenview, Ill.: Scott, Foresman.

Schneider, Elizabeth M. 1986. "The Dialectic of Rights and Politics: Perspectives from the Women's Movement." *New York University Law Review* 61:589.

Schopenhauer, Arthur. 1965. *On the Basis of Morality,* trans. E. F. J. Payne. Indianapolis: Bobbs-Merrill.

Scott, James C. 1985. *Weapons of the Weak: Everyday Forms of Peasant Resistance.* New Haven: Yale University Press.

Selznick, Philip. 1969. *Law, Society, and Industrial Justice.* New York: Russell Sage Foundation.

Shapiro, Martin M. 1990. "The Presidency and the Federal Courts." In *Classic Readings in American Politics,* ed. Pietro S. Nivola and David H. Rosenbloom. 2d ed. New York: St. Martin's.

Silbey, Susan S. 1985. "Ideals and Practices in the Study of Law." *Legal Studies Forum* 9:7.

Silbey, Susan S., and Austin Sarat. 1987. "Critical Traditions in Law and Society Research." *Law and Society Review* 21:165.

Silverstein, Helena, and Robert Van Dyk. 1989. "Social Movements in the Courts: Power and the Problems of a Legal Strategy." Paper presented at the twenty-fifth anniversary meeting of the Law and Society Association, Madison, Wisconsin.

Singer, Joseph William. 1984. "The Player and the Cards: Nihilism and Legal Theory." *Yale Law Journal* 94:1.

Singer, Peter. 1975. *Animal Liberation: A New Ethics for Our Treatment of Animals.* New York: Avon.

———. 1976. "All Animals Are Equal." In *Animal Rights and Human Obligations,* ed. Tom Regan and Peter Singer. Englewood Cliffs. N.J.: Prentice-Hall.

———. 1978. "The Fable of the Fox and the Unliberated Animals." *Ethics* 88:119.

———. 1981. *The Expanding Circle: Ethics and Sociobiology*. New York: Farrar, Straus, and Giroux.

———. 1990. *Animal Liberation*. 2d ed. New York: Random House.

Sitomer, Curtis J. 1989. "Animal Rights." *Christian Science Monitor*, January 26, 13.

Sorauf, Frank J. 1976. *The Wall of Separation: The Constitutional Politics of Church and State*. Princeton, N.J.: Princeton University Press.

Spaeth, Harold J. 1979. *Supreme Court Policy Making: Explanation and Prediction*. San Francisco: W. H. Freeman.

Sperling, Susan. 1989. *Animal Liberators: Research and Morality*. Berkeley: University of California Press.

Spiegel, Marjorie. 1988. *The Dreaded Comparison: Human and Animal Slavery*. Philadelphia: New Society.

Stevenson, Richard W. 1989. "A Campaign for Research on Animals." *New York Times*, January 20, sec. C, p. 5.

Stewart, Richard B. 1975. "The Reformation of American Administrative Law." *Harvard Law Review* 88:1669.

Stille, Alexander. 1990. "Animal Advocacy." *National Law Journal*, April 16, 1.

Stone, Christopher D. 1972. "Should Trees Have Standing: Toward Legal Rights for Natural Objects." *Southern California Law Review* 45:450.

———. 1987. *Earth and Other Ethics: The Case for Moral Pluralism*. New York: Harper and Row.

Subar, Loran. 1987. "Out from Under the Microscope: A Case for Laboratory Animal Rights." *Detroit College of Law Review* (1987):511.

Tarr, G. Alan. 1977. *Judicial Impact and State Supreme Courts*. Lexington, Mass.: D. C. Heath.

Thomas, Brenda L. 1986. "Antinomy: The Use, Rights, and Regulation of Laboratory Animals." *Pepperdine Law Review* 13:723.

Thompson, E. P. 1975. *Whigs and Hunters: The Origin of the Black Act*. New York: Pantheon.

Trubek, David M. 1977. "Complexity and Contradiction in the Legal Order: Balbus and the Challenge of Critical Social Thought about Law." *Law and Society Review* 11:529.

———. 1984. "Where the Action Is: Critical Legal Studies and Empiricism." *Stanford Law Review* 36:575.

Tushnet, Mark V. 1984. "An Essay on Rights." *Texas Law Review* 62:1363.

———. 1986. "Critical Legal Studies: An Introduction to Its Origins and Underpinnings." *Journal of Legal Education* 36:505.

———. 1987. *The NAACP's Legal Strategy against Segregated Education, 1925–1952*. Chapel Hill: University of North Carolina Press.

Vogeler, William. 1990. "Free Speech May Protect Animals." *Los Angeles Daily Journal*, May 10, 7.

Voltaire. 1932. *A Philosophical Dictionary*. 2 vols. New York: Coventry House.

Vose, Clement E. 1959. *Caucasions Only: The Supreme Court, the NAACP, and the Restrictive Covenant Cases*. Berkeley: University of California Press.

———. 1986. "Litigation as a Form of Pressure Group Activity." In *Courts,*

Judges, and Politics: An Introduction to the Judicial Process, ed. Walter F. Murphy and C. Herman Pritchett. 4th ed. New York: Random House.

Waldron, Jeremy. 1987. *"Nonsense Upon Stilts": Bentham, Burke, and Marx on the Rights of Man.* London: Methuen.

Warrick, Deborah M. 1989. "Wolves and Dogs: Canine Cousins." *Animals' Agenda* (December): 18.

Wasby, Stephen L. 1970. *The Impact of the United States Supreme Court: Some Perspectives.* Homewood, Ill.: Dorsey.

———. 1983. "Interest Groups in Court: Race Relations Litigation." In *Interest Group Politics,* ed. Allan J. Cigler and Burdett A. Loomis. Washington. D.C.: Congressional Quarterly.

Wells, Ken. 1989. "If Star Witness Croaks, Will Case Then Be Dismissed?" *Wall Street Journal,* November 6, sec. A, p. 1.

White, James Boyd. 1985a. *Heracles' Bow: Essays on the Rhetoric and Poetics of the Law.* Madison: University of Wisconsin Press.

———. 1985b. "Law as Rhetoric, Rhetoric as Law: The Arts of Cultural and Communal Life." *University of Chicago Law Review* 52:684.

Williams, Lena. 1989. "Wardrobes Tailored by Social Concerns." *New York Times,* March 29, sec. C, p. 1.

Williams, Patricia. 1987. "Alchemical Notes: Reconstructing Ideals from Deconstructed Rights." *Harvard Civil Rights–Civil Liberties Law Review* 22:401.

Wise, Steven M. 1992. "The Legal Activist: When Do People Have Legal *Standing* to Sue on Behalf of Animals?" *Animals' Agenda* (March): 19.

Wittgenstein, Ludwig. 1962. *Philosophical Investigations.* New York: Macmillan.

Wright, Robert. 1990. "Are Animals People Too?" *New Republic,* March 12, 20.

Wynne-Tyson, Jon, ed. 1985. *The Extended Circle: A Dictionary of Humane Thought.* Fontwell, Sussex: Centaur.

Yngvesson, Barbara. 1988. "Making Law at the Doorway: The Clerk, the Court, and the Construction of Community in a New England Town." *Law and Society Review* 22:409.

Zak, Steven. 1990. "Why Prosecutors Shouldn't Let Animal Abusers off the Hook." *Los Angeles Daily Journal,* September 20, 6.

Zemans, Frances Kahn. 1983. "Legal Mobilization: The Neglected Role of the Law in the Political System." *American Political Science Review* 77:690.

Undated Pamphlets

Animal Legal Defense Fund. *Objecting to Dissection: A Student Handbook.*

Fund for Animals. *Furs: Who Really Pays?*

Humane Society of the United States. *Fur Shame.*

International Society for Animal Rights. *The Argument for Abolition.*

National Anti-Vivisection Society. *A Change of Heart: Former Defender of Animal Researcher Reconsiders His Positions.*

———. *National Anti-Vivisection Society.*

People for the Ethical Treatment of Animals. *Animal Rights: Why Should It Concern Me?*

―――. *Cosmetics Testing.*

―――. *Dissection: Your Right to Refuse.*

―――. *Let's Talk about Animal Rights.*

―――. *Silver Spring Monkeys: A PETA Casework Report.*

―――. *Travelling Animal Acts.*

Progressive Animal Welfare Society. *Animal Rights: Speak for Them.*

―――. *PAWS.*

Trans-Species Unlimited. *Animal Rights: What's It All About?*

Index

Action for Animals, 247

Activists in the Lafayette Animal
Rights Movement, 256n.15

Adams, Carol J., 70, 77, 245, 246

Administrative Procedures Act, 144

American Anti-Vivisection Society,
58, 244, 246

American Medical Association, 154

Amory, Cleveland, 246

Animal care committees, 140, 150–51,
178–80, 196, 267n.41, 269n.16,
269n.18. *See also* Freedom of
information laws

Animal law, 132–33, 141–44, 189–
91
enforcement of, 123–24, 133–34,
143, 189, 264n.3, 265n.19
limits of, 123–24, 143
See also Environmental law; Litigation, direct effects of; Litigation, indirect effects of; Litigation, limits of; Standing

Animal Legal Defense Fund, 265n.21,
271n.15
and litigation, 123, 140, 154, 176,
179, 205
and rights, 67, 69

Animal liberation, 30, 48, 68, 94, 111,
233, 263n.24
versus animal rights, 88, 90,
115–16, 118, 234

Animal Liberation Front, 152, 202,
272n.3

*Animal Lovers Volunteer Association,
Inc., v. Weinberger*, 138, 182

Animal rights
absurdity of, 51, 72, 87, 93, 234,
259n.47, 262n.13
and compassion, 75–76, 255n.3
in court, 19, 98–100, 124, 133, 154,
158, 193, 207, 211
versus equal consideration, 44, 116,
118
perceived as extreme, 18, 91–92,
118
philosophical foundations of,
27–28, 38–54
popularity of, 88
uniting welfare and rights, 36–37
versus animal liberation, 88, 90,
115–16, 118, 234
See also Animal rights movement;
Human Rights; Legal mean-
ing; Rights

Animal Rights Direct Action Coalition, 200

Animal rights movement
case study selection, 16–20
composition of, 34–37, 77–78,
228–29
divisions within, 94
historical development of, 29–33
and identity, 232–33
and legal meaning, 16–20, 24–26,
28–29, 86
and the media, 71–75, 261n.13
revising the meaning of rights, 18,
25, 28, 50–53, 66–71, 75, 81–82
See also Animal rights; Animal
rights movement, connections